Y0-AQM-161

Praise for *Six by Ten*

"The voices heard in this powerful collection are haunting. As these men and women make inescapably clear, the practice of removing human beings from everything that makes them sane and stable—keeping them for days, months, and years in utter isolation without light, touch, sound, space, and hope—is unimaginably cruel. *Six by Ten* is a deeply moving and profoundly unsettling wake up call for all citizens. The use of solitary confinement is deeply immoral and we must insist that it be banned in all of our nation's prisons. Immediately."

—Heather Ann Thompson, Pulitzer Prize–winning author,
Blood in the Water: The Attica Prison Uprising of 1971 and Its Legacy

"Some of the people in *Six by Ten* were convicted of crimes, but this book convicts the United States of an incomparably greater crime: blighting the lives and searing the souls of untold hundreds of thousands of men, women, and teenagers by a practice that more enlightened countries consider inhuman. You will not find a more riveting indictment anywhere of our reckless use of solitary confinement, nor one told through such a variety of moving, poignant voices."

—Adam Hochschild, author, *King Leopold's Ghost*

PRAISE FOR *SURVIVING JUSTICE*

"*Surviving Justice* is a necessary truth telling that amplifies the voices of the countless wrongfully incarcerated sons, lovers, husbands, fathers, mothers, and daughters who languish in America's prisons. These oral histories give insight into the nature of the injustice to which they have been subjected, but also offer a way forward. I never could have written *An American Marriage* without the brave and thoughtful testimonies in this book."

—Tayari Jones

Additional Interviewers
Sameer Jaywant, Steven Lance, Hope Metcalf

Transcribers
Victoria Alexander, Pablo Baeza, Corey Barr, Emma Cogan, Brittany Collins, Charlotte Edelstein, Katie Fiegenbaum, Justine Hall, Miriam Hwang-Carlos, Mary Beth Melso, Ariela Rosa, Barbara Sheffels, Annie Stine, Paul Skenazy, Lucy Wallitsch

Research Editor
Annie Stine

Research Assistance
Charlotte Edelstein, Kaye Herranen, Miriam Hwang-Carlos, Joe Stephens

Fact-checking
Hannah Murphy

Copyeditor
Brian Baughan

SIX BY TEN

Stories from Solitary

EDITED BY
TAYLOR PENDERGRASS
AND
MATEO HOKE

Haymarket Books

Chicago, Illinois

Narrator portrait illustrations by Christine Shields
Cover design by Michel Vrana
Cover photograph © Richard Ross, juvenile-in-justice.com

Published in 2018 by
Haymarket Books
P.O. Box 180165
Chicago, IL 60618
773-583-7884
www.haymarketbooks.org
info@haymarketbooks.org

Free curricula is available at voiceofwitness.org/education/lesson-plans.

ISBN: 978-1-60846-531-6

Trade distribution:
In the US, Consortium Book Sales and Distribution, www.cbsd.com
In Canada, Publishers Group Canada, www.pgcbooks.ca
In the UK, Turnaround Publisher Services, www.turnaround-uk.com
All other countries, Ingram Publisher Services International,
IPS_Intlsales@ingramcontent.com

This book was published with the generous support of Lannan Foundation
and Wallace Action Fund.

Library of Congress Cataloging-in-Publication data is available.

10 9 8 7 6 5 4 3 2 1

To everyone working to tear down cages

CONTENTS

INTRODUCTION

Part 1: Stories that Needed Telling

TAYLOR PENDERGRASS

From where I was living in New York City in 2010, it was about a seven-hour drive north to the small town of Malone, New York, right on the Canadian border. I'd made the trek with my colleague Scarlet Kim the day before. Now, as the sun was coming up over the Adirondacks, the two of us were standing in chilly fall air behind rows of fencing and concertina wire staring at Upstate Correctional Facility, a massive New York state prison where on any given day about a thousand men are held in solitary confinement in what New York calls "Special Housing Units" or "SHUs."[1]

Even from where we stood behind the fence, separated from the prison grounds by at least a couple hundred yards of grass lawn, we could hear a tremendous clamor: men yelling, hooting, and simply screaming. As a lawyer working with the ACLU on criminal justice issues, I'd been in numerous jails and prisons before, but I'd never experienced anything like this. At Upstate, the people kept in the SHUs were allowed one hour

---

1. SHU can also stand for "security housing unit." The nomenclature varies by prison system. Whatever the name, a SHU refers to a solitary confinement cell unit. Prisoners and guards commonly refer to "the SHU" as a single word rather than initials, as in "the shoe."

a day out of their tiny cells. That hour was spent in an even smaller "recreation cage" attached to the cell—basically a concrete patio with a thick metal grate on one side providing some access to sunlight and air. The door from the cell to the recreation cage is released remotely by prison guards, sending dozens of people out to their patios all at the same time.

The cacophony of voices we were hearing was the sound that a large group of human beings will make when in earshot of one another after spending twenty-three hours in an isolation cell. We knew that some of the men we were about to talk to had been living this daily routine for years. We listened for another minute, and then walked toward the nondescript front entrance of the prison.

The night before, we'd stayed in a small bed-and-breakfast in Malone. That evening we settled into the den and accepted the husband and wife owners' offer of a glass of wine. After some polite small talk, we learned that he had just recently retired after working for decades as a counselor at Upstate. We told them who we were and that we were planning to write and publish a report about the use of solitary confinement in New York state prisons.

He and his wife exchanged glances. Over the next hour or so, he slowly opened up to us about his experiences over the years trying to counsel the men held in solitary confinement. In this company town with a population of under fifteen thousand, where the three big prisons in the area are the major local employer, the man used hushed tones even in the confines of his own home. "Where we live, it's a large farming community," he said. "We have laws on the books against cattle being confined to these huge, huge barns. The Department of Agriculture watches for that type of abuse. Yet when it comes to human beings, we are keeping them in cages that wouldn't be fit for our cows."

Over the next year, we spoke with dozens of men and a handful of women held in New York's solitary confinement wings. We published our report, gave testimony to the United Nations, filed a federal lawsuit, and are currently in the process of monitoring a multiyear settlement to reduce the use and severity of solitary confinement in the New York state prison system.

During those initial interviews at Upstate, it became apparent that there was no way to possibly convey all the complicated dimensions of this practice in a report or lawsuit. The stories were too big and too complex. Solitary confinement is the little-known dead end of the US criminal justice system. To understand that system, people need to understand and wrestle with what is happening in America's isolation cells.

◆◆◆

In the winter of 2014, Mateo Hoke had a stopover in New York City and stayed with me and my wife for a few days. I had first met Mateo in 2002, when we were both students at the University of Colorado in Boulder. We formed a quick and lasting friendship that revolved around campus activism and a shared love of hip-hop. Sitting on my couch in New York, we talked for hours as snowflakes fell outside. I told him about the limits of my work as a litigator and how I continued to be haunted by the stories of the people I'd spoken with in solitary. I'd followed Mateo's work as a journalist and oral historian. He suggested that we work jointly on a book about solitary confinement for Voice of Witness. This, I thought, was the work that needed doing. These were the stories that would never be told in a lawsuit. That conversation with Mateo eventually led to the stories you hold in your hands.

Since my first visit to Upstate Correctional Facility, public awareness of the use of solitary confinement has grown. As you'll read in these pages, states around the country have started scaling back the use of solitary confinement. At least one state, Colorado, has reformed the practice to such an extent that it can reasonably lay claim to having abolished long-term solitary confinement throughout its entire prison system. But as narrator Steve Blakeman said to me, "The punitive default is resilient. The punitive norm is self-perpetuating." As national legal expert Amy

Fettig discusses in one of this book's essays (see appendix V), meaning-ful reform is happening, but policy change does not necessarily alter the underlying societal values that led to these practices in the first place. To the contrary, changing policy by tinkering at the edges of the core problem—for example, by tackling only the easiest cases, the people who *obviously* do not need to be in solitary confinement—can be a way of avoiding a harder conversation.

Solitary confinement is unlikely to change significantly in America unless there is a corresponding transformation in the underlying values that led to its creation. Unless a shift occurs, including how we view the hardest cases involving serious violence and harm, solitary confine-ment is likely to continue to exist in some form, however relabeled or repackaged.

In engaging with the stories here, we hope to delve beyond the sur-face and look at some of the harder questions that implicate our individ-ual and collective values. How was an individual impacted or influenced by life's events long before they ended up in a solitary cell? How do we hold people accountable for causing grievous harm, and how do we keep one another safe? Can we accomplish both these goals without resorting to putting humans in isolation cages? These stories provide an essential context for these questions as we evaluate the efficacy and morality of a system that heaps on endless punishment in the form of isolation.

PART 2: THIS IS AMERICA

MATEO HOKE

If there are men and women anywhere among us who need to have their condition looked into in an enlightened, sympathetic and helpful way; if there are any whose very helplessness should excite our interest, to say nothing of our compassion as human beings, they are the inmates of our jails, prisons and penitentiaries, hidden from our view by grim walls, who suffer in silence, and whose cries are not permitted to reach our ears.

—Eugene Debs, *Walls and Bars*, 1927

This book, being about solitary confinement, is by its very nature about violence—against the spirit as well as the body and mind. But at its heart, this is a book about America.

In the following pages you'll read the stories of people whose lives have been deeply impacted by solitary confinement in the United States. And while each narrative does its part to paint a comprehensive picture of contemporary solitary confinement, these stories are more than mere accounts of prison trauma. They are intimate portraits of people you might encounter in the grocery store or at your neighborhood park. They include families and friends, childhood memories, and questionable decisions.

Various stories that follow, like Shearod McFarland's and Levi Stuey's, show us how ordinary kids can find themselves becoming so-called criminals. Other stories, like Vernesia Gordon's, pinpoint where our mental health and juvenile justice systems fail. Each of the narratives, in its own way, tells us as Americans how to do better.

These stories cover the United States from Alaska to Florida, from Connecticut to California, and from Michigan down through Colorado,

Texas, and Louisiana. They come from the family members of people who've been locked in some of the darkest corners of detention centers and from the people themselves. We've also included two narratives, from Steve Blakeman and Travis Trani, of people who've worked in these units, in hopes of complicating our readers' thinking by presenting numerous views from within prison walls. In addition to the narratives we collected, we're including a primer to help readers understand what we're talking about when we talk about solitary confinement, as well as appendix material, which includes a list of actions readers can take to get involved and essays by Amy Fettig of the ACLU and Yale law professor Hope Metcalf.

And while we've worked hard to put together a complex representation of life in America's isolation units, it's worth noting that there is an inherent limitation to producing a book like this. The people most affected by solitary confinement are generally unable to be interviewed. They're frequently too traumatized by the experience to speak about it, or they've lost, or never had, the mental capacity to accurately recount their stories. Or they are simply locked too far away to be reached, or they are forgotten, or dead. What that means is that you'll be hearing from people who survived their solitary confinement experiences with their bodies and minds more or less intact.

Another challenge Taylor and I encountered is that it is tremendously difficult to interview people currently in solitary confinement. Those in power don't want the stories of people in solitary getting out, so they make it extremely challenging to collect stories from individuals housed in isolation. It can be impossible to bring a recording device into facilities, even when meeting prisoners housed in general population. When prisoners are in solitary, these difficulties multiply. In fact, most prisoners confined in solitary aren't permitted visits at all, much less an opportunity for meaningful interviews. Many don't even get mail.

To navigate these obstacles, we spent years corresponding with those inside through letters and email. We visited prisons with pen and paper, and we worked with attorneys who interviewed incarcerated people we otherwise would not have had access to. We also found survivors on the outside who shared vivid stories of what they dealt with inside and how those experiences lingered in their lives.

For many people in the United States, it may seem easy to dismiss or condone solitary confinement when incarcerated people are thought of as "criminals," or the "worst of the worst," who are getting what they deserve. But as we found through our interviews, it's not just those who are in solitary confinement who suffer. Solitary can mean a complete lack of communication, and, as you'll read in chapters like Heather Chapman's, not knowing if one's child or spouse is alive, dead, or losing their mind has a profound effect on those on the outside.

The US public, however, knows very little of how the damage of solitary confinement reaches far beyond prison walls into homes and communities, and even less about what that damage looks and feels like for thousands of Americans returning home each year. Upwards of 95 percent of all people who go to prison in the United States will be released. How they're treated while inside has a huge impact on the communities they return to.

Though each story is unique, the following narratives weave together a larger web of prison abuses, showing that solitary is not a singular abuse happening separately from the violence and dehumanization of everyday prison life. In fact, as we see with Aaron Lewis's description of corrections officers chaining him in stress positions, or with Davon Mosley being denied medication, solitary is often one of a litany of abuses that incarcerated people face every day in America. Isolation just turns up the volume.

As evident in many of the following narratives, solitary drives people to do disturbing things to themselves and others. When locked in isolation, behavioral similarities arise—people self-harm and smear feces in Louisiana just as they do in California. Faced with walls that feel like they're closing in, identities atrophy in Alaska just as they do in New York. The similar accounts you'll find in these pages are not coincidental. Isolation everywhere does terrible things to the human machine.

However, it's worth noting that some of the people you'll meet in these pages say solitary was tolerable, even desirable, because it was a respite from the violence and chaos of being housed in a prison's general population. Read that again. A punishment the United Nations classifies as torture can be a respite. Such are the conditions of being incarcerated in the United States.

Yet while solitary units remain hidden behind structures of immense power and bureaucracy, we found the human spirit perseveres in profound ways. People like Maryam Henderson-Uloho are literally making flowers from toilet paper to keep their bodies and minds occupied. People are sharing food with one another to make sure everyone eats. People like "Zah" Dorrough are reading and writing and exercising to keep their minds sharp and their dignity intact while locked in a place that is designed to dull one's senses and destroy one's poise.

We hope these stories will prove valuable to anyone wanting a truer understanding of American incarceration and American notions of liberty and justice. As Eugene Debs said nearly a hundred years ago, those hidden behind grim walls well deserve to have their conditions viewed in an enlightened and sympathetic way. In fact, the very health of our communities depends on it. So while tens of thousands of people continue to linger in solitary units throughout the United States, it is our hope that by amplifying some of the voices of those who've survived long-term isolation, as well as those of their family members, we honor the thousands whose stories remain yet untold.

SOLITARY CONFINEMENT: A TEN-POINT PRIMER

1. **Long-term solitary confinement meets the legal definition of torture.** According to the United Nations, long-term solitary confinement for more than fifteen days constitutes torture and violates fundamental human rights. The UN found, as early as 1992 and on several occasions since, that solitary confinement amounts to "cruel, inhuman, and degrading treatment or punishment." In 2012, the United Nations Special Rapporteur on Torture concluded that solitary confinement under the conditions noted above—twenty-three or twenty-four hours in a cell with little human contact—should never be used for more than fifteen consecutive days—regardless of the reason.

2. **The United States leads all other industrialized nations in both volume and rates of incarceration.** Every year, around seven million people cycle through the prisons and jails of the United States. On any given day, about 2.3 million people are sitting in US prisons and jails. The United States has just under 5 percent of the world's population yet over 20 percent of the world's prisoners. It incarcerates about 700 people for every 100,000 Americans. (Compare that to rates of 114 for every 100,000 in Canada, or 130 for every 100,000 in England and Wales.) The statistics for people incarcerated don't capture the churn of incarceration. Americans go in and out of jails over eleven million times in a single year.

3. **Solitary confinement is everywhere in the United States today, in every part of the country.** Exact numbers are hard to come by (which points to a major problem: no one actually tracks solitary confinement usage), but most scholars and advocates believe that upwards of a hundred thousand people are in some form of solitary confinement at any moment in the United States. The pervasiveness of the practice means that the number of people exposed to solitary confinement over the course of a year is probably ten times higher. Solitary is used in all types of detention facilities, including civil detention facilities for immigrants, in small county jails holding people accused of crimes before trial, and in juvenile detention facilities. People are held in solitary confinement in the dank and filthy basement cells of US prisons built in the nineteenth century, and they are confined in multimillion-dollar, state-of-the-art prisons built expressly for solitary confinement within the last decade. At least forty-four states and the federal government have freestanding solitary confinement prisons. States spent hundreds of millions of dollars to build these prisons and currently spend hundreds of millions of dollars more annually to operate them.

4. **Solitary confinement units look different from prison to prison, but the basic principle is universal: maximize deprivation and isolation.** People in solitary are held in tiny spaces generally no larger than a parking space—ranging from about sixty to eighty square feet—for twenty-three or twenty-four hours a day. Access to sunlight and fresh air is limited or nonexistent. In places where an hour of recreation is permitted outside of the solitary cell, it often occurs in another barren concrete room. Personal property, like a book or a deck of playing cards, may be forbidden or extremely restricted. There is little or no meaningful human contact. Often, the only human contact a person will have in solitary is with staff through the cell door or

while being handcuffed to be moved to recreation. Visitation and other contact (telephone calls, letters) with loved ones are not allowed or severely limited. There is nothing to do, no one to talk to, nowhere to go—for days, weeks, months, and even years. Prison terms for modern-day solitary confinement vary widely. Prison officials generally refer to solitary units as "segregation," "restricted housing," or "special housing," and use a variety of acronyms to denote specific solitary confinement units. Solitary also goes by slang terms like "the hole" or "the box."

5. **Solitary confinement isn't always solitary.** Some prisons put two people in a solitary confinement cell, a practice generally referred to as "double-bunking." Prison officials may "double-bunk" people in solitary because they have run out of room in their solitary confinement units or because they have designed isolation units that are purpose-built to hold two people in the small cell. Double-bunked prisoners are subject to all the same deprivations as others in solitary confinement. Many prison officials assert that "double-bunking" lessens the severity of isolation in segregation units. Many people who have been subject to double-bunking consider it a special form of torture, oftentimes worse than being alone in a solitary cell, to spend twenty-four hours a day in a small concrete box with a stranger. Assaults often occur between "bunkmates" or "cellies."

6. **People are placed in solitary confinement for a variety of purported reasons.** In US jails and prisons, there are basically three official reasons that people are put in solitary: (1) as punishment for a certain length of time for breaking prison rules ("disciplinary segregation"); (2) for an indeterminate amount of time because prison officials have "classified" a person as being too dangerous to be held in the general prison population ("administrative segregation"); or (3) to protect vulnerable people

from threats from other prisoners ("protective custody"). In practice, if a corrections officer wants a person in solitary confinement, he can almost always find a way to put a prisoner there. Any corrections officer can write a disciplinary "ticket" that will be ruled upon by other corrections officers, who almost always find the target "guilty" and impose punishment. People may be "classified" as dangerous and put into solitary on the basis of flimsy evidence or no evidence at all.

7. **Long-term solitary confinement can pose a risk to mental and physical health.** In the mid-1980s, psychiatrists first studied a group of prisoners living in extreme isolation in the Special Housing Unit, or "SHU," of a Massachusetts prison and identified a variety of negative physiological and psychological symptoms exhibited by the prisoners. The now well-recognized symptoms of solitary confinement include social withdrawal; anxiety and nervousness; panic attacks; irrational anger and rage; loss of impulse control; paranoia; hypersensitivity to external stimuli; severe and chronic depression; difficulties with thinking, concentration, and memory; and perceptual distortions, illusions, and hallucinations. For people with pre-existing mental health issues, solitary confinement can be devastating, and even deadly—rates of suicide and self-harm are higher in solitary units.

Solitary confinement can also lead to a host of medical problems that can be painful, permanently debilitating, and lead to premature death. People held in long-term isolation can experience dangerous levels of chronic hypertension. They commonly suffer from problems with vision. The lack of free movement can atrophy muscle and exacerbate joint pain and arthritis. For inmates with mental illness, segregation often means being subject to the most extreme conditions of confinement. For more on this, see *Locked Up and Locked Down: Segregation of Inmates with Men-*

tal Illness, a report by the AVID Prison Project: Amplifying Voices of Inmates with Disabilities, at www.disabilityrightswa.org.

8. **There is no good evidence that the use of solitary confinement improves safety in prison.** Prison officials have long argued that solitary improves safety by deterring future bad conduct and by removing dangerous or vulnerable people from the general prison population. These claims were never supported by evidence when the use of solitary confinement first exploded in the United States, and it appears increasingly likely that long-term solitary confinement provides no net safety benefits. A person thrown into the box for weeks as punishment for petty rule breaking, like stealing a candy bar, may come out of solitary even more likely to engage in disruptive behavior than when they first went in. When it comes to the smaller number of people held in solitary who have committed serious acts of violence, the most promising approaches involve intervention and programming, like intensive mental health and substance abuse treatment, and restorative justice processes that require the individual to accept meaningful responsibility for the harms caused by his or her actions—none of which occur in solitary units.

9. **There is evidence that solitary is bad for public safety and community health.** To the extent that prison officials realize any short-term safety benefits by warehousing dangerous individuals in their solitary units, they are only shifting the ultimate risk onto the public. Around 95 percent of people who are incarcerated are released. In many cases, prison officials are releasing their most dangerous prisoners directly from solitary confinement to the streets, after having done nothing at all to address the risk that these individuals could be suffering from solitary-induced mental illness and engaging in antisocial be-

haviors. Time in solitary has been shown to increase the risk of recidivism. Placement in solitary confinement cuts people off from contact with family, which is consistently shown to be the single-best predictor of success in society after release.[1] People in solitary confinement lose access to educational or vocational training that may help them get a job upon release. It is unclear if solitary does anything to make prisons safer, but it is certain that it damages the communities and families to which people held in solitary return.

10. **Change is happening.** The harrowing experiences of solitary confinement survivors, which have previously been all but hidden, have now been thrust into the public's view in unprecedented ways. Ten years ago, media reports about solitary confinement were scarce and wide swaths of the public knew little or nothing about these practices. In the last few years, however, solitary confinement has been the subject of an increasing number of public education campaigns, lawsuits, investigative reports, TV shows, documentaries, and even theater productions. Numerous states have dramatically reduced the use of solitary confinement in response to pressure from prisoners, family members, lawsuits, and legislation, and they are doing so at the initiative of corrections leaders. Many more states and the federal government have indicated an intention to reexamine the practice. There is no denying that change is occurring and that there are clear alternatives to solitary confinement. The only question is how far those changes will actually go.

---

1. See, for example, Julie Poehlmann, Danielle Dallaire, Ann Booker Loper, and Leslie D. Shear, "Children's Contact with Their Incarcerated Parents: Research Findings and Recommendations," *American Psychologist* 65, no. 6 (2010): 575.

EXECUTIVE EDITOR'S NOTE

The thirteen narratives in this book are the result of oral history interviews conducted over a two-year period between the spring of 2016 and the spring of 2018. With every Voice of Witness narrative, we aim for a novelistic level of detail and (whenever possible) a birth-to-now chronologized scope in order to portray narrators as individuals in all their complexity, rather than as case studies. We do not set out to create comprehensive histories of human rights issues. Rather, our goal is to compile a collection of voices that (1) offers accessible, thought-provoking, and ultimately humanizing perspectives on what can often seem like impenetrable topics; and (2) can meaningfully contribute to the efforts of social justice and human rights movements.

In order to honor our narrators' experiences, Voice of Witness oral histories are crafted with the utmost care. Recorded interviews are transcribed and organized chronologically by our dedicated team of volunteers. Then, narrative drafts are typically subject to three to five rounds of editorial revision and follow-up interviews, to ensure depth and accuracy. The stories themselves remain faithful to the speakers' words (we seek final narrator approval before publishing their narratives) and have been edited for clarity, coherence, and length. In a few cases, some names and details have been changed to protect the identities of our narrators and the identities of family and acquaintances. All narratives have been carefully fact-checked and are supported by various appendixes and a glossary included in the back of the book that provide context for, and some explanation of, the history of solitary confinement in the United States.

We thank all the individuals who courageously, generously, and patiently shared their experiences with us, including those whom we were unable to include in this book. We also thank all the frontline human rights and social justice defenders working to promote and protect the rights and dignity of all people throughout the prison systems of the United States. Without the cooperation of these advocates, this book would not be possible.

Finally, we thank our national community of educators and students who inspire our education program. With each Voice of Witness book, we create a Common Core–aligned curriculum that connects high school students and educators with the stories and issues presented in the book, with particular emphasis on serving marginalized communities. Our education program also provides curriculum support, training in ethics-driven storytelling, and site visits to educators in schools and impacted communities. Visit the Voice of Witness website for free educational resources, behind-the-scenes features on this book and other projects, and to find out how you can be part of our work: voiceofwitness.org.

In solidarity,
Mimi Lok
Cofounder, Executive Director, and Executive Editor
Voice of Witness

MARYAM HENDERSON-ULOHO

AGE: 61

BORN IN: Pine Bluff, Arkansas

INTERVIEWED IN: Arabi, Louisiana

Maryam Henderson-Uloho says she runs her Sister Hearts Thrift Store "like a marine captain." She's tough and direct and committed to helping her employees learn and grow in ways they haven't been able to for a long time. At Sister Hearts, "Ms. Mary" hires formerly incarcerated people, and if they have nowhere else to go, she houses them in a separate area above the store. For someone recently released from years or decades of incarceration, an opportunity like this can mean the difference between a new beginning or a quick return to crime and prison. Working at the store gives her employees a chance at economic independence and a place to transition back into a society where jobs for formerly incarcerated people can be very difficult to find.

Sister Hearts is currently located in a 17,000-square-foot warehouse packed with furniture, clothes, and knickknacks. It's big, organized, and clean. During

our visit Ms. Mary wears a burgundy Sister Hearts T-shirt and jeans. When she's
not sitting down to talk with us, she's setting up for an event she's hosting later for
formerly incarcerated women to showcase the creative cooking skills they learned
behind bars.

Louisiana is often called the incarceration capital of the world, and Black
people there are more than four times as likely to go to prison as white people are.[1]
Ms. Mary herself spent nearly thirteen years in a Louisiana prison, seven of them
in segregation. When she went in, she was a successful real estate investor. She says
she was targeted in prison and sent to isolation because she's Muslim and refused
to take off her hijab.

I WAS SO SCARED, I WET THE BED

You know, sometimes I say to myself, I have all the ingredients to be a
failure. All the ingredients. But here I am.

I was born January 23, 1957, in Pine Bluff, Arkansas. When I was
fifteen months old, my mother moved us to Fort Worth, Texas. That's
where I grew up. My father passed when I was three. He was in prison
for robbery and something happened with his kidneys. He got very sick.
He got let out on medical release and went home to his mother's house
in Pine Bluff and that's where he died. He was a serious gangster. I was
told he never went anywhere without his .45. People always told me I
look just like him. I don't remember him, but I remember the funeral
like it was yesterday. My father was lying in a gray casket with burgundy
crushed-velvet lining inside. I wanted him to get up and he wouldn't get
up. We went to the cemetery and they lowered him into the ground.
They threw dirt on him. I didn't want them to throw dirt on my father.

Up until the age of about sixteen I had extremely hard crying spells
over my father. Being his only child, I longed for him. And my brothers
and sisters weren't very nice to me at times. My mother worked all the
time. So I didn't have anybody, I felt like I was just so alone.

---

1. Prison Policy Initiative, 2010 US Census data.

When I was younger I didn't socialize with people. I didn't like to be touched. I didn't even want my mother to touch me. She used to ask me at times if she could hug me, and sometimes I'd just cry. I couldn't play with other children. Intellectually I was very advanced. But I didn't know how to socialize. I had no friends. When I would go outside to play I would take a book and sit under a tree. I could read very well. I had a favorite tree, a peach tree, in front of our house. I used to climb that tree and pluck the peaches and eat them. That was pretty fun.

There were eight of us kids. Six boys and two girls. We all had different fathers. Let's see, my fourth brother and my sixth brother, they had the same father. My mother was somewhat promiscuous—my oldest sister and my second brother had the same father, but after that everybody has different fathers. My mother has a third-grade education. She cooked and cleaned people's homes to take care of us. And she had many "friends."

My sister Rosemary was very mean. She had short, thin hair. I have very long, thick, coarse hair. I was tender headed, and Rosemary would take Mama's big brush and beat me in the head with it, so I didn't like for her to comb my hair, and I didn't get my hair combed a lot. Other kids would make fun of me and call me "Little Nappy Head." I was always called names. The kids, they laughed at me because they said I was ugly, that I had rat teeth because I had a gap between my teeth.

Me and Rosemary shared the same bed. She was like seven years older than me. She used to go out and get men and bring them back in at night and she would have sex with them, in the same bed that I slept in. She would make me get down at the foot of the bed. One time Rosemary had this white man in the bed. He wanted to play with me, but my sister said, "No, don't touch her." I was so scared, I wet the bed. I started crying, but I couldn't cry aloud because I was scared. When I got up the next day my sister told Mama I wet the bed. But I couldn't tell Mama why I wet the bed 'cause if I did, I was gonna get a worse beating from my sister. So I just took the beating from my mother instead of having to take it from Rosemary.

HIS CONFIDENCE WAS JUST SO INTERESTING

When I was eleven, my mother married my oldest brother's father, and moved all of us to Dayton, Ohio. I liked my stepfather and he liked me. But he was mean to my mother, and they fought a lot. One time, when I was twelve, he was lying in bed and my mother tried to shoot him with her .38. She missed him, but it definitely wasn't 'cause she wasn't trying to hit him.

When I was about fourteen, my mom left my stepdad and we moved into the projects in Dayton. I didn't do a lot of socializing. So, being in the projects consisted of me mainly staying in the house. Because we had a big family, we got a duplex with four bedrooms. I looked after my brothers. The projects were violence, abuse, more violence, more abuse. You had to mind your own business.

Then when I was sixteen I went to my first party. I went with my friend from high school. She was very promiscuous, but I didn't know because I was very naïve. It was a basement party, and we were having fun, dancing. Well, there were a lot of Nigerians at the party. They were older—grown men.

So I'm dancing, and this man came walking down these steps. He was so interesting to me because he had on these big high-heeled shoes—when men used to wear big high-heeled shoes—and he had on bell-bottoms and stripes and flowers and plaid and polka dots. And he wasn't matching no-where. He had zits all over his face and he was so ugly! Well, my mother told me not to say the word "ugly," so—he was different looking. But he acted like he was the handsomest thing in the room. I thought that was just the most comical thing—his confidence was just so interesting. He asked me to dance with him, and I said no. Well, I didn't know that his father was like a king, and people actually bow down to him. You know the movie *Coming to America*? Well, where he was from in Nigeria, he was used to people actually bowing down to him wherever he went. But we don't have kings and queens in the projects.

His name was Augustine. Eventually I danced with him and we danced very well together. He wanted my phone number, but I wouldn't give it to him, so he bribed my girlfriend, and she gave him my phone number.

I realized he wasn't all bad, you know, he was a lot of fun. And then we started hanging out together and he started buying my mother all kinds of gifts and presents.

We had sex for the first time when I was sixteen. He'd invited me over and was cooking food, and he started messing around with me. I told him I wanted to go home, but he started guilting me, telling me I owed him this once, that he knew it was my first time, but I shouldn't be scared, and that my mother wanted us to be together, that I didn't want to disappoint her. I was so humiliated and ashamed.

The thing was, I didn't even know I was pregnant before he did. He figured out I was pregnant and he told my mother and together they made all the arrangements for me to get married. He picked me up from high school one day and took me to the justice of the peace and that's where we got married. I cried like a baby. The judge said, "She don't look like she's real excited about being married." Augustine put his arms around me and said, "She's so excited, that's why she can't talk. She's just overjoyed." I never said, "I do." I never said "yes." I never opened my mouth because if I'd started crying I would have gotten hysterical and I wouldn't have been able to stop. And my mother told me, "Well, you're going to learn to love him."

When I got married in 1973, at first I tried doing what I had been used to seeing my mom do in her relationships. But my husband, he was older, and he quickly told me, "You will not yell at me. You will not curse at me. Those are not things you will do because that is not how a wife treats her husband."

My son Augustine Jr. was born nine months later when I was seventeen. He was born May 5, 1974. After that I had three more boys—Greg in '75, David in '76, and Lucky in '78. Basically one every year.

My marriage initially felt forced but not abusive. I did not love him, but I did respect him. He was very patient with me, and he was very good with the children. He worked two jobs and went to college to make sure me and the kids were provided for. He was my husband, but really he was my guardian. So year after year of him being patient with me, I developed a sense of love for him as a father and husband and as a man. Enough so that I moved to Nigeria with him.

Maryam and the boys spent the next nine years living in Nigeria with Augustine. She describes the years as mostly happy and filled with wealth and status beyond her imagination, complete with chauffeurs and multiple houses. In 1984, Maryam moved back to Dayton alone after what she describes as severe abuse and threats from Augustine. Her children then joined her in Dayton, where they lived in a car for a brief period before Maryam was able to fully get on her feet.

I ENDED UP IN THE HOSPITAL

I started going to Sinclair Community College, and after two years I got a degree in property management and real estate. Then I started working for the housing project, developing programs.

The first property that I bought of my own was a duplex in Dayton— three bedrooms on each side. My kids and I lived on one side and I rented the other side out. We stayed there for a few years and then I started buying other houses. In less than eight years, I'd bought dozens of properties. I had a major real estate investing business, Uloho Investment, with millions in assets. And during that time I raised my four boys and had three more kids, two boys and a girl—Adrian, Robert, and TaQuilla.

Unfortunately, I became public enemy number one with some detectives in Dayton. You see, detectives working in my neighborhood, they wanted to use some of my properties for sting operations. Some of the clients in my real estate business were "pharmaceutical dealers." Some of them were less than honorable citizens with criminal backgrounds, drug convictions, the whole nine yards. But some wanted to turn over a new leaf and help women with children get into their own homes or help senior citizens. I felt like that was a good thing and I was in support of it. The police wanted me to help raid these guys, and I wouldn't go along with it. So I became a problem.

In 2000, my business was raided. The police didn't find anything because I wasn't involved with drugs. But when they raided the office they left the building open. The property was robbed and vandalized. Everything was gone. I had a $15,000 printer. I had computers. It caused sort of a nervous breakdown for me. I didn't understand how the police could raid my place and then just leave the business unsecured. I started spiraling down and I ended up in the hospital. They put me on medication that had me not thinking straight. On TV I saw that Mardi Gras was coming up and I just booked a bus ticket. That was not like me. I had every intention of coming right back, but it didn't work out that way. In February 2001, I left my youngest kids with their brothers, who were in their thirties, and I went on a vacation to Louisiana.

I FELT LIKE I WAS AMONG SAVAGES

Maryam says that while on vacation in Louisiana, she met a man with whom she stayed during her trip. Because he is still fighting his case from prison, Maryam asked not to use his name. On March 3, 2001, the two were driving in Lafitte when they were pulled over by the police. The man was suspected of perpetrating an armed robbery of an armored car and was arrested. Maryam was also arrested and charged with armed robbery and aggravated battery. She pleaded innocent, and no witnesses put her at the scene of the crime. Though the armed robbery and battery charges were dismissed, Maryam was convicted of obstruction of justice for refusing to turn state's evidence. She was considered a two-time offender because of an aggravated assault charge she had previously pleaded guilty to in Ohio and sentenced to twenty-five years. She maintained her innocence throughout the trial.

When I was first arrested in 2001 and taken to Jefferson Parish Jail, it was a really scary experience for me. Now, here I am, this professional woman, never in my life have I been in a holding cell, or a holding tank, so I had no clue what to expect. One woman had lice. And these women would just steal each other's food. I felt like I was among savages. And if you go to sleep, I mean, only God knows what'll happen, so I couldn't sleep.

I was held in jail for eighteen months while I was waiting for a trial. It wasn't unusual. Some women were there five years before their trials. I was concerned about my younger kids back home, but I wasn't too worried about them because I knew their older brothers would take care of them. And my mom was in Dayton too. One problem was, the detectives from Ohio who had raided my business asked Jefferson Parish to deny bail and hold me. I couldn't get out on bail, so I just had to wait.

Inmates and guards would find ways to mess with me. One time the guards sent three women to fight me, and they stood on the other side of a window and watched. Another time six or seven guards kicked a mentally ill woman until I saw blood coming out of every hole in her head. They beat her unconscious, then took her to a room and strapped her down and kept her there. And these were supposedly Christian people. I was a die-hard Christian, but I actually turned to Islam partly because the guards and inmates who were Christians could be so cruel. I didn't want to be affiliated with it. So I converted there in jail. I needed peace, and I found it in Islam.

"TAKE THAT RAG OFF YOUR HEAD!"

I was convicted and sentenced in February 2003. Then a few months later, that's when I was moved from jail to prison, to St. Gabriel.[2] The guards came and got me early in the morning and told me to pack up my stuff. They chained me into the back of a van with no windows with some other prisoners. I felt like a slave on a slave ship.

And then when we got to the prison, I think there were about eight of us prisoners, and everybody rolled out and went to the building for

---

2. St. Gabriel is the Louisiana Correctional Institute for Women, located in St. Gabriel, Louisiana, seventy miles northwest of New Orleans.

the new commits. A new commit is a person who's just coming into the prison. So we get there, and I have on my hijab and the officers tell me to take the rag off my head. I said, "No, I can't do that. I'm Muslim. I don't know where I am. I don't know if there's men around here, and I'm not taking my scarf off." As Muslim women, we keep our heads covered, especially in the presence of men, because we're taught that you don't expose your beauty to strange men, you just don't do that. The guards weren't hearing any of that. They thought I was being rebellious.

So, they took all the other women to process them. I had to stay in a tiny corridor locked between two doors. I stood there for about two hours while they decided what they were gonna do with me. No one knew, so they eventually put me in handcuffs and shackles, very tight, and a woman guard ordered me to go with her. She was angry, but I didn't let it click with me, I just kept smiling. Actually, my first impression was that prison was the most beautiful place I'd ever seen in my life. They had the most beautiful plants, and trees, and flowers, and greenery, and the lawn was manicured perfectly. So I kept commenting on the flowers, and the guard was confused that someone could express joy around so much anger. She told me to just keep walking, and she put me in a cell by myself. I was in the hole.

I was the only woman in the prison who was Muslim, the only one who wore a headscarf. When I got out of solitary after those first two days, I took my scarf off to let them see I wasn't hiding anything. I didn't want confrontation. I told myself, *Mary, we're gonna try to get along here, we don't want anyone thinking we're terrorists, we're gonna try to keep the peace.* When I was in jail, I had a lot of trouble because of my headscarf with guards and also other inmates. I'd had to fight because of it. I didn't want to do that in prison. So for the moment I kept my scarf off.

But then a week later there was an incident when the prison deacon was handing out prayer books, and women were lining up for them. I got in line for a book, and when it was my turn, the deacon asked me if I was Christian or Muslim. I said I was Muslim, and he refused to give me a book. He said, "They're only for Christians, and you can't be both. You'll have to choose." So I walked down the hall, put my scarf back on, and from that day forward it was war.

There was a chaplain there that I'd met when I first went in. He looked like Santa Claus, he really did. But he hated me because of my religion. He told me, "Before I allow you to infest this compound with Islam, you will do your entire time in the hole on lockdown." He meant that. He went out of his way to try to get me locked up on many occasions.

When my family sent me my prayer rug, it went to the chaplain's office first. It was in his possession because he was the chaplain, rightfully so. He called me and gave it to me, and then he flipped the script and told the administration that I stole it, that he didn't give it to me, that I'd gone in his office and taken it. That was a serious infraction. But, the deacon happened to be there, and he saw everything that was going on. He stepped up to the plate and he says, "She didn't steal that. He gave it to her. I saw him give it to her." I was able to escape that one. This deacon protected me from the chaplain, but after the deacon got fired, I was at the mercy of the chaplain.

All the time, guards would see me with my scarf and just say, "Take that rag off your head, fool! Are you crazy? Are you stupid? You know you can't wear that rag here." I'd say, "No ma'am, I won't. Can't do that." And then they'd lock me up, put me in the hole. I'd be in for ninety days at a time. Then eventually they'd let me out, but it would happen again. The longest I'd stay out was two weeks or so.

In 2004, I was in general population and I got called to see the chaplain. He was with a guard. He told me that there'd been an accident, that my son had died. I didn't know who he was talking about, so I asked the guard. It was my first son, Augustine. He'd died in a motorcycle accident. I called my second son, Greg, and asked him to bury Augustine, since I couldn't be there. I was devastated. Losing a child is something you can't imagine, but not being able to be there with my family was a whole other level. I was so distraught for the first time, I asked to go to the hole, since

I didn't think I'd be able to control myself around other people. I stayed there a few days.

AFTER A WHILE, YOU START TO LOSE HOPE

I got used to the hole. I developed a mentality of survival. Once I realized these people were trying to tear me down mentally, I strengthened my mind. Only my body was imprisoned.

All of the buildings at St. Gabriel are named after zodiac signs. Like the Gemini building is for mentally challenged prisoners. The solitary cells, they're in Leo. The cells are a little bigger than a bathroom. Maybe nine feet long and six feet wide. The walls are made of cinderblock. The door is made of metal bars. On the left side is a bed made out of steel. On that steel bed is a mattress wrapped in thick, heavy plastic. The pillow is wrapped in the same thick plastic. There's a small window at the back, about six inches square with metal mesh on it, and a little round knob you'd turn to open it. In that same corner there's a steel sink and a steel toilet. Beside the toilet, a step or two away, is a steel desk fixed to the wall. On the floor is a steel stool. You can reach your hand out from your stool on one side of the room and touch the gate at the front. The fluorescent lights are always on. It was something I got used to. But not everyone could do solitude.

You had the hole. But then you had the hole inside of the hole. Even when you're in the hole, you were in a hallway with twenty other cells, so we could pass things from cell to cell through little openings, so we still had contact with each other. But there's another door at the end of the hallway with two cells that are separate that are even smaller, and they're under twenty-four-hour surveillance. A lot of the time if you get sent back there, you're back there by yourself. I could do the hole inside the hole, because my routine didn't change. But it does get to you. I hallucinated all the time in solitary. I'd see a little boy out the window. I'd think it was my first son, but I knew that couldn't be right, that he'd passed.

When my mind would start to slip, I'd hear him say things: "Mommy, stay strong mommy, I'm here mommy. I'm here for you." I didn't feel so alone when I saw him. I'd start to sing, sometimes I would dance. It would make me happier.

If you want to know how I felt, put yourself there. You put yourself there and you visualize that to be you. You visualize how you enjoy hugs and being treated warm and kind. But now put yourself inside a cell or a cage where the trash and the garbage can has more regard than you as a human being, and then you tell me how you feel. I mean, even the trash gets out, but you don't.

You don't see nobody, day after day. You get an hour on the rec yard, but if it's raining, you can't go out. You have ten minutes to take your shower and clean your room, take your trash out. Sometimes it's not enough time. Then you have to be back in your room, in your cell. If you don't make it, you get another report. If you get a report while you're already back there, you have to do an additional ninety days. Your world becomes consumed inside a six-by-nine prison cell, year after year after year. You're just in complete despair. After a while, you start to lose hope. You feel helpless. You just sit there, and you sit there, and you sit, day after day. What kind of life is that for a human being?

Women who were thrown into solitary, it affects us so horribly, mentally. A lot of them just went completely insane. You go to an animalistic level that I never witnessed before until I got to prison. One girl was eating her feces and throwing urine. She was a young girl. I saw her eat her feces then smear it all over her body and the walls and the bars. The guards restrained her and gave her Haldol and then just kept her sedated. Then they made other inmates go in and clean it up.

A lot of women didn't make it out of the hole. I remember one young girl in the hole, she was twenty-six. I'd known her mother too, and her mother got out, and I'd kind of promised to look after her girl. This girl would come to me sometimes, like when she was sick, or when she needed wisdom. Well, she ended up in the hole within the hole, and it was affecting her. When I was able to talk to her, she told me, "Ms. Mary, I can't take the hole anymore. It feels like the walls are closing in on me." She was talking in a way that I knew she was getting to a breaking point. So I asked a guard, "Could you let me go back there and take her cell and she can come in mine? She's at a breaking point and I don't think it's going to turn out good if she's back there by herself." And the guard said, "You don't tell me what to do, you don't run nothing around here! You think you're runnin' shit, but you don't tell me what to do. I'll check on her when I'm ready to check on her." So to spite me, she didn't even look in on her. And the girl hanged herself. She didn't survive. And I took that real, real hard.

I was angry. I was beyond the point of being able to respect any of the guards. I was saying things like, "Y'all murdered her, and you know you did. I told you all to go check on her and you refused out of spite." Because of that, they put me in the tank. The tank is worse than the hole inside the hole. In the tank, they strip you buck naked. They take all your clothes, put you in a smock, take your mattress and pillow, and give you a blanket/mattress thing and a roll of toilet paper. You can't make phone calls, can't get mail, you don't have communication with anybody. If they want to punish you real bad, they put you in there. And you know if you go in the tank, you might not come out alive. I went in not expecting to come out. I was in there two weeks. I kept my mind busy making flowers out of the toilet paper. My whole cell was filled with flowers. I was able to get a magazine from the guards, and I'd leach the ink out of the magazine pages to color my flowers. There were flowers all over the head and foot of my bed, the sink, the floor. That's how I made it through two weeks.

But that was the hardest time for me. I was losing hope of ever coming out. I was losing my will to live. I felt like I had no purpose, that my purpose for being on earth was over. I understood though that those were the kinds of thoughts I was being programmed to have, and that's when I kind of fought back to get control of myself. But that's what happens to the mind in isolation.

I didn't get many visits in prison because my family was so far away, but I got a visit once while I was in the hole from a Muslim sister, and I got letters while in solitary. The only reason I got out, I think, is my son Greg kept contacting the prison wanting to see me. They didn't have an official reason for keeping me in the tank, so that forced them to let me out.

I WANTED TO TAKE AWAY THEIR POWER OVER ME

It went on like that for years. The rule was women couldn't cover their hair at all for the first three years I was there, and so I spent a lot of time in the hole. Around 2010, it got to the point where I got a medical order from Earl K. Long hospital that the hole was detrimental to my health, and they could no longer put me in the hole. Then I spent more time in general population.

In the compound, in general population, I didn't get very close to my roommates—that's what cellmates were called. I had a routine, and I was disciplined. I'd get up early, I'd make prayer, read from my Quran, go get food, come back and do yoga and writing. Some of my roommates weren't so disciplined and wanted to spend their days talking about what this one was doing down the hall, and I wasn't interested in any of that. I didn't socialize much.

I didn't spend as much time in the hole after the first seven years. But things would happen. One time, a girl tried to take my Scrabble board, and so I fought her. Her friends joined in, and I grabbed a chair to defend myself. That's what I went to the hole for, for assault with a weapon, even though I was just defending myself.

Once I realized that this was the worst that they could do to me, I wanted to take away their power over me. I began to find solace inside solitary. I had my Quran and my prayer rug. I could also read other Islamic books, other books under the umbrella of religious artifacts. Otherwise, all there was to read was just paperback novels—all kinds of rubbish, but nothing to feed your brain.

SISTER HEARTS

I honestly think they let me out because I was so much trouble. I mean, I made it so they had to let people observe their religions, even the Wiccans. And let me tell you, the prison did not want no witches having a service. I was released April 21, 2013. Usually they give you $10 or $20 and a bus ticket, but they didn't do me like that. They put me in a van and chauffeured me to New Orleans, they wanted me out of their hair so bad. They brought me to this place called the Exodus House. It's a facility for people in substance abuse recovery and with mental disabilities. I was going there as a dorm mother. I was supposed to look out for the women in one of the buildings. My first night there, I go into the apartment. It's a four-bedroom apartment. It smelled like a dump and it was just as filthy. That's where I was supposed to stay. I said, "Okay, I'm going to deal with this because this is where I have to stay. I'm just going to make the best of it." I cleaned the place up, started cooking for everyone. I worked for my room and board. I was there three or four months. I would have stayed longer, but my supervisor started making advances on me, and when I turned him down, he told me it was time for me to go.

Reentry for women and senior citizens in this country sucks. Being free was overwhelming. I didn't know which way to go. I second-guessed myself. I didn't know how to think. I had been looking for apartments, but they were all so expensive. I wasn't making any money and I didn't have any money. I went to this apartment on Amelia Street where I'd seen a "For Rent" sign, but it was filthy. Roaches were everywhere, falling down in my hair when I opened the door. It smelled horrible. The window was broken. But when Exodus House put me out, that was where I went, since all I had in my pocket was $40 I'd made selling drinks and chips at Exodus House. I became a squatter in that apartment. I remember my first night. I slept on my clothes. And then I started cleaning and fixing up the place. When the owner found me there a month later, he was so impressed with how I'd fixed the place up he let me stay. And he paid me to fix up other apartments.

During that time, Imam Rafeeq NuMan and some Muslim brothers from my mosque used to come and get me on weekends. They would take me to a flea market across the river and drop me off. I would get things at the flea market and then resell them. I'm an excellent salesperson. And that's how I started making money again. It helped me pay my bills in my new apartment and get things that I wanted. At first I would go to thrift stores and buy stuff and I'd put it in a suitcase that had wheels and I'd roll it up and down the street, you know, how bag women do with the grocery cart? The only difference was I had a suitcase and inside that suitcase I would sell my little wares and I would get my profit and I kept turning—I'd flip that money and flip that money. And that's how eventually I built my business, Sister Hearts. Last year I did well over $150,000 in sales.

When I tell people I started my business with $40, they look at it like, *unbelievable*, but I really did. All the employees here are ex-offenders. If someone out of prison comes in and says, "I need a job," I'll do an interview on the spot. But if you just want a job, then this is not the place for you. It really isn't. Because a job means I'm gonna tell you everything you need to do. And you gonna do whatever I tell you to do. This is more of a program than a store. This organization is one that promotes mental and emotional rehabilitation and transition. It's about learning skills to take care of yourself after prison.

The name "Sister Hearts" comes from the way I felt about some of the other women in prison. I can't use the word "friends" because it's too loose. Those were the women who held me when I cried. When I was hungry, those were the women who stole food out of the kitchen for me to eat. When I was sick, those were the women who went to the medicine line and hid pills under their tongues to bring back to me. Those were the women who sometimes lied for me and stole for me and fought for me and fought with me and stood beside me, Black and white. Saying "sister heart," is very intense for me. Every time the words "sister heart" rings off someone's lips in this free world they're remembering my sister hearts in prison.

BRIAN NELSON

AGE: 53

BORN IN: Chicago, Illinois

INTERVIEWED IN: Chicago, Illinois

Before he was even a teenager, Brian Nelson was living a life straight out of The
Outsiders *or* West Side Story *as a member of the Simon City Royals street gang on
the North Side of Chicago in the late 1970s. In the early days, Brian's gang life largely
revolved around partying, trying to meet young women, and getting into fistfights
with rival gang members. When handguns started appearing on the scene, however,
a lifestyle that might have once been possible to romanticize from afar quickly turned
deadly. Brian became a "gunner" for his gang, and a close friend was murdered. The
violence escalated rapidly. In 1983, Brian was charged and convicted of murder, and
he was sentenced to twenty-six years in the Illinois Department of Corrections.*

*Once in prison, Brian was placed in various forms of solitary confinement,
but it wasn't until 1987, when he refused a prison warden's request to mediate*

an in-prison gang feud, that his nightmare really began. Brian was put on "the circuit," an unofficial program employed by prison officials for individuals they deemed to be most troublesome. Prisoners on the circuit were continuously shuffled to and from solitary confinement units across the state without any explanation or sense of where they were. Brian was also subjected to tremendous physical abuse on the circuit, including being used for live training exercises for Illinois correctional officers. The circuit was exposed in part by a federal civil rights lawsuit brought by Brian. He was taken off the circuit in 1993, although he continued to be subjected to other forms of solitary afterward. He was released from prison in 2010.

Brian now works as a paralegal for the nonprofit legal services organization Uptown People's Law Center in Chicago, where he regularly corresponds with people currently incarcerated in Illinois jails and prisons—many of them in solitary confinement. Brian speaks about his torture at the hands of the Illinois Department of Corrections, why many days he feels like he is worse off now than when he was released from prison seven years ago, and how answering prisoners' letters is a form of therapy.

DOING THE BASIC THINGS THAT KIDS DO

I think I was fourteen the first time I was put in solitary. I was locked in solitary because I was so small, they didn't think I could be around the other kids. I don't remember what that time was like. I've put walls up about that. Me and my doctor talk about it, and she worries for me, that the walls will come tumbling down, and I'll hurt myself remembering.

I was born in 1964 in Chicago and I grew up on the North Side. I have one brother, two sisters. My older brother is Roy, my older sister is Kelly, and my little sister is Wanda. And we're all one year apart. Mom and Dad had a handful. My dad, Robert, he worked at a printing company and my mom, Patricia, worked in the garden industry her whole life.

We grew up during the late sixties, early seventies doing the basic things that kids do—playing football in the street, softball in the parking lot, fast pitch against the brick walls. Went to St. Benedict for school. I'm white, and the neighborhood I grew up in was predominantly German,

Italian, and Irish. We had a huge house, big backyard. Back then, in our neighborhood, we all knew each other. And it was sort of a Saturday ritual when my mom made homemade pizza. A lot of our friends would be on the front porch stairs in the summertime waiting for it—everybody loved my mom's pizza.

In most of the neighborhoods, everybody hung out with each other on the street because there were a lot of middle-class families. There were maybe twenty-five kids just on one block that were all similar ages, and then next block over were other friends of all the same ages. We were riding bikes and playing tag in the alleys, on the garage roofs, around the train tracks and everything. We didn't have the worries of drive-bys or all the craziness. It was more innocent stuff.

I JUST STARTED GETTING IN TROUBLE

In elementary and middle school I was more the "sitting in the back of the class just watching" type of student. And then, I want to say sometime in sixth, seventh grade, in the mid-seventies, I screwed up and got involved with gangs. I started hanging around some guys in the neighborhood who were into the street life, sitting around in the park partying, chasing the girls.

I don't remember the first time I decided to hang out with those guys. We just grew up in a neighborhood, and they were part of it. I remember hanging out and some guys from another neighborhood came in messing around, and we just started a "rumble" fight. The rumbles were with these little baseball bats you'd get at Wrigley Field. That was one of my first big fights.

Soon I was more aware of there being different neighborhood gangs, the Bel-Airs and all these different street gangs. We were the Simon City Royals. Simon City was started from Simons Park. It's a park on the northwest side of Chicago. The Royals were another group, and they merged and formed the Simon City Royals.

One gang would be on one block and one would be on another block, and they would just fight over something stupid, but most of it was over a girl—"Hey, what did you say to my sister?" I was never the one doing the fighting.

At first, when I started hanging out with those guys, my parents had no idea. And gangs were not prevalent back then, there was no awareness of what wearing certain colors meant or that sort of thing. When I got arrested, cops explained to my mom and dad what I was involved in. And of course my parents tried to talk me out of it, but it was too late.

The gangs weren't racial. There was no racial identity with the organization or anything like that. Basically we just wanted to party, go to rock concerts, smoke our weed, do our acid, and hang out. But every once in a while, these other groups would come in and try to intimidate us, or tell us we couldn't do this or that, or beat us up at school.

There were times when we were kids that the cops shut up a park where we would fight a different gang. They'd know there was a feud going on between the two streets. So the police would say they're gonna set up a football game with the two gangs. And basically they were just setting it up for a fight. But there's no weapons involved, and everybody just beats the crap out of each other and gets it out of their system. Everybody's just sitting on the ground all whipped and tired, ready to sort of laugh about it afterwards.

Winter was like a truce period because nobody wanted to be outside. Chicago gets mighty cold in the winter. And there were times we all partied together, go to the lake and go smelt fishing together, drink beer, race cars and motorcycles.

IT WAS A GAUNTLET

It was about this time when guns started coming into play a lot more in Chicago. In the late seventies and eighties. One minute we were rumbling, and the next minute there were guns everywhere. I don't know what happened. Maybe guys returning from Vietnam.

I started holding the guns. At my age—twelve, thirteen—if I got caught, it'd just be a night in the police station or juvenile hall, not prison. So all the older adult guys would say, "Here, hold this gun for me." I did what they said.

I was maybe five foot two, maybe a hundred pounds. They called me "Mousey" because I was so little, and I was the last person you'd expect to be walking around doing this stuff. The first time I shot a gun I was the little kid sitting in the tree holding the guns in a bag. My job was to drop the guns down from the tree when a certain group came into the neighborhood, and we knew they were coming and expecting 'em. Instead of me dropping the guns down, I took one and just opened up on the car, just shot the car up. I know three people got shot. Nobody died. I was maybe thirteen years old.

It was weird because the girls in the neighborhood were attracted to that stupidity. And then it was really disgusting because it was like you became a hero for this stuff. I look at it now like, *Wow, were we idiots . . .*

Within a week of the first shooting it got more serious, 'cause one of the older guys was like, "Okay, well, we know he'll pull the trigger, now send him on a mission." And they drove me into a certain neighborhood and said, "Hey, walk up there real close and just open up on everybody." I did not point the gun at the group I was supposed to, I actually shot at the ground. I was thinking, *What am I doing?* The very next day they took me again and said, "No, no, this time do it right." And so I did it right the next time. I would've been violated if I didn't. Back then for a violation you walked the line. It was a gauntlet, and everybody beat the crap out of you.

I think I was fourteen the first time the police caught me carrying a gun. They just stopped me and it was like, "What is that?" I had a pistol sticking out my back pocket. Just walking down the street like it was nothing. They arrested me and I had to spend the night in the Audy Home before they cut me loose to my parents.[1]

---

1. The Cook County Juvenile Temporary Detention Center, popularly referred to as

Around that time my parents separated. And the weird part is they were separated, but my dad lived upstairs after a while. My mom busted her butt to raise us, and put us all through Catholic schools and did everything. My dad helped as much as he could, but then things changed because he developed really, really bad arthritis and bone problems, had trouble working, and became an alcoholic.

At that point, I was also just not listening. I thought I knew the answers, and I didn't know shit. Walking around with dumb people just made it dumber for me.

"YOU'RE TOO SMALL FOR GEN POP"

It got real serious after another gang killed our friend, Tommy. We went for revenge. We were jumping on them every time we saw them. We were so mad, and it just escalated from there.

We were all at funerals wearing gang sweaters, gang T-shirts. I know that had to piss off the parents because their son had just died because of our stupidity.

I got picked up by the police all the time, usually for disorderly conduct. There was one time, swear to God, I got picked up like six or seven times in one day. We would get taken to the police station, and then our parents would pick us up and we'd go back out.

Then I ended up going to juvenile hall. The police alleged that I tried to shoot a cop. The facility was St. Charles. It was a very different world than the Audy Home. At the Audy Home, it was more quiet. There's a dayroom with a TV, everyone out there at the same time. But at St. Charles, it is a big building, with no one really watching over. A lot of

---

the Audy Home, after Superintendent Arthur Audy, who ran the juvenile hall in the 1940s, is a massive juvenile detention facility that at the height of its population was referred to as "the largest juvenile jail in the world." Facing widespread allegations of deteriorating conditions and staff abuse, it was the subject of numerous lawsuits, including a class action lawsuit that resulted in a federal court monitor from 1999 until 2015.

chaos, a lot of fights. The "St. Charles Shuffle" is what they used to call it—kids learning how to fight.

Like I mentioned, at fourteen, I was way smaller than other guys my age. So when I was sent to juvenile, one of the first things that happened is that I was put in a cell by myself. For my own protection, the guards said. I felt shocked that they locked me up in solitary, but they're like, "We can't let you out. Look how little you are, you're too small for gen pop." And I'm like, "So you're locking me in a room by myself? I didn't do nothing wrong." It was a solitary cell—ad seg.

I was in solitary for almost two months. I know I couldn't see out the window 'cause the window was up way high, so I had to stand on the bed. And I was too little to sit there. There was a window on the door, but all I could see was the bathroom.

I remember scratching my name into a wall, pacing the floor. You remember when you were a kid how you used to fold a piece of paper to make the little triangle football? I remember doing that and flicking that around the room, playing football. And then just doing little things like that to pass the time. At first I didn't even have a book, and then I finally got one—it was a Louis L'Amour book and I still remember it. Louis L'Amour writes a lot of historical westerns, but the one that I got was a little bit different, it was like a sailor, the guy from England getting in trouble coming over here to America. And I think I read it three times when I was there.

After two months, they released me to my parents. So I got out for a while and I don't know how long it was, but then I got arrested again, and I ended up eventually at a detention facility called Valley View. That's where I first had my interactions with big street gangs and the African American street gangs from the South Side of Chicago and all of that.

I was at Valley View on and off, maybe eight, nine months. Every time they turned around I would jump the fence and run away. I'd get all the way back to Chicago, and they'd pick me up in the neighborhood.[2]

2. The Illinois Youth Center facility, also referred to as "Valley View," was located in Kane County, in the western suburbs of Chicago.

The neighborhood cops knew immediately who I was. They'd see me and just say, "Let's go." There was a lot of times my mom and dad didn't even know I'd escaped and been sent back! But after nine months or so, I was sent home and stayed out for a while.

I SAW MORE DRUGS IN STATESVILLE
THAN I EVER IMAGINED I'D SEE

I finally went to adult prison when I'd just turned seventeen. A fence got shot after he ripped off some guys who brought him some stolen goods. He got murdered, and it was alleged that me and another guy went in and executed him. I got twenty-six years.

The first prison I went to was Statesville in 1982, '83, right around the new year. So, I'm on the bus and I'm feeling shock. I'm thinking, *What is this gonna be like? Where am I going? What am I gonna face?*

When I walked in it was a shock. I mean a shock like you could not imagine. There was no whites, anywhere, except the guards with the guns. It was mostly African American, maybe some Latinos. The first people I met, one was named Bo Diddley and the other one's name was Skull. Both of them had to be six-four to six-six, 250 pounds pure muscle, like, "What you be, white boy?" I'm like, *Oh my god, what did I do?*

The way Statesville is organized, it's a big, round house. There is a single tower in the middle of the cell house. And everybody's out of their cells walking around. The only guard I saw was at the front door and in the tower. And they assigned me to my cell. I was put up in cell 452.

The whole cell house was like the Muslim gangs and the large African American gangs. And, Statesville at the time, everybody said it was run by the gangs. Really the administration used the gangs to run the prison.

There was a guy there, in 1983 or '84, he got caught with nine guns in his cell. This is in prison. *Inside the prison.* And one of them was a shotgun! The administration basically allowed it. And I'm like, *What the fuck did I do to get put in here?* I saw more drugs in Statesville than I ever imagined I'd see in my life. And I had never been exposed to heroin, cocaine, or any of that kind of hard stuff. It was all over Statesville.

I got a job assignment working in an M&M shop, the mechanical and maintenance shop. While I was working there, two guys got in a fight, and they stabbed each other. We were there when the fight happened and all got put in controlled seg, which is solitary. It was a special unit above the hospital. When a serious stabbing or something happens, or a murder, that's where they put the guys while the investigation goes on.

The cells there were crazy. They're roughly twenty feet high, maybe about eight feet across, made of old limestone with a huge steel door. And it's like a soundproof box. They call it "controlled seg" because they control everything about you.

We didn't even have our property. Only thing we had was a bar of soap and toothpaste. At one point I had memorized every ingredient on a tube of toothpaste. I just paced back and forth in my cell. All day. No showers, no yard, we were just literally forgotten. We were fed, but there was no paperwork, so there were no rules saying when we'd get out to the yard, when we'd get moved to regular segregation or anything. We were just left there. So all we could do was just pace or sleep. We were in our cells twenty-four hours a day. Never got out.

Finally, the assistant warden came through, going cell to cell, talking to each person in seg about, "Why are you here?" We're like, "We don't know."

"How long have you been here?"

We said, "Almost two months." And we got out within like ten minutes. He's like, "What the fuck?" It turns out that the two guys who got in a fight came back from the hospital and admitted we weren't involved. Somebody never did any paperwork on me and the two other guys, and we were just forgotten for about forty-five days. The administration had just forgotten about us, and we were left in a cell.

July Fourth weekend, 1984—I'd been out of solitary for a while by this time—I escaped from Statesville. Me and two other guys built a ladder with scraps from the M&M shop, climbed over the wall, got away, then got caught. And I was again placed in solitary confinement for a brief period of time.

This segregation was nothing compared to controlled seg. You had your TVs, your books, your radio. You talked to the guys in the cell next to you, you went to the yard together. The prison had some guys work the seg units as workers who were not in seg—cleaning the gallery, serving food, what have you. And the guys who worked the gallery sat in front of your cell, and they played chess with you right through the door, the open bars. So it was like, *This is not too bad.*

I did maybe nine months in Statesville seg and then they shipped me to Pontiac, in the middle part of the state. I was immediately put in solitary confinement because I was an escape risk. In Pontiac at the time, solitary confinement was with death row. I was put with guys who all had death sentences. It was very hard 'cause they didn't want to talk to me—I wasn't one of them. They didn't know if I was a stool pigeon or what. It was just a whole different world.

At this point I was pacing a lot. Getting depressed and anxious all the time. Just trying so hard to keep track of time. When you lose track of time it gets harder. I don't know how to explain it.

A SORT OF PSYCHOLOGICAL EXPERIMENT

After four months in solitary at Pontiac I got released into general population. And I was the only white guy in the entire general population—four thousand inmates and I'm the only one in pop. Again, mostly African American, but more Latinos than Statesville.

In general pop, I got caught carrying two homemade shanks. They brought a new criminal case against me for that, for having weapons. My defense was, "I was the only white inmate." At the time, the gangs were trying to extort me because I wasn't associated with the big street gangs. And the jury found me not guilty, basically because they believed that I needed the shanks for self-defense. I mean, even all the guards were like, "Hey, we carry a knife, Nelson's the only white kid in there, he should have one too." After I beat the case, and after they immediately transferred me out of Pontiac back to Statesville for about ten months or so in general pop, they sent me to Menard for the first time.[3] This would have been around 1987.

That year, there was a riot between the Black and white gangs. Big riot. Approximately two weeks later, the warden called me to the office and told me they wanted me to find out what the issues were. They're like, "Both sides. We want you to talk to them to find out what's going on." I'm like, "Ain't no way in hell I'm gonna do that." That makes me a stool pigeon and puts my life in danger. I refused to do it.

Because I wouldn't be their informant or mediate a gang war, they put me on "the circuit." I didn't know what it was at the time, but it was sort of a psychological experiment. Being on the circuit meant I was constantly being transferred. I would eat one meal in one facility, the next in a different prison, and the third in a whole new facility. I was being driven around the state every day, and after every meal I just got in the car and they took me somewhere else. I was moving three times a day! Every time I got done eating, I'd get right back in a car and keep going. That went on for three months.

After that, it changed, I'd be moved like once a week, every couple of days, every two weeks. For the first four or five years, I never stayed longer than thirty days in any prison. At any time day or night they'd say, "Let's go," and put you in a car and you're gone. My family rarely knew where I was. I was let out of my cell maybe an hour a week.

Part of what I came to understand later was that they were moving us to different prisons so that the tactical teams could practice on us.

---

3. Menard Correctional Center is a maximum-security prison holding about 3,500 people that was first opened in 1878. It sits on the Mississippi River in the southwestern part of Illinois on the border with Missouri.

They were using "circuit riders" to train these new teams that they were creating as they were opening up all these new prisons because "truth in sentencing" was filling up the prisons.[4] We were their guinea pigs.

Here's one of the games they would play. You'd come in new to a prison, and they'd give you a strip search in the shower. Toward the end of the strip search, one of the correctional officers would make a disrespectful comment like, "Turn around and show me that cute little ass on you, boy." I'd say, "What?" But it was all a setup. The cell right across from the shower had like eight officers in riot gear waiting for this. As soon as I said, "What?" the officer pulls the shower door open, and these guys run in and beat me up because I was "refusing to follow a direct order." I was beaten so bad. I was beaten, wow, maybe sixteen different times while I was handcuffed and with leg irons on. One time I was beaten and woke up in an outside hospital three days later. Yeah, I deteriorated. I became, at times, violently insane. *When does this stop? When does this stop?* And nobody ever had an answer for me.

I got out of my cell one hour a week. That was it. There was no "twenty-three and one." There was six days of complete lockup and I got one hour out a week and that was for my yard and shower. It all had to be done within an hour, and then I'm locked back up. I wouldn't have had access to books if it wasn't for my mom sending them to me, and sometimes I got them, sometimes I didn't. But she was always sending me packages of books. There's books I've read thirty, forty times, just because I needed something to keep my brain active. There were a lot of times, my mom and sister would drive to a prison to visit me and I just wasn't there no more by the time they got there.

There were COs who showed me humanity and disapproved of the way I was being treated. There's a few of them like, "Man you need to sue

---

4. "Truth in sentencing" refers to legislation popular in many states and incentivized by the federal government from the mid-1980s through the 1990s that aims to abolish or curb parole so that people convicted of a crime must be incarcerated for all or most of the prison term to which they have been sentenced.

and find out why they're doing this." I started doing the hunger strikes to demand a copy of the rules for the program I was in. And officers would tell me, "There are no rules for this program. This program doesn't exist. You're not here." And I'm like, "What do you mean?" They would tell me point-blank I was not allowed to be in their prisons because I'm a high-escape risk. I was a maximum-security prisoner. I was not supposed to ever be in a minimum-security prison.

In Danville Correctional Center they built a solid steel box. And I mean solid steel, the entire cell. So cold in the wintertime, if your skin touched it, it was like being burnt. And that's where they kept me for like a month at a time. When I went to Danville this was the special cell for me. And those other guys on the circuit would be put in there too. Every prison was different. There were no rules for this kind of solitary confinement at all. Every one was different. Some places called it "the circuit," some places called it "solitary," some called it "maximum-security detention," some called it "temporary disciplinary rooms."

During that whole time I was probably transferred like thirty times a year, all over the state—East Moline, Dixon, Hill, Danville, Lincoln, Logan, Taylorville, Graham, Centralia, Illinois River, Big Muddy, Shawnee, maybe some that I missed. I would file grievances, hundreds of them, and not one of them would ever call it the circuit or anything. That's why I was shocked that they finally answered the grievance saying I was part of a psychological experiment for more than seven years. That was at Shawnee Correctional Center. I think somebody just screwed up in putting it in black and white.

I started reading *The Prisoners' Self-Help Litigation Manual*. To me that's one of the best books, next to the Bible, that's ever been written. It taught me so much. I think I've read it, cover to cover, maybe ten times and looked at it fifty or more. Over and over I read that book. Started taking paralegal courses, started filing lawsuits to find out what this circuit program was. All these people say I'm a circuit rider. But there's no rules or programs for the circuit program. I only got off it because of a lawsuit settlement. I filed that case myself, and then they appointed a lawyer to represent me and joined it with a case from another guy, Anthony Wilson.

Eventually we went through three days of full trial in Chicago. I'm on the stand and allegedly everyone is all done asking me questions, and I turned to the judge, Judge Zagel, and I said, "Judge, how come no one is asking me about the circuit?" And then we ended up talking, just me and the judge, for like two hours about what they were doing to me on the circuit. It was like I was the court's witness. And he was appalled! Everyone, even our lawyers, thought we were making it up, but we didn't have to make it up. It was just that evil, what they were doing.

The DOC made a deal. After seven and a half years on the circuit, they took me off, gave me a bit of money, and left me alone for a little while. About the same time, there was another guy, Tommy Ortiz, also on the circuit, who got like $750,000 in damages because they beat him so bad. It got national attention. We had exposed the circuit, and they modified it so that guys could stay for six or seven months in one place before being transferred. They added access to a law library. They stopped most of the physical abuse, the tactical team training. Guys could go to the yard together sometimes. Basically, not *so much* solitary confinement no more.

A HUNDRED DEGREES IN THIS BOX

After the lawsuit settlement, I finally got off the circuit and was in general population for a while. Then they sent me down to New Mexico, sent me out of state, never found out why. I was in a minimum-security prison. I made the officers' uniforms. This sounds weird for being in prison, but I finally knew what it was like to have a semi-life, I guess. I had a job. I was able to go to church. I was able to have visits. Even though I was in New Mexico and my parents were in Illinois, I was able to talk to my mom when I wanted, for the first time since I was locked up. I spent a year, maybe two, in New Mexico.

Then, in March 1998, all of a sudden, US marshals come running into the prison, weapons drawn. They chained me to a dolly cart, put me in a van, put me on an airplane in Albuquerque, and transferred me to Tamms.[5]

At Tamms I had nothing. I was in a gray box, and there was one time in Tamms where I was in a cellblock all by myself. Just left on B1 by myself, no property—all I got is two pairs of underwear, two pairs of socks, one jumpsuit, and shower shoes—and they would take my weight every week because I got so small. I mean I looked like I'd given up. I had no appetite. Nothing. I just wanted it to end.

It was like, *I just can't do this, I can't do this no more.* I mean, my whole life you've put me by myself, I'm just tired. I think it might've been six months before they forced me to see a mental health professional. I might've been there nine months before they started putting me on medication. And I was tired of life. I was tired of being in a box by myself.

I spent my last two years in prison begging them for help, "My out date is coming, I need to get ready, I need help." And instead of helping me they kept giving me more and more medication. As my release date got closer, I got transferred out of Tamms to Menard, and they wrote me a disciplinary report saying that I was a threat to the safety and security of Menard. And they put me in a building by myself in Menard for my last twenty days in prison. No soap, no toothpaste, no shower, no yard, no nothing. A hundred degrees in this box, and that's how I spent my last month in prison.

I was on five types of psychotropic medication. But when I walked out I had no medication, no prescription, nothing. So not only am I shocked by being out, I have to cold turkey from medication, and I'm scared shitless out here.

---

5. Tamms Correctional Center, located in Illinois, was a supermax prison with five hundred solitary confinement beds that opened in 1998. After years of allegations of brutal conditions, lawsuits, and a public campaign to close the prison, Tamms was shuttered in 2013.

I DON'T FEEL LIKE I BELONG OUT HERE

I got out June 29, 2010, and I was terrified. My mom drove up to get me. I was basically a caveman going into society.

The trip home, I had been out maybe fifteen, maybe ten minutes, we stopped to get ice cream, and a guy walked in behind me, and I started shaking. I became so scared and enraged just because he had gotten in line behind me. And my mom was looking at me like, *What the fuck is wrong with you? What did they do?*

In solitary, there were times where I completely lost track of time. I have maybe a hundred watches now. I've got some very expensive watches, but most of them are ten-, twenty-dollar watches. I have one watch on, I have a pocket watch, and I have the clock on my phone. I have time everywhere around me, because I'm afraid of losing track of time again.

I'm worse off now than when I first got out. There's a lot of days that I don't feel like I belong out here. Talking to other solitary survivors, they feel the same way. It's real messed up to feel like that. Like, it's not our world out here. I wish I could have like just a week without it coming up, without a nightmare, without that garbage.

I've been seeing a psychologist regularly for four or five years now and also talking to a trauma specialist. The sad part is, the doctors out here don't know what to do for me. They don't know any ways to treat it. They know how to treat the guys inside in prison, but they don't know what to do for me out here.

Out of most of the other guys I know who came out of solitary, I'm the only one who has a job. They are on social security for post-traumatic stress. They can't handle working around people, or being around people.

I hear people say, Let's save the whales, let's make sure the doggies don't get hurt. Well, what about the human beings? You know? If you can't sit in your bathroom for three days with none of your gadgets, you can't understand what they did to us. I did something wrong, I deserved to go to prison. But I didn't deserve to be tortured.

I once tried to write a book about it. And when I read what I wrote, I was disgusted at myself. Because I was talking to the cell *like it was a person*. And how lonely the cell has to be without me there. I was shocked that I had even written something like that. It is a gray box, a cement box. *It is not a person*. But the sad part is, when I was in there, it was. It was my chess partner. When I was talking to myself, I would be talking to the cell. I'd be like, *What, you're not going to answer me now?* It's screwed up, but it was my reality.

What is helping me though is reading prison letters all day and trying to figure out a way to respond and help the guys inside. I read sometimes a hundred a week, sometimes two, three hundred. I track the trends in all the prisons.

Sure, they closed Tamms, but now they have mini-Tamms in the medium prisons—Pontiac, Menard—where people are still in solitary. The conditions are maybe slightly better, but it is still horrible. Torture. All that's gonna stop is they're not gonna call it solitary confinement. They're just gonna change the name. Like *the circuit, temporary housing, maximum-security housing, the SHU*, they'll just keep changing the name and have it hid somewhere in the system.

It is sorta like my own therapy, doing this work and answering letters from family members and people on the inside. There are times when I want to stop doing the work, but I can't stop. I've got friends in that box. I'm not going to forget them.

AARON LEWIS

BORN IN: Stamford, Connecticut

INTERVIEWED IN: Northern Correctional Institution,
Suffield, Connecticut

When Aaron Lewis was growing up in the streets of New Haven, Connecticut, in the 1990s, Connecticut's prison population was ballooning.[1] A prison population of six thousand in 1986 grew to sixteen thousand in 1996 as a result of the "war on drugs" and other tough-on-crime policies. Instead of reforming those policies, Connecticut—like a lot of other states—simply started building more prisons, especially harsh "supermax" prisons like Northern Correctional Institution that soon became synonymous with abusive and inhumane conditions.

In 1999, when he was just a teenager, Aaron was arrested and incarcerated

---

1. Narrator's name and other identifying details have been changed at his request.

at the height of this prison boom. In 2000, Aaron arrived at Northern while he was still awaiting trial. He was seventeen. Aaron would spend ten of the next twelve years confined there, the vast majority of that time in solitary confinement. In these conditions, litigation became a means of resistance and survival. Though Aaron had never done well in school and was without a high school diploma, he taught himself the law and filed and won his own cases, and for years he's assisted other prisoners with their legal challenges.

At thirty-five, Aaron's spent half his life behind bars. He faces the prospect of remaining in prison until at least 2035. We first meet Aaron in the fall of 2016 at MacDougall-Walker Correctional Institution in Suffield, Connecticut. The room, past two steel sliding doors that slowly and loudly grind open and close, is small and nondescript. We sit at a metal table bolted to the ground.

A LOT OF THINGS THAT HAPPENED
IN MY PAST, I JUST FORGOT

The only thing I remember about my childhood is getting in trouble with the law. Everything else, I don't remember none of that. It's probably there, I just don't remember it because I pushed all of that out.

That's part of what comes from being confined. When you're numb to emotions, your memories of emotional experiences start to fade away. You suppress them and you start being bitter and you care less about things. The more I became bitter, the more I pushed things out my mind like family, childhood, friends, and all that. I haven't been in tune with my emotions, save for anger, in eighteen years.

This numbness blocked me from revisiting my childhood days when I felt happiness, joy, love, appreciation. I only remember things from my past that I could identify and associate with what I'm feeling in my present. I figure this is why I could remember how frustrated and pained I felt growing up. Being bitter and fixated on such bitterness, pain, and hate, I haven't focused on anything that makes us human. This fixation accounts for why my memory of my childhood is a blur.

Actually, my vision of most of my adolescence is a blurred one. I'm pretty sure there are happy days in my family history growing up; I just don't remember them.

I was born in Stamford, Connecticut, on April 18, 1983. My mother's name is Connie. My father's name is Aaron. I really don't remember nothing about growing up in Stamford, but that's where all my family is from. All my pain comes from growing up in New Haven and Rockview Circle. That's the projects. That's where I basically grew up.

I've got five sisters, and I'm the youngest, the only boy. My aunt's kids came to stay with us for a while. My cousin, Winter, she's like another sister. Then my mother had a boyfriend and his daughter, Serena, was with us for a period of time too. So, it was a household full of girls, and that basically drove me crazy. My other little cousin, Iroquois— that's my aunt's son—he was always under me. He was a year younger than me. Everything I did, he wanted to do. I always treated him like a little brother. I knew he looked up to me.

At our place in New Haven, my mother was harder on me than she was on my sisters. She was more punitive with me because she said she was scared. I don't know what she was scared of. Probably growing up in the projects, and me being her only boy. One day I remember, when I was littler than twelve, I told her, "I'm going into the army." She said, "*Hell* no. I'm not losing my only son." Growing up, we all had chores and my sisters would try to get out of doing them. They'd try to get me in trouble because they knew my punishment would be to clean the whole house. So it was a battle and my mother always took their side.

My father didn't live with us. He lived all the way in Stamford. He was a man of few words. I would see my father whenever my mother took us to Stamford, which probably was a few times a year. Besides giving me life and money, he never gave me too much of anything else. I really don't remember my mother like that during my childhood. The only thing I remember of my mother growing up was that she was associated with discipline. Which meant "trouble." I could only remember my mother in the times I got into trouble. Since I associated her with trouble as a kid, I tended to want to avoid her. So I did. As much as I could, I avoided her growing up. I had more of a mother–son relationship with my aunt Amy. She passed away of a heart attack from complication with diabetes in March. It hurt me when my aunt passed away. It still hurts me to this day. It will hurt me for the rest of my entire life.

I got in trouble in school some. My first time in juvenile detention was for something petty. I had a BB gun and I let one of my friends see the BB gun, coming from basketball practice at school. We wouldn't let another kid at school that we weren't friends with see the BB gun, so that person told on us. So I got a "facsimile of a firearm" charge and got sent to juvenile detention for a month, waiting for resolution of the BB gun charge.

Juvenile, for me, wasn't that bad. I've always been a little taller for my age, so I wasn't really vulnerable to other kids based on my size. I was more protecting the vulnerable from the bullies. It didn't feel like being in jail. But you don't realize how much you miss home until you go to juvenile. At home, you always feel like you want to get away. But you go to juvenile, you feel like, *Home is better than this shit right here.*

For the BB gun charge, I was sentenced to some probation time and twenty-four hours of community service. I had to wash the windows of the New Haven Juvenile Courthouse. My mother made sure I did that community service. After I did the community service, I went to school, and then afterward I'd be running the streets with my friends, especially my best friend. We did everything together. Everything. He got me smoking weed. He had brothers. All his brothers, they were like my brothers.

We moved out of the projects to Sherman Avenue in New Haven in '97, but I'd still go to my best friend's house in the projects. You couldn't separate me and him. We'd do little petty crimes. We'd steal car stereos and sell them for $40 and buy weed with it. We'd go get some Subway, we'd eat, and we'd get high. Flirt with some girls. All that came to an end quick because my best friend moved out of the projects to some-where else in town.

I was away from home for a while in the summer of '97. One night I stayed out too late, and I didn't want to go back home because I didn't want to get in trouble for having stayed out all night. I was planning to go back and face the punishment, but the next day I was like, *nah.* Then it became two days, three days, then I felt like I couldn't go home. I just stayed out and lived with friends.

The police picked me up in Fair Haven. I was with somebody else who was selling drugs. When they picked me up, I wasn't holding any money or drugs, but they had me down as an "86," and I asked the officer, "What's an 86?" He was like, "A runaway." *A runaway? I ain't a runaway.*

I called and asked my mother if she called the cops and said that I ran away. She was like, "Yeah, yeah." I told her that I didn't run away. She was like, "You didn't come home. You haven't been home all summer. What am I supposed to think?" I'm like, "Alright, Mother, you win. If you want to put it that way, I guess so." But that was the first time I real-ized I wasn't home all summer.

JUST SEND ME THEN AND GET IT OVER WITH

The cops knew that I wasn't holding drugs when they picked me up. I had no money on me or anything. But the other kid that I was with at the time had been caught many times with drugs. When the cops brought me in, they wanted me to say the drugs were the other kid's. But I wouldn't say what they wanted. So they took me down for conspiracy to possess narcotics.

I was in detention for four months, and my lawyer, he just kept say-ing, "They're thinking about sending you to Long Lane."[2] I said, "Just

---

2. Long Lane School was a juvenile correctional facility for boys and girls age eleven through sixteen located in Middletown, Connecticut. It originally opened as the "Connecticut Industrial School for Girls" in 1870 and functioned as a home for girls in state custody for a century, housing both children incarcerated for crimes and

send me then and get it over with." He said, "Alright." And so I entered Long Lane on December 21, 1997. My mother was pissed because they didn't ask her about anything. She didn't even know that I pleaded guilty. The police had to tell her. They gave me eighteen months.

At Long Lane, they didn't call us inmates. They called us "YJOs," youthful juvenile offenders. Or "SJOs," serious juvenile offenders. Or they just called us by our names.

My time in Long Lane was—I cannot describe it. It was difficult. All of us in there just felt like it was preparing us for Manson Youth Institution as the next step, even though none of us had been to MYI.[3] We just heard stories. If you were being kept at Long Lane, you could earn passes to leave the grounds or get furloughs. But I didn't want any passes, I didn't want any furloughs. I just wanted to do my time, get this over with, and go home.

We lived in cottages on the grounds. At that time, Long Lane was like a college campus. You had dorms, a medical center, a swimming pool. We could move around where we wanted, but if we got in trouble, the officers there would serve us with misconduct reports. Sometimes with a report we'd get confinement to our rooms. If it was serious, then the officers would take us to what was known as "the unit"—isolated confinement.

I was in and out of the unit, usually thirty days in the unit. If you were in a unit, you'd wear a jumper. You were in a cell by yourself, and you cleaned your own cell. The windows were glass with a mesh grate on the inside. You could hear the kids outside—it wasn't like soundproofed or nothing. In the unit you came out four hours a day to go to the gym and class—two hours in the morning, two hours at night.

---

children taken by the state due to perceived home neglect. Long Lane became coed and something closer to a detention and custody facility in the 1970s. After decades of building decay—and the investigation of a suicide of a fifteen-year-old girl in 1998— the facility was closed in 2003.

3. Manson Youth Institution is a detention facility for males ages fourteen to twenty-one located in Cheshire, Connecticut.

The majority of the people at Long Lane were Black. There was only one white kid there that I can remember. There was one Asian guy, that was my boy. The rest were Black and Puerto Rican. All the staff was Black, with only a few white people, like the chaplain, the director. And the administrative staff—case workers, case managers—they were mostly white. The teachers were all white women. The substitute teachers were Black—like they wasn't good enough to be regular teachers, right? We never seen the warden. The security force was mostly white guys.

I remember once I got into a scuffle with this officer. I was coming from the bathroom and I think I opened somebody's door to look in, and the officer jumped on me from behind. I'm like, *What are you doing?* He banged my head on the ground. And they sent me to the unit for that. I don't know what his problem was.

After the scuffle, I had a big knot on my head from where he banged me against the ground. I'd had a staff member once tell me, "Listen, whenever they do something wrong, write them up." So, after my scuffle with the officer, I wrote a grievance that he'd banged my head against the ground. It was a big investigation and they even called my mother in. I think they called her in to tell me to withdraw the grievance. That's what she said—"Stop writing these people up. Stop being mad." It worked, though. I got out of the unit early because they found the officer hadn't acted the right way. That experience kinda prepared me for some of the bigger fights down the line. I had learned the process of filing grievances.

I DIDN'T LIKE MY CELLIE ANYWAY

Aaron was released from Long Lane in June 1999, and returned to live at home. Six months later, on December 13, 1999, sixteen-year-old Aaron was arrested in connection with a shooting that occurred several days earlier outside the apartment complex where his family lived. One man died in the shooting. Authorities placed him into Walker Correctional Institution, a maximum-security adult prison, to await trial.[4]

---

4. The MacDougall-Walker Correctional Institution, in Suffield, Connecticut, is a maxi-

Aaron was ultimately convicted of manslaughter in the first degree and a weapons charge, and sentenced to thirty-five years. He continues to maintain his innocence.

Walker was a new experience for me, and I remember spending some time in segregation there. The first ticket I caught was because I didn't get out of the shower in time. I was showering and the guards said, "Recall." I didn't know what that meant. I guess I was supposed to get out, but I didn't. I get out eventually and the guards said, "You're getting a ticket." I didn't even know what that meant. I said, "So?" I didn't know what none of that meant. Then my cellie told me, "Ticket means they are going to write you up."[5] And I am still like, "So? What's that going to do?" It meant I was going to be confined to my cell.

There was another time, after getting in a fight with a white gang. In New Haven, where I was growing up, there wasn't no gangs. If there was, I didn't know, because I wasn't with the gangs growing up. It was just us, me and my friends, doing what we do. And I didn't know nothing about Aryan Brotherhood, white supremacy. The only thing we heard about was the Ku Klux Klan, because we learned about them in school and in my projects. We had these community leaders, they'd come and show us films of how it was in the sixties, and the KKK and all that. That's it. So Walker was a brand-new experience.

One day me and one of my friends from New Haven were playing basketball in the yard. The ball happened to roll over to these two white dudes and they snatched the ball up. So my boy said, "Let's get this ball." The white guy said, "No." My boy said, "Man, give us the ball," and the white dude threw the ball and hit him in his face with it, and then they rushed him. They started jumping him. I'm like, "What?" So, I jumped in it. We all ended up in segregation units, and the two white boys were shouting from their cells, "You fucking niggers. You dirty nigger," and I am like, *This is crazy.* In my mind, I'm not thinking that they are racist.

_____

mum-security prison for adult men. It is the largest correctional facility in New England.

5. *Cellie* is slang for cellmate.

I am just thinking, *These dudes is crazy.* But I was actually glad to be in segregation; I thought, *That's fine, I didn't like my cellie anyway.*

From December 14, 1999, to February 2, 2000, I was at Walker. Then I was sent to Manson Youth Institution, MYI. At one point early on at MYI, me and this other guy my age were arguing, and the other youths was instigating us. It got to the point where we both wanted to fight. We were in different cells, though. The older guys in the cells next to us told us if we wanted to fight, to tell the guards that we were "gonna hang up," which means threaten self-harm. If we did that, we'd get sent to the Hartford MHU block, the mental health facility. They said the COs—correction officers—would transfer us.

So me and this other guy got ourselves sent to the psych ward on purpose. I talked to a nurse and told her I was hallucinating, seeing frogs jump out of the toilet and that kind of thing. I was just making it up. But when I got down there, I couldn't take it. Hence, me and the other guy never was put in the same holding cell. Therefore, we never fought.

It was a stupid idea looking back; I don't even know why we were so mad at one another. I was in a room by myself with nothing but a paper gown, and there were people down there that really had mental health issues, medicated all day, banging and screaming. They had a light on all day, and a camera in the cell. A hard metal bed, no sheets, no nothin'. It was cold. I couldn't take it. I tried to get back out by acting wild, but that just made it seem like I was more crazy. I caught three tickets just trying to get out of there. So then I chilled out for seven days. Finally, they sent me back to MYI. But isolation at Walker and MYI wasn't anything like where I went next.

"ARE YOU BROKEN YET?"

In June 2000, the state sent me to Northern Correctional Institution, the supermax, while awaiting trial. This is maximum security, with the most violent and dangerous inmates. I didn't feel like I was a dangerous

inmate. I committed no assault on nobody. I got sent to Northern because I caught too many minor disciplinary tickets.

I could feel the overly aggressive nature of the Northern environment instantly when I got there. I'm seventeen at this time, but that has
no effect on the staff. Coming into Northern, everyone's treated the
same: big, small, young, old, it doesn't matter. It was like a culture shock.
When I first come into Northern, they stripped me of all my clothes—
my drawers, socks, T-shirt—and put me in a jumpsuit. They chained
me up with leg irons, handcuffs behind my back, and then a tether chain
and padlock connecting the handcuffs to the leg irons. They marched me
down the hall, like ten COs and a lieutenant. They want you to know
who is running the show. They letting you know like, go ahead, try something. When you chained up like that, and you're naked, it actually para-
lyzes you. You feel vulnerable in the presence of force. You feel defeated.

What got me about Northern was how everything was glass and
metal, and it's all reflective. You feel like you're in a spaceship. The second thing that got me was how they do the recreation. You rec in kennels, like dog kennels, like a big cage. That's it. That really made me
feel depressed: *This is it, life in a cage.* It felt like everywhere you go, you
were still in a little cage. You go from your cell to the shower, and the
shower is enclosed—another cell. You're not in no type of open area.
You're always in some type of closet, or you're in some type of locked
confinement. Even when you're out your cell for that one hour, you still
feel like you're locked down. It's really no movement. All that takes a
toll, especially if you constantly pay attention to it.

They put me in a cell with a Puerto Rican dude named Angel. The
cells at Northern, everything is gray. The walls are all dark gray with
holes in it—it's all made out of Quikrete. When I got to Northern all
the cells were double-bunked. The bunks are steel and a bluish-green.
The toilet's steel. Everything's steel. Everything is gray. The cell is about
six by eight; if I stood and spread my arms I could touch wall to wall. If
I stand on my tippy-toes, I could touch the ceiling. It's narrow. The cells

were designed for one person, but they're double-bunked. So it's two people in that little room.

Angel and I were getting manipulated by some of the older prisoners. They kept telling us there were women and potato chips and all this other good stuff down in the mental health wing. I didn't really believe them, but I guess they were persuasive. They convinced us. So we told the COs we were going to kill ourselves, and they took us down there. It was on Friday. There's no windows in the reformatory at Northern. You have a mirror, sink, toilet, shower inside the cell. The door is all glass. And they only give us a paper gown and paper slippers. They don't give us no type of bed linen, no sheets. You could take a shower, but there was nothing to dry off with. We were down there all weekend. On Monday the doctor comes, and we tell him we don't want to kill ourselves, we tell him anything to get out of that situation.

After I come back, one lieutenant asked me, "Are you broken yet? Are you broken?" So that's why I know this is a bigger game plan in place. So from that point on, I seen everything as them trying to break me. The feeling of being in Northern? You feel isolated. You feel hurt. You feel mad. You feel bitter. You got all these different emotions running through you at the same time.

I STARTED WILDING

One day I went to court, I came back, and my whole cell is flooded. The toilet is overflowing. There's toothpaste spilled all over the place, and bologna and potatoes everywhere, and my cellie Angel is missing. The guards just put me in there anyway. I'm hearing yelling and thudding from below my floor, and I found a note from Angel saying he'd eaten all my commissary food. I'm hearing yelling, crying, and it's Angel. I can hear him through the vent.

Once the guards left I could talk to him through the vent. He said he couldn't take it anymore, that he had to get out. He said they had him strapped down to the bed on "four-point." It's the first time I'd heard of that. I didn't see Angel again for a while, they moved him to another block. I found out "four-point" is where they chain you down to the bed, with your legs and arms handcuffed to the four corners of the bed.

My next cellie was someone I'd met at Long Lane, who'd been in with me for a while. One day the guards were in a cell downstairs from mine, chaining up another inmate. I was at the door trying to figure out what was going on, and a guy on the other side of me named J Scar was kicking the door, screaming about whatever was going on. I guess he was objecting to someone being restrained. But the guards thought it was me doing the banging.

A lieutenant came to my cell and told me to turn around and "cuff up." I told him I didn't do it, and the guy in the cell next to me even said the same thing, that it was him. But they didn't care. They put me on in-cell restraints. In-cell restraints are different from four-point. With in-cell restraints, they put you in handcuffs, leg irons, and a tether chain between the handcuffs and the leg irons in the front, and then wrap the tether chain around the handcuffs three times, so you're bent forward at the waist. You can lie down, but you can't really stretch your legs out, because you're in a cramped position. You're just constantly twisting and turning to try to get comfortable. You just cramp up. They left me like that for twenty-four hours.

After that incident, I started wilding. I wasn't adjusting. I wasn't complying with the rules and regulations. I was always at it—covering the windows, basically acting up, acting out. It helped me not pay attention to the psychological effects of the environment. That it was affecting me. That it was affecting everyone. But some people were wilding because they were mentally ill; others because they were upset. I was wilding because I was following the crowd and it was something to do.

From that point it just got worse and worse for me. First, it was about twenty-four hours in-cell restraint, then it got to be two days, then three days, then it was five days one time. Then they got the black box. The black box is this thing they put over the handcuffs and then they got the waist chain, the tether chain, the leg irons so you don't have any range of motion, nothing. You chained up like Houdini in a magic show. They left me like that for three days in the black box. Then they took the black box off and the waist chain and left me in the in-cell restraint setup for two more days and took me off. After five days straight of being chained up.

From that day on, I've been determined to change this barbaric, abusive, humiliating, insane, and every-other-word-that-connotes-torture practice.

THEY'RE TRYING TO GET YOU TO ACT OUT

You know they're trying to break you, you know they're trying to get you to act out and you really don't want to give them what they want, because it's a battle, it's a fight, it's a war. If I give them what they want, they're gonna win, but if I don't give them what they want, they're still gonna win, so how can I level this playing field? I'm gonna give them what they want until they tell me they don't want it no more. And that was what my first two years was like adapting to that new plantation called NCI Supermax. You try everything in your power to basically make them feel how you feel—defeated. And that's why I stayed in Northern from 2001 to May 2002.

I went on trial in 2002 from May 31 to July 3. I was in New Haven county jail then. May, June, July, I wasn't at Northern. And getting away for those three months, I realized that things are different there. When you in an environment, you're wilding, and everybody's wilding, and you think it's normal. But when you leave an environment and you look back at it, you start to see yourself differently. Especially seeing other people in other environments. When you're around other people, you see that they are looking at you like you're not normal. You see that your behavior ain't normal. After the trial I went back to Northern, and I started seeing that everyone is not normal. I saw the elements that cause psychosis—the colors, the restrictive environment, the lack of environmental stimulation, the slamming doors, the restraints. I was able to see all the things that cut you off mentally from society, and influence the development of your brain.

FOCUSED ON RETALIATION

Then after my sentence, on September 11, 2003, I was back at Northern all the way to 2013. I lost count of all the times I was chained up. I'd say about twenty would be a good estimate.

That whole time, I felt angry, destructive, violent, bitter, sad, mad, depressed. I felt anxious and defeated. I felt painful and mistreated, and experienced institutionalized racism, but of course at that time I couldn't identify exactly what I was going through. I heard cries for help. And that's the best way I could describe what being back at Northern was like. You're cut off from the outside world.

At Northern you remain bitter and frustrated, mad and angry. You're focused on retaliation. You're always trying to get back and you're always trying to, basically, reciprocate the feeling of being defeated.

ONCE I LEARNED THE LAW

I didn't start to calm down, so to speak, until I met Andre Twitty in 2005. Andre is the one who made me realize my whole incarceration from beginning to end was a violation of my rights. He helped me start learning how to do something about it. He introduced me to criminal law and helped me find websites that a lady friend of mine who was going to school at University of Massachusetts could go to and download a case and send it to me.

I met Andre at Northern when we were on the three-cell tier. He more or less taught me certain things about the law through discipline. I had no knowledge of the law whatsoever at this time, completely legally bankrupt. Now I think I know something. With Andre, my question would be answered with another question, which frustrated me. But it also challenged me to find the answer myself. So it was a process of getting me to think.

I'm a fast learner. From reading so much, I started understanding general concepts—due process of law, failure to protect. Where's the court's holding at, what the facts are. I started to know how to read criminal cases. I never had access to a law library or the internet. I used to write the New Haven Law Library and ask them to send me cases and pay for them myself. They'd tell me how much a page. I'd send them the money. I learned through reading cases. Everything started from reading case law. Then I got the annotated version of the statutes. From that, I got the cases that supported the annotations. Reading the criminal law introduced me to the civil law.

Once I learned the law, the authorities didn't know how to deal with me. They're trained for dealing with violent inmates, not litigious inmates. When I was aggressive and frustrated, and acting out of those emotions, they were right there, front and center, with their shields, masks, mace, dogs, batons, whatever. They could deal with that. They train twice a year for that. But now that I ain't dealing with that no more, now that I'm seeking to change things through the court system, they don't know how to deal with me. They call their attorney at the state attorney general's office to deal with me.

The more I felt confident with the legal system, the calmer I got, and the closer I got to getting out of Northern's "administrative segregation" program, which was set up around three levels or phases. If you catch a ticket, you'd go to phase one for 120 days. You have just one fifteen-minute phone call and one half-hour visit every week, limited commissary and full restraints wherever you go. Then you go to phase two where you get more commissary, and just handcuffs when you're taken out of your cell for the first thirty days. After ninety days there without a ticket, phase three.

I almost didn't make it out of phase three in March of 2003. I ended up catching a ticket right at the door when I was about to be transferred. I was given a *Georgetown Law Journal* from another inmate, and for that I got a Class C ticket. They ordered me back to phase one for that, but I challenged the ticket and got it overturned on appeal.

I thought, *They ain't ever sending me back.* I was free. *Boom.*

IT SEEPS DOWN INTO YOUR DREAMS

Aaron was sent back to Northern Correctional Institution later in 2003 for the same reason he had been sent there in 2000—a combination of low-level Class A and B disciplinary reports. During this ten-year stint at Northern, Aaron was charged and designated as a member of a "security risk group," that is, a gang member. He vehemently contests this designation. He was transferred out of Northern in 2013.

Now I'm at Walker, in Security Risk Group. I'm here because they say I'm a gang member. The physical structure is different—Northern is designed to maximize the isolated effect. Walker, where I am now, wasn't built with that effect or objective in mind. Here, you're not really that isolated by the physical structure of the building in the SRG unit. But here it's still twenty-three hours in the cell and one-hour rec. It's still no TV, lack of programming, lack of social contact, et cetera.

But before I got moved to SRG at Walker, I was in an SRG block at another prison, Corrigan, where they had TV. It was the first time I'd seen a TV since I'd been sent to Northern. I remember once watching something on my cellie's TV. It was *Rosemary's Baby.* I think it was a scene where she was in a lot of pain, and I started crying. I'm like, *Why am I crying? Why am I getting so emotional?* I can't control it though. I'm tearing up. Somehow the TV reconnected me to my emotions. I pushed all those emotions back. I suppressed them. Now I'm confronted with them again. What a time.

But that doesn't happen very often! Northern makes you bitter and emotionless. It makes you hard. That's what isolation does. It seeps down into your dreams. That's how deep it go. That's how real it is.

I had one dream recently. In it, I'm watching a conversation. There was an inmate, and he's at the table with his mother. He has a low haircut, chubby face, nappy hair. And he's walking back and forth, and he shakes his head in a circular motion, like he's saying "yes." And only thing I can understand is he was explaining to her how much pain he was in. I'm listening and watching the conversation, but I'm not there. I can hear them talking. I'm listening to him say he's in pain. She's weeping, she's crying, saying she wants to help him, but she really can't. He is shaking. She says something and whatever she told him, it caused him to fall over weeping.

The dream shifts. I'm at dinner, at a restaurant. I'm with the inmate and his two sisters. We talking about the situation, and I'm asking them, "How did he end up in solitary confinement?" The sisters are saying, "It was nothing. Tax evasion." I'm like, "No, not why he went to jail, what he did in jail to be put in solitary confinement. Ask him, what rule did he break?" He's not answering. He's just rocking back and forth. I'm like breaking it down. "I can file a motion to get him out of segregation. I can file an injunction. But I have to know what he did that made them put him in segregation." They're not understanding. They're saying, "Nothing, nothing. He didn't do anything."

Then the dream shifts again. I'm walking on a college campus with one of the females who was at the restaurant. We're on campus, but we're on a bridge. And beyond the bridge is a beach. I can see the sand. From the bridge, I can see the water. Clear blue water and white sand. It's crazy. We're walking and looking over the railings. I ask her, "What are you studying?" And she laughs, looks back at me and says, "Why, what are you here for?" And I wake up.

There was a time when I could see no end to the abuse being perpetuated upon me by staff at Northern. I could see no way to make it out of

Northern. All that changed when I was blessed with the ability to humble myself and quiet my environment, listen to Andre Twitty, and learn the law. The law has been my shield and my way to articulate the need for prison reform and for my release.

If it wasn't for my family, friends, associates, Andre, and even certain CT-DOC officials, I'd probably be stuck in my old ways, more bitter and angry. My family and friends have been my cornerstone, though. They've come see me when they could, even at Northern. They write. They encourage me. They buy me books when they can. Inetta, my sister, thinks I could be the president of an African country.

What happens to people in Northern who finish their bid is this: it can radicalize a person. They create this hardened person and then they release him to the community, and that person is doomed for destruction.

But what keeps me alive is my family. When I'm released, I can't go back and live the street life. That'd be selfish. They did this bid with me. They've always been there, but I haven't been there with them at times. I haven't been able to be there with them, but they never gave up.

In the spring of 2017, Aaron was sent back to Northern because of alleged gang activity. He remains there today.

VERNESIA GORDON

AGE: 25

BORN IN: Pontiac, Michigan

INTERVIEWED IN: Anchorage, Alaska

Vernesia Gordon has her hands full. She's a young mom of three and also works full time at an elder care facility. She makes time to talk with us in the evenings while taking care of her small kids and often some of her two brothers' kids as well. She fixes dinner and snacks while disciplining and joking with the kids, and she recounts the love she shared with her fiancé, Davon Mosley. Davon dealt with mental illness for much of his life and was in and out of jails in California before he and Vernesia decided to start their lives anew in Alaska.

When we meet Vernesia in Anchorage, she's coming from work, on her way home to take care of the kids. She wears white scrubs with a frog pattern, burgundy glasses, and gold hoop earrings, and her hair is in a single long braid. She says she loves her job but that she's planning to go back to school in order to become a nurse. Before her current job she worked part time at Toys"R"Us while taking phlebotomy classes. Her mom, Khenisia, joins us, telling us she's concerned about her daughter's recent weight loss and that the stress Vernesia carries means she doesn't know how to slow down.

HIS EYES TOLD ME SOMETHING DIFFERENT ABOUT HIM

One day in October 2009, I was walking to the apartment complex where my family lived in Bakersfield, and there was a boy leaning over the second-floor balcony of the complex.[1] I think he was leaning over trying to see who I was. He leaned so far over he fell off. He literally flipped over the balcony! Yeah, he got my attention.

The next time I saw him I was sitting on the stairs of the complex talking to my brother, and the guy who had fallen off the balcony earlier came down to talk. His name was Davon, and he was friends with my brother. I was seventeen at the time, and he was sixteen. When I first met him I was looking at him thinking, *He's so weird.*

We just started a conversation and ended up hanging out all weekend. We went to the movies. We walked to the park, and just talked about us and our lives. We ate at the park and stayed until the sun went down, looking at the stars and the moon.

The first thing I liked about Davon was his eyes. His eyes told me something different about him than everybody else's did. When we talked I learned that Davon had bipolar schizophrenia. I believe he was fourteen at the time when he was diagnosed with it. His sickness didn't change anything. I didn't judge him. I just kind of liked him.

HE DIDN'T SHOW HE WAS SCARED

I was born on August 11, 1992, in Pontiac, Michigan. But my family only lived in Michigan until I was five, and then we moved to Arnold, Penn-

---

1. Bakersfield is a city of 375,000, located in central California, roughly 120 miles north of Los Angeles.

sylvania, and then New Kingstown, Pennsylvania, for about five years. I
don't remember too much about my early childhood, but I remember my
mom's family being in Pennsylvania, so we were around her family a lot.

Then when I was close to turning ten, we moved to Lancaster, California. My mom's sister lived out there, so we moved out to be around
her. That was 2001. We didn't have much more extended family in California, so it was just me, my mom, and my three brothers, two older, one
younger. Even in California we moved around a lot, on almost a yearly
basis around Lancaster. I don't know why we were moving around so
much—sometimes it was because my brothers would get into fights in
school, and my mom would want to get them out of there.

So we were moving around Lancaster, and then my family moved to
Bakersfield. This was around the time I was in high school. At that point
I was doing well, so I didn't want to move to a new school again. So we
worked it out that I would stay with a friend in Lancaster to go to school,
then visit my family on weekends and days when I didn't have school.

Eventually I ended up coming back to Bakersfield and staying with
my mom. Davon was a big part of the reason why I came back and stayed
in Bakersfield. He would always leave school and come home with food.
I love to eat, and he knew that, so he would always surprise me with
burritos from the Mexican stand down the street. I literally was always
at Davon's house. I would go downstairs to my mom's house to change
clothes, take showers, stuff like that. We were inseparable until he went
to jail. Then when he got out of jail we were inseparable again.

I didn't know if things were serious, but not long after I started staying in Bakersfield, I got pregnant. It caught us by surprise because it was
very soon after we met. I missed my menstrual cycle, and Davon and I
walked to Walgreens and bought a pregnancy test. Two came in a pack.
I took the first one and I set it down, and when the timer went off, I had
him read it. And he just stood there like, "You're pregnant." I'm like,
"You're lying. Don't lie." I took the second test just to make sure, and it
turned out I really was pregnant. That's when my life changed.

It was all a bunch of feelings at once just rushing in. But for the most part, I was really scared. Davon, he was happy about the pregnancy. His mom was happy. His dad, though, would say things like I was just using Davon to get pregnant, to get welfare, that Davon should get a paternity test, those kinds of things. Davon always protected me from his dad though. Davon used to tell me he didn't think his dad loved him.

When Davon was seven his older brother, Carlton Jr., was killed. Carlton Jr. was in a car and he was shot in the head in Bakersfield. I think it was a setup. Davon felt more of a dad connection to Carlton Jr. than he did to his own dad. He took it hard. They were all mixed up in gangs.

I think my presence changed Davon in many ways. He used to be out in the street. But Davon slowed down completely to the point to where his parents were like, "You saved our son's life." They used to think Davon could get killed any day. But when me and Davon got together, he never went out. It was always me and Davon together. And when I got pregnant, he became a family man.

My pregnancy was miserable. It was so hot! I was hospitalized because my placenta ruptured. All the complications with the pregnancy were very scary, but Davon was at the hospital the whole time. He spent nights at the hospital, went to school, came right back to the hospital or he would go home, get fresh clothes, and then come right back to the hospital. He was there every day. He probably tried to keep his emotions to himself, like that he was scared or worried for me. He was always there, reassuring me, "It's going to be all right and you're going to be all right. It's nothing to worry about." I believe he was scared because the doctors were saying our son might not make it. I know Davon was scared, but he didn't show it. He kept it to himself.

Davon Jr. was born on August 10, 2010. I was happy, nervous, emotional. But for the most part, I was really scared. When I had my son, he wasn't getting any oxygen. His umbilical cord was tied in a knot. So they had to do an emergency C-section and take him out. The doctors said if he stayed inside any longer, he would have died.

A lot of people put me down, saying, You're not gonna finish school. You're stupid, you shouldn't have the baby right now, you're not even eighteen. I didn't listen to them, and I still have my baby now! I never dropped out of school, I always had straight A's, I always did everything I was supposed to do. Even after I had my son, I still graduated from high school, and I'm going to graduate from college.

WALKING DOWN THE STREET WITH AN AX

Davon and I went through a lot together very quickly in our relationship—getting pregnant, having a complicated pregnancy, Davon being a bipolar schizophrenic. So dealing with Davon and his illness, it was stressful, but he was always there for me during my pregnancy. I was always there for him, too, every step of the way.

In the beginning of our relationship, he'd pick and choose when he wanted to take his medication and I had to tell him, "You can't just do that. You have to actually take it every time," but I also understand why he wasn't taking his medicine. It's lithium, and out in Bakersfield it was so hot. Lithium is salt, and it would always make him pass out. He was dehydrated.[2] He'd be walking outside and just pass out. He kept constantly passing out.

We would call his probation officer and tell him Davon isn't taking his meds. His probation officer was aware of his illness, but the officer would say, "Oh well, you have to wait until he does something. We can't do anything because he's not doing anything wrong right now."

One time Davon was walking down the street with an ax. He was literally just walking down the street with an ax and that's when his dad first called the probation officer, and they were like, "He's not doing anything." He's walking down the street with an ax! What do you mean

2. Lithium compounds are psychiatric medications commonly prescribed as a treatment for bipolar disorder. Side effects include increased thirst, dizziness, and fainting, among many others.

he's not doing anything? They said we had to wait.

Because of the side effects of lithium, Davon was telling his doctor that he wanted a different kind of medicine. But instead of giving him a different medication, she just took him completely off everything.

Not long after, Davon had an episode. It was September 2011, a little after my son's first birthday. He was arguing with my brother D'Aire and got a machete from under his dad's bed. He was actually just going crazy. He was hitting the walls with his machete. D'Aire's arm got cut really bad. The machete almost hit D'Aire's artery. And my bother Durrell got a cut too trying to calm Davon down.

This is why Davon ended up going to Wasco State Prison—assault with a deadly weapon. I believe he was supposed to get nine years, but the then mayor of Bakersfield intervened and said Davon's probation officer should have done something when our family was calling and asking for help. So Davon was sentenced to two years, and he served fourteen months.

A FRESH START

I hardly got along with Davon's parents. I guess his parents didn't like the way I spoke my mind, and I just didn't let them talk to me like they do everyone else. It also seemed like when Davon was away from his parents, he was more calm. It was stress free. My mom had left Bakersfield again, this time moving up to Anchorage, Alaska. Davon and I were living with his brother, right next door to his parents.

So in August 2013, my mom invited us to come up to Anchorage to visit for my birthday. I could be around family, and I could be happy. I wasn't even sure we were going until we bought our tickets like two days before.

Davon and I went up there for a weekend. Unfortunately, Davon's parole officer visited his brother's house to check in on him, and his brother told the officer Davon was in Alaska. Davon wasn't supposed to have left California. So the parole officer put a warrant out for his arrest. All that led to us deciding to stay in Alaska, for a fresh start, and so Davon wouldn't go to jail when we went back. We just stayed. Davon put in job applications and got hired at Toys"R"Us, and that was that. We were staying with my mom, and I was putting in apartment applications.

My second son, Davontae, was born a few months later, on November 29, 2013. Davon was a good dad. He'd hold Davontae, watch TV with him, talk to him, read to him, play video games with him. He'd prop Davontae against a pillow, put a controller on his lap, and Davon would be playing a game as if Davontae was playing with him. He'd be like, "Hey, bug. You see that? We winning." I'd be like, "Shut up." It was cute though.

But it was hard. I had postpartum depression. My mood was all up and down. I was always tired. My mom was saying that I was going through too many emotions at one time and she told me I should go get checked, to make a doctor's appointment and basically see what was going on. The doctor prescribed some medication that wouldn't affect the breast milk because I was breastfeeding at the time.

The medication helped, but my doctor thought we might need couples and individual counseling. Davon and I were on a waiting list to get couples counseling and that's when it started, that's when everything happened.

HIMSELF AGAIN

In February 2014, Davon had an episode. His dad and I were arguing over the phone and then Davon got on the phone, and either his dad called me a bitch or he called me something that made Davon get mad. He hung up on his dad, and his dad called back. It was going back and forth.

Davon ran to the kitchen and grabbed a knife. I'm not sure why he got the knife, but whenever Davon had an episode, he would go grab a weapon. He jumped over the balcony and basically just stood outside. I guess he was talking to his mom on the phone, and I believe his mom called the hospital and told them what was going on. When they sent officers from the Anchorage Police Department out, they spoke with

Davon outside and Davon basically told them that he had a warrant in California. I guess they asked him what was going on and what happened, and Davon told them. The police asked me if Davon was on parole in California, and I said yes. They were like, "Well, he's very forward with us, and he let us know that he had a warrant out for his arrest and he just wants to get help." The police took Davon to Alaska Psychiatric Institute. The police were telling us that they would assign Davon an officer so that if he were to have an episode in the future, that officer would come out and deal with it. That's what they were supposed to do for people with bipolar, schizophrenia, or mental illnesses.

We had been scheduled to have our first couples counseling appointment, but we missed our appointment because Davon was at the psychiatric hospital. He was there for four days. I went to visit him every day. He'd get an hour visit. I'd bring him food and we would talk. He was doing better and back on his medication. I feel like the medication was helping him. He was himself again. The hospital gave him lithium and Seroquel and he was able to take the lithium because Alaska isn't hot like it is in California. So he was actually able to take his medicine without being sick or having any of the side effects that he did in California. When Davon was released from the psych hospital, the police contacted his parole officer and they were told that they could let Davon go, that he could be released to come home.

NEVER HEARD FROM DAVON AGAIN

I was still struggling with my postpartum issues, but I didn't even really get to deal with my depression because everything happened so fast with Davon.

In March 2014, Davon and his father were fighting again. Davon was telling his dad he didn't want to have anything to do with him. That's when his dad called the police in Anchorage and told them he had a warrant in California. That's when they came and got Davon, and he went to jail.

We were at Motel 6 to have some space from my mom. The kids were sleeping, and we hear a knock at the door, and I go to answer the door. It was the police, and they asked, "Is Davon here?"

They arrested him on the warrant in California. He went to jail on March 16, 2014. When he went to jail, the Anchorage police said the California police have a certain amount of time to decide whether they were going to come get him. After the police left and took Davon, I called his mom, and I told her what happened and that's when she said they had just called the Anchorage police to check on him. They weren't supposed to take him to jail. That's when I told her, "Well, they said you guys called and said he had a warrant."

I think I talked to him once or twice that day. I would ask him every day, "Did you take your medicine?" He said no. He said they still hadn't given it to him in the jail. I had to put a request in. He told me he still didn't have it. And that's when he told me that California had until April 3 to come get him or Alaska had to drop everything and let him go.

While in jail Davon had punched a wall, like a brick wall, and broke his hand. I guess someone in a booking tank with him said something. I'm not even sure what was said, but something was said and instead of hitting the guy, he just hit the wall and he messed his hand up. I'm honestly not sure what really happened to his hand because Davon wasn't taking his medication.

Then I heard from Davon that he'd been put in solitary confinement because he basically told a police officer that he wanted to fight him. Davon was moved to confinement because he had a towel on his head and the officer said to take the towel off his head, and Davon didn't want to. I guess because his hair was wet. So he basically got into a confrontation with the officer and he told the officer that he'd fight him in his cell. He told him he wasn't shit without his badge, and told him to take his badge off and "Let's fight." So the officer had him moved to solitary.

I was able to talk to Davon up until March 20, which is when they put him in solitary. The last time I talked to him I was on my way to church.

Davon said he'd been asking for his medication, and they weren't giving it
to him. He was talking about becoming a hawk and that he's Lucifer, things
like that. That's when you know Davon hit a point where he's really manic,
where he's not even Davon anymore. I knew Davon was having an episode.
I was scared. And I was upset they weren't giving him his medication.

Davon told me to have a good day at church and he told me to pray
for him. Every time before we got off the phone, we always told each
other "I love you" and "See you later." We never said, "Bye." We always
said, "See you later." And that was our last conversation. I literally never
heard from Davon again.

So when I still hadn't heard from him the following day, which was a
Monday, I called the jail to see why he wasn't being given his medication.
When I called, they said that he couldn't have visits. He couldn't talk on
the phone. I asked when he would be able to have visits or talk again, and
they basically told me to call every day to see when I could visit. I believe
that's when things started spiraling. I called every day, and every day
they told me that he couldn't have visits or phone calls.

I WAKE UP AND I'M AT THE JAIL

The jail wasn't supposed to hold him past April 3, but they held him past
his extradition time. The court had sent the paperwork to the jail to release him, but the jail said they lost the paperwork. On Friday, April 4,
I was headed to the jail to find out what was going on and why he wasn't
being released. On our way down to the jail as I was leaving the house,
I literally got this energy vibe through my body. I was nervous and I was
looking at my mom, and I told her, "Mom, I just got this whole energy
jolt from the top of my head all the way down to my toes." I felt cold, like
I had a whole energetic chill or something. I don't know. I was throwing
up that morning too.

When I got to the jail, all of a sudden the guards at the reception
were like, "Oh, he can have a visit." This was at 1:47 p.m. But they told

me that the visiting period was full, so I should come back in a couple of hours. The only reason I didn't go back that day was because I didn't have a way to get up to the jail. My mom wasn't back in time to take me during the later visiting hours.

Later that day, I was in my room talking to my little brother and my sister-in-law. My mom's friend had passed away that winter, and we were all talking about how someone could be here and then the next day they could be gone.

During that conversation, Davon's brother called me. He just said, "They got him. He's gone." I was like, "What are you talking about?" And that's when he told me that Davon died, that the Alaska authorities called and told them that they found Davon slumped over in his cell.

This whole time, I kid you not, I'm thinking it's a joke, like he's playing. It's the beginning of April, not April 1, but I'm still thinking he's trying to play an April Fools' joke. I don't know. I just probably wasn't trying to believe what he was telling me, but he was basically like, he's gone. He's dead. I don't know. From the time that I got that phone call, I remember screaming, "You're lying!" I remember falling on my floor. "You're lying. Don't say that. You know that's not true. That's my baby, he can't be gone and stop lying." I remember walking downstairs, going outside, like I guess I was ready to walk to the jail, but that's all I remember. From there everything is a blank. I blacked out, probably for a whole hour.

I wake up and I'm at the jail. My mom, my brothers, my stepdad all took me there while I was blacked out. My pastor met us up there. I remember the officers telling me that he's really gone and that it was from natural causes. I'm thinking, *There was nothing wrong with Davon. He's perfectly healthy. How did he die of natural causes? When did he pass away? Because someone told me to come here today for a visit and that Davon was fine.*

That same day, I'd been throwing up a lot. My mom asked what was wrong and I'm telling her I don't know. She had seen that I hadn't really been eating and then when I threw up, she wanted to go home and do a pregnancy test. I took the pregnancy test and found out I was pregnant.

Later on I found out from people that were in jail with Davon that they said he was actually talking about having some kind of feeling that I was pregnant. When I found out I was pregnant, it hurt. I was in shock, but when I first found out, I was in the bathroom for at least twenty minutes just crying. It was heartbreaking. It was surprising. The whole thing of me finding out I was pregnant that same day Davon died was very emotional. Very, very emotional. At the same time it was a bittersweet feeling, like he's supposed to be here.

SCREAMING THAT IT HURTS

We weren't getting any answers about what actually happened. I still didn't believe it. I didn't believe it until I saw Davon's body. That was the following Tuesday. Davon died the previous Friday. I later found out that he had passed away between 11 a.m. and noon. Literally, when the jail told me to come back for a visit Davon had already been dead for a couple hours.

Honestly, I don't remember what happened after Davon passed away. I remember people from the church coming over, bringing food. My pastor was there. They were going to ship Davon's body to California so he could be identified by his mother, next of kin, but I paid for his mom to come to Anchorage. She came that Monday night and then we went to identify the body together. They were supposed to wait to do the autopsy until she got here to identify him, but they told us that they had done Davon's autopsy without his mom's signature and had identified his body through his fingerprints. Until Tuesday, our knowledge was just that he had died, that he just stopped breathing. We didn't know why he stopped or anything like that.

My mom had had a car accident not long before and she had hired a lawyer who did traffic incidents. When Davon died we called him for help and found out he also specialized in wrongful death lawsuits, so he became our lawyer for this case too. On Tuesday we found out that Davon had died of fourteen bleeding ulcers. We didn't understand how he could possibly get fourteen bleeding ulcers. Our attorney hired another medical examiner to do another autopsy and the examiner said Davon was bleeding internally through his small intestine. Basically he was in a hyper-manic state, which can include high blood pressure. We had to go to the funeral home to see his body, and he had so many marks and bruises all over his body, and I'm like, *What the heck? Why is all this on his body?* He had really big knots all over his head. He had deep cuts where the handcuffs were. The skin was gone. You could see the white underneath. And you could tell he'd been dragged. He had drag marks from his toes to his knees. He was all scratched up. And on his ankles the cuff marks looked like they would if you dragged a dog.

Either that Wednesday or Thursday after Davon died, I met with my attorney. We started building our case. I had to get my call logs, like all the times Davon and I talked while he was in jail. That's when I wrote down everything that happened from the day that Davon went to jail until the day Davon died. We had a memorial service for Davon here in Anchorage and then when we took his mom back home, she took part of his ashes, and we had another memorial service for him out in California.

We had to keep fighting for more information about what had happened to Davon. A couple people who were in segregation with Davon ended up getting in touch with me through the reporters who wrote about Davon's death. One of the guys told me that Davon was screaming for help all the way up until he died. He was basically just screaming that it hurts, help, I need to go to the hospital. My stomach hurts. They have cameras all throughout the jail and we decided to fight to get the video of his time in jail released.

WHAT AM I SUPPOSED TO TELL MY BABIES?

I cried the whole month of April, then May, then June. I was emotional. But at the same time I couldn't let myself fall apart because I had the babies. It was very hard. It's gotten a little bit better because I've learned to deal with it through the last several years, but even to this day it's still very hard to deal with.

At the time Davon died, I wasn't working. My second son, Davontae, was four months and Davon was working before he died so I didn't have to. I didn't start working until July of that year. I ended up moving out of my mom's apartment into a place downstairs from her. My brother D'Aire moved in across from me, and my other brother Durrell moved in across from my mom. My mom is able to help out some with taking care of my three kids. I have a good support system here, but it doesn't change the fact that Davon's never coming home and that we will never see him.

After Davon passed away, I was trying to get grief counseling for me and Davon Jr. My son was almost four when Davon passed away and was able to get counseling, but then that stopped last September. He's seven now. I think he still needs counseling because every time March and April come around, he starts acting out. He does things he usually doesn't do. He's been lying a lot and he's not been himself starting in March.

When I found out I was pregnant the day that Davon died, I was like, *What am I supposed to tell my babies?* That's one of the reasons why I fought so hard. I would have fought hard regardless for Davon, but it was more like when my kids want to know what happened to their dad, I want to have answers for them. I want to be able to explain to my kids why he's not here.

THEY PEPPER-SPRAYED HIM
WHILE HE WAS NAKED AND HAD HANDCUFFS ON

We had to wait almost a whole year to see the videos of what happened the day that Davon died. We went to court in June 2014. My attorney was married to a legislator in Anchorage, and they were actually involved in getting the video released. Everyone came together to help because they knew something went wrong. We couldn't pinpoint what happened or anything like that until after we had the videos, but we all knew that something wasn't right. In Davon's case, it seemed like the guards kept him from calling me to tell me he was being beaten and pepper-sprayed.

When we finally got the video, it showed the guards throwing food at Davon through the slot in the door. You see it in the video. They just throw it in there like he's a dog or something. And they pepper-sprayed him through that slot in the door. You see these long shots of pepper spray going in. Then they took him out of one cell and put him in another. The video didn't show anyone beating him, but it does show five officers walking out of his cell, walking down the hallway high-fiving and laughing. When they brought him back he was naked. He was beat, and they just throw him in.

Then they cut his water off, and they pepper-sprayed him while he was naked and had handcuffs on. They pepper-sprayed Davon in two different cells. Each time, they took Davon out and had another prisoner go in and clean the pepper spray off the walls. One of the guys who was in his cell after him got in touch with me after he was released and said that there was so much pepper spray on the walls that he could barely breathe, that he was coughing the entire thirty or forty minutes that he was in there cleaning. The guards said they pepper-sprayed him because he was in a manic state, which he was. I mean, you guys weren't giving him his medication, what do you expect?

In the video you see Davon using the water that was in the toilet to rinse his face after the pepper spray because his water got cut off. You see him walking back and forth in his cell. It gets to the point to where he couldn't even walk to get water. When he was telling them his stomach was hurting, they were throwing his food in, and then it was like he couldn't open his milk carton, he couldn't even hold an apple.

I'm still looking into getting his death certificate changed because he didn't die of natural causes, and on his death certificate it says "natural causes." That's false information, and I've been saying that since the beginning. The Department of Corrections never admitted to anything, but they had to pay our kids $625,000. After attorney fees I think each kid has about $150,000 in a trust.

Honestly, I don't think I would be able to fully get over it or start to heal until someone is actually held responsible. I mean you guys paying my children is still not bringing their dad back. Still not getting justice for their dad. Period. Y'all can have that money back if y'all could bring Davon back, but y'all can't do that, can you? The people who took him need to be held responsible. All those guards walking down the hallway high-fiving and laughing, what kind of disciplinary action is being served to them for what they did? Until they're held responsible, I don't think I will honestly be able to fully heal from them taking Davon.

I SOCK HOLES IN MY WALL

I know I have major depression problems. I was telling the doctor. And stress. I've lost seventy-eight pounds. I eat like crazy and still don't gain weight. I work a lot and go to school. I don't do anything else. I go to work, come home, cook, go to sleep. I can't be still, I can't be in a place by myself. If it's just me in a room and I'm just sitting there, I'm going to cry. I'll be going crazy to the point I'm crying and I sock holes in my wall. I'm just angry.

Davon was my heart. He was my soulmate. He's always gonna be in my heart, with me. I look at pictures of Davon all the time. His pictures are all over my house. I touch his face, I tell him I love him every day. The kids wake up and tell him, "Good morning." Davon Jr. talks about his dad all the time, says he misses him all the time. I've had conversations with him and he'll say he doesn't like the police, things like that. He doesn't really sleep at night. He'll wake up in the middle of the night crying. Then he'll say he wants his dad. I tell him that his dad is in the sky, that he'll always be with him, that he's always watching over him. He kind of gets the concept of what death is.

We have Davon's ashes in the living room. I have a mantel with Davon's pictures and his ashes. So I try my best to keep Davon Jr. knowing that his dad is here. He'll ask me, "Why did they do that?" And I'm like, "Baby, I don't know." To this day, he'll go up to the fireplace and say, "Daddy, I miss you. Why can't you come home?" It hurts my heart! It hurts because there's nothing I can do to bring his dad back. There are times when I tell Davon Jr. to go talk to his dad and his dad will send him answers in some kind of way. I tell my kids, "Your dad lives through you." I try my best to let my kids know, "Your dad is here and this isn't a choice that your dad is gone." Justice is two now. She is the daughter we had always wanted. That's the way she came. It's like, Davon was gone and then I got her. That's why I named her Justice, for Davon.

MOHAMMED "MIKE" ALI

AGE: 40

BORN IN: Navo Nadi, Fiji

INTERVIEWED IN: Hayward, California

The knuckles on Mike Ali's hand spell out "F-I-J-I" in fading tattoo letters, a subtle clue to his former life as a young gangbanger. But these days, "Crazy Mike" lives a relatively quiet life. He works full time at a hospital taking out trash and collecting linens, which he says pays well and provides solid benefits. He lives with twelve members of his extended family in a four-bedroom house. It's cramped, but he's hoping to move out soon to get more room for himself and his brother's four kids, whom he looks after. Mike's brother is serving a sentence of fifteen years to life for the kidnapping and torture of the boys' mother.

Mike came with his family from Fiji to the United States as a child and turned to gang life in the 1990s as protection from being bullied in school. He spent much of his teens and early twenties between juvenile hall, jail, and prison before being

detained for deportation at age twenty-four. Mike experienced long stretches of iso-
lation in a privately run immigration detention center and struggled to maintain
hope with an uncertain sentence and the threat of deportation hanging over his
head for over four years.

The United States maintains the world's largest immigration detention in-
frastructure, with upwards of four hundred thousand people detained each year.
Many of the detention facilities that house these prisoners are privately run. These
facilities typically earn a fee from the federal government for each night a detainee
is held. In order to minimize costs and maximize profits, facilities are often over-
crowded, and medical and mental health care go lacking.

Mike has shining dark eyes and a round face. His short-cropped hair is going
gray. His body carries severe scarring from the life he's led, but his cheerful person-
ality means he laughs a lot during our conversations, even when telling us about
getting beaten up, stabbed, or shot multiple times with a shotgun.

A BIG OL' GANGSTER PREDATOR

Immigration detention is fucked up, man. More fucked up than prison.
With prison you got a date to come home. With immigration, you don't.

My name is Mohammed Ali, but everybody calls me Mike, or "Crazy
Mike." When I was younger, Mike Tyson was famous, so everybody started calling me Crazy Mike, from me fighting too much. It stuck with me.

I was born in 1978 in Fiji, in a little village called Navo Nadi, and I
grew up there until I was ten, in '89. That's when we came to the US. We
landed in San Francisco—me, my big brother, two sisters, and my mom
and dad. We had our green cards already. We came as permanent residents
and were sponsored by an aunt. My mom's family was here, which is why
we ended up coming here. I think we would have had a better life in Fiji.

I was okay when I first got here. You know how you get wowed when
you first land—'cause Fiji don't have high-rise buildings, nice bridges, all
that stuff. At first it was like, *Wow, this is cool.* And then after living here
for a while I was like, *Damn, this sucks. I should have stayed in Fiji.*

We lived in Oakland for a year, then we moved to Hayward.[1] My mom worked as a housekeeper and my dad was a chef. In Hayward we were the minorities. Me and my sister were the only Fijis in the whole elementary school. We got bullied a lot. Then we went to junior high at Winton, and we were getting bullied again. And then we moved to South Hayward and went to La Vista Junior High, where there were four other Fijis. The majority of kids were Mexicans. There were Blacks, whites. The Mexicans didn't like us and were always bullying us 'cause back then we didn't know about deodorant. In our houses we were cooking with a lot of curry, so we all smelled like that. They used to jump us, so me and my four homeboys, we made our own gang and we start beating them up too. We were like twelve years old and we were all Fijis, all from South Hayward. We didn't have no outsiders. Four or five guys would hit us, but then we'd grab one and beat the shit out of him. And then things just kept on escalating.

After that, me and my homeboys were just gangbanging. I was gangbanging all the way out. It was like the coolest thing to do. If you were a gangster, you were the coolest cat in the street, in school, everything. I first went to juvenile hall in '92. I pulled a gun on somebody at school. We got into it, and I happened to have a gun on me I got from one of my homeboys. It was a Smith and Wesson .32. But I didn't know how to use it. If I'd tried, I probably would've ended up accidentally shooting myself.

I was in juvie for three months. It was hell, man. Everybody who goes to jail the first time, they bust out and cry. I cried in front of my mom. My older homies in juvie were like, "Man, you can't do that shit in here. You gotta swallow your emotions. It makes you weak, it makes you our prey." So it just kind of made me tougher.

When I got out of juvenile hall everybody started looking up to me. I was the coolest cat in the whole group because I'd done time. That time

---

1. Hayward is a city in Alameda County, California, located fifteen miles south of Oakland.

in juvie made me a predator instead of a prey. A big ol' gangster predator. I came out with more knowledge. Now I knew how to structure a gang, right? Like hey, this is what we can do, this is how we get away, if we did a drive-by, we need to throw this, this, and this away.

Around '94, when me and my homeboys went to high school, we started claiming Bloods as our gang. We called ourselves the Red Blood Fijians. We carried red rags. We imitated the way the Mexicans dressed. We wore Dickies and white T-shirts. We got more into it. Like, really more into it. Before we were like 40 percent, 50 percent, now we're 90 percent into it. Getting bullied meant we had to watch our backs. We were the minorities back then.

At fifteen, my cousin gave me a line of speed, and it was like the best fucking high in the world. I'm telling you, man, it was a rush you could never get from anything else. When you're running down the street, fighting all the time, it was like a totally different high. It enhanced my rage, you know? If you have that anger and hate inside of you, that drug just blows it out of proportion. I started having a drug problem in '94. I was like Speedy Gonzalez, man, always going. That year, I went to juvie again. I'd pulled a knife on a principal. And then Hayward PD came to the house and got me and took me to jail. I went to juvie, did six months or something.

Later that year, I got jumped and was almost killed. We had problems with the Indians; we didn't get along. But I was dating an Indian girl, and she's the one who set me up. She called me to come outside my apartment and the only thing I remember is getting hit. A group of Indian guys jumped me with baseball bats. They broke my jaw, cracked my head open, stabbed me. My sister found me on the concrete inside my apartment complex, and I made it to Saint Rose.[2] They saved my life.

I met my wife, Janet, in '94, when I was sixteen, and my son was born in '96. I was there at the hospital when he was born, and it was one of those feelings you never get in life, you know? A one-of-a-kind feeling. It was just amazing the way he looked. He was so cute and adorable. His

---

2. St. Rose Hospital is a major emergency care not-for-profit in Hayward.

name is Mohammed too. But just because you have a kid doesn't mean you're a father. You have to be around. I wasn't around. I was always on the streets or I was locked up. I went to jail like every six months. And shit, I didn't know nothing about being a dad. It just happened. I was a baby myself, and I was always on drugs, so having a baby didn't make a difference to me. My wife, she tried. She was like, "Hey, man. Get your shit together." I tried, too. But I was so much into the gang life. I got more deep into it than I realized. I kid you not, my heart was into it, and I couldn't leave no more.

I got shot in '97 by some dudes we were having trouble with in Berkeley. They hit me with buckshot from a sawed-off shotgun. And I got stabbed a couple of times after that. I have a loud mouth. People would get intimidated, think I'm trying to punk them, and then things would go from there.

SANTA RITA WAS LIKE COLLEGE

I went to jail in 1999, when I was twenty-one, for drugs. Got caught with an ounce of dope and a scale. They sent me to Santa Rita.[3] I watched too many fucking movies, so I was like, *Damn, I'm gonna get raped here!* I was small, motherfuckers in there were like fucking twice my size. I'm in Santa Rita scared shitless like, *Fuck! This is gonna be all bad in here.*

But I didn't realize going in that people from my city who I knew were there doing time. And they're all the ones that I'd sold dope to or that I did dope with. So I got to my pod, and this homeboy from Hayward is like, "Man, what's up, G? What's up, dog? Hey man, what you doing? Why don't you come and kick it with us?"

I think I was in Santa Rita six months. Janet never came to see me. My mom had just passed away, so I was in a rage, and nobody wanted to come see me. I didn't expect no one to come visit me. I messed up all my relationships. All of them.

---

3. Santa Rita is a jail operated by the Alameda County Sheriff's Office.

The whole time I was at Santa Rita and prison, I absorbed every bit of knowledge. You know how you go to school and you observe? Imagine not going to college, right? Instead, you choose to be a gangster. A dope dealer. You're in junior high at juvenile hall. You got this junior high knowledge and you graduate. You go to high school, right? From high school, now you graduate and go to college. Santa Rita was like college. And then your whole goal is to graduate from college. You get pointers on how to be a real gangster. How to be a real dope dealer. How to be a real hustler. How to do all the stuff you didn't think you could do. Remember, you were in there for petty shit compared to all the other people been doing time for ten years, fifteen years. They taught me how to be a man—how to fight better than before. Like I said, man, in high school I was a rookie. Now I'm a pro, you know?

After that I kept getting arrested every six months. Possession, stealing cars. I ended up going to San Quentin and then Folsom. I came home in 2003 from Folsom. They were supposed to hold me there because I had an immigration hold.[4] But they fucked up and misfiled the hold, so they released me to the street. After a month on the street, I went to immigration to pick up my green card, and that's when they picked me up again.

It was me and maybe fifteen other inmates. They took us to Marysville County to sleep in a holding tank. Next day, we went to Oakland Airport, then LA, San Diego, then to Florence, Arizona, and from there a bus took us to Eloy, which is migrant detention.[5] They were going to try to deport me.

Immigration said my crimes were deportable, so that's why they picked me up again. The drug cases are what sent me to immigration

---

4. An immigration hold is a request by Immigration and Customs Enforcement that local police hold people until they can be turned over to ICE.

5. The Eloy Detention Center is a private prison operated by the Corrections Corporation of America, now called CoreCivic, which is one of the largest private corrections companies in the United States. In 2015, CCA reported nearly $2 billion in revenue. Eloy is located in Pinal County, sixty miles southeast of Phoenix.

detention, even though I never got convicted for transporting, just possession. Immigration said I was transporting. So that's why I got sent to Eloy, to await deportation.

NEVER COMING BACK TO THIS COUNTRY AGAIN

Eloy was loud. We were secluded from the world in a desert. There's sandstorms, and when we had to go to the cafeteria during a sandstorm, we'd walk outside and the sand would be so thick you couldn't see the guy in front of you. The sand and dust would come through the vent. We'd get spiders and scorpions in there. It was cold at night—we'd have to wear our beanies and jackets. The water was harsh—it was well water, and it tasted like chemicals. We'd melt ice down and drink that instead. Some of these guys they'd bring in off the street would have bad odor. There's two prisoners per cell so if one smells, they make your whole cell smell bad.

Going to prison and going to an immigration detention center are two different things. Prison is more structured. Immigration has all these people who come and go. In prison, you know your sentence, how long you've got left. But in immigration detention, they'll hold you until they can deport you. And that's for life. You're never coming back to this country again.

Going back to Fiji might sound nice to some people, but remember, going on vacation and getting deported are two different things, right? If you go back in shackles, it's a whole different ball game. You wouldn't get the same respect or treatment. People in Fiji would see you as a criminal. I didn't want to go back. I decided I'd fight my case as long as it took me.

Also, there's a lot of people in Eloy who came to the US so young that growing up they thought they were US citizens. I thought I was a citizen. I didn't know I was only a permanent resident until I was trying to get a driver's license after I got out of prison in 2003. Shit, I thought I was a citizen!

In immigration detention, everybody was fighting for their lives but in different ways. In immigration you didn't know when you were getting out. You knew you might not ever see your family again. There's dudes I met that were just picked up at home after living their whole lives in the US. There's one cellie I had, a buddy from Vietnam. He was at home with his kids eating dinner when immigration came for him, came in the house and cuffed him in front of his kids. He'd been in the US twenty-four years. Turned out when he was eighteen, he'd gone joyriding in a car that a guy he knew had stolen. He didn't do nothing, but they found him twenty-four years later, came to his dinner table, cuffed him in front of his kids. He was in Eloy for six months. They don't deport people to Vietnam, so he ended up going home.[6] But people put in that situation are really stressed out, and at Eloy everybody's stressing out.

Janet left me in 2004 while I was at Eloy. We had never got married legally, which was a good thing. I found out when I called my dad's house from Eloy. He said Janet was there, and that she's getting remarried. I was mad, but I couldn't do nothing about it. I didn't know if I was going to get out in the US or get shipped back to Fiji.

I was looking for a way to vent. I got segregation a lot for the fighting, especially with guys who'd never been in prison before. But I wasn't the one starting the fights. See, there's a difference between *convicts* and *inmates*. Inmates don't know prison rules. There were a lot of guys in there for immigration reasons who hadn't really served time. Maybe they'd done thirty days, a few months before, but they'd never been in a prison structure. Convicts like me had been in prison before, and we knew there's rules, there's respect, there's ways to act to avoid conflicts.

Honestly, the inmates, the guys who'd never been in prison before, they're the ones that started the most shit. They started race shit, tried to call the shots. But convicts don't put up with that. You don't kick off

---

6. Before 2008, the United States and Vietnam had no repatriation agreement, so deportations to that country were not legally possible.

shit when you're a convict, you sit down and talk. You're supposed to understand the situation. We're all trying to go home to our family.

Unfortunately, the COs allowed these conflicts to happen by putting everybody together, maximum-security convicts with the inmates. So hell used to break out. The COs would run around like little girls when fights broke out because they didn't know what to do. The problem was, these COs weren't well trained. It was probably the highest-paying job in the area, and they'd just grab guys off the street to work in this private prison. Otherwise the area in Arizona where Eloy is is just crops and cattle. The people working there weren't used to prisons. They'd go on a little power trip to make up for it. They'd try to bully us and intimidate us. They didn't realize some of us had nothing to lose.

They should have separated us convicts from the other inmates. In prison you might know when you're getting out, but over here, you get deported, you're never going to see your family again. You don't know how long you're in, and you get into a fight, and the chances of getting deported go up. So these guys come in and mess it up for everybody. Some guys know they're gonna get deported and just want to fuck things up for everybody.

SEND ME BACK TO FIJI

I first came on the SHU for fighting in 2003, right after I got to Eloy. I got into it with a Southern Mexican from LA. I did two months before I got out. I went in and out of SHU, but eventually they put me in SHU indefinitely because we had a riot, and they said I "called the shots." They thought I set it up, but they couldn't prove it, I was like, *I didn't*. I didn't say nothing, man. It was a fight, then *bah!* The riot started, and I was just sitting back and watching.

At Eloy in the SHU, they got you alone in a cell. And you got to learn to live with this now. You're confined in a six-by-nine cell with a solid steel door that has a metal screen in it so the guards could look inside and see what you're doing. You get three meals a day. You get yard for one hour three times a week, then a shower. Every time you move you gotta get shackled up.

In order to survive, you gotta structure yourself. Gotta get up, work out, take a shower. Pray. Eat. Stay up all night and sleep all day because when you're up all night you pass the days quicker. A lot of people are backwards. You gotta get a couple of good books, you gotta read books, you gotta keep yourself busy. Soon as you're thinking, *Aw, man. Shit, I ain't got nothing to do.* Now your mind's wondering, *What's going on in the streets?* Now your mind's wondering what's your wife doing. Now your mind's wondering how's your kid doing, how's your mom and dad doing, right? Soon as you start thinking more, you start stressing. As soon as you start stressing more, you start tripping out more. So then you start tripping out more, now the walls are tripping on you, right? You start getting delusional. You start seeing all this shit that's not there, because your mind's fucking running wild. You can't sleep 'cause you close your eyes, but your mind's still running.

You think you see shit. I was seeing a young girl running around the hallway of the pod. It went on a couple of weeks. I'd look out and see her running around at night. I asked if other people saw that. They said no. At one point I thought there was a dude in the cell next to me looking at me. I asked about him, and the guys in the other cells were like, "No, nobody's in there, you're tripping."

This happened to me, but thank God I got it under control. But it happened. It happened. Being in the SHU is like being a dog tied to a pole with a ten-foot chain. Imagine leaving a dog like that for months at a time. He could eat, drink, shit, you know, take a shower and everything, but just in that space right there, ten feet. He can't go anywhere besides that ten feet, you know? Imagine what he's going through. For thirty days, two months. Eight months. Ten months. Imagine.

A lot of people died in the SHU. The medical attention was horrible. One Fijian guy I knew had high blood pressure and it wasn't treated, and he had a heart attack. People cut their wrists with razor blades. Hung themselves.[7] There were mentally ill people who weren't medicated. I saw two people straight up lose their minds in there and go crazy. They fucking just lost it, dude. If you're not strong-minded, and you don't have that strong will, you're screwed. Eventually that cell is gonna get to you, is gonna start eating you up and making you crazy.

There was this Haitian soldier, his name was Baptiste. He snapped. He was smearing shit on his windows and putting soap up his ass. I knew the dude before the SHU, and he flipped out in the SHU. He straight up lost his mind. He just lost it. That place got to him. His cell was across from mine, so I saw it firsthand. Even after I moved cells I could still smell his shit 'cause we were on the same pod. Each pod is ten cells, with five on each side, so everybody had to smell his shit. Even the COs. He'd be screaming for help, and they never gave it to him. Even when he got out of the SHU he wasn't the same.

Three days a week you get to leave your cell. And what I remember most was how it enrages you. It's like being a kid and you look out the window and see everybody playing and having fun, and you can't join them for some reason. You start to get angrier and angrier, and you have all this hate for everybody. If you don't know how to release it, when you finally do come out, you come out angrier than before.

Still, some things I actually liked better about being in SHU. I got to read a lot of books. I got to actually read the Quran and understand it. I got to freakin' have the peace of mind to think, work out, you know? When you were in mainline, which is another way of saying general population, you couldn't let your guard down. When you're in the SHU, you can relax, kick it, hang out. You could talk to the guy across from you, you know, and don't trip about, *Aw, man, did I say something wrong?*

7. Eloy is one of the deadliest detention centers in the country. At least fifteen inmate deaths were reported since Immigration and Customs Enforcement was created in 2003, including at least five suicides. Eloy's death total is twice that of any other immigration detention facility, and its suicide rate is at least five times that of other detention facilities.

In a pod you can't do that. What you say, who you associate with, all this other stuff you gotta watch. When you're in the SHU, you don't. You don't got to worry about none of that shit.

But after a while it got to me. We have to act all tough and put up this front, but I got wore out. At one point I cried. I just thought, *Send me back to Fiji, I can't take it anymore.*

I BROKE DOWN AND CRIED LIKE CRAZY

I spent most of my four years at Eloy in the SHU for fighting. One time I was just singing that song that goes "shake it like a salt shaker" and they sent me to the hole for that. I was miserable. But in 2003 I got connected with the Florence Project, which helps with legal cases in immigration centers all over the area. Florence Project comes into Eloy to do pro bono work, so that's how I met my two lawyers, Rachel and Holly. They encouraged me to fight my case.

I'd just about given up fighting, but I remember what changed things for me was that I broke down and cried in front of my lawyer, Rachel. I think that was the biggest thing—when I broke down crying in front of her. It took a burden off my chest. I think that changed me. It just—like all the pain and stuff you hold inside, it broke. I broke down and cried like crazy. And I think that helped. I started growing after that. I wasn't thinking about going back to the streets and all my grudges anymore, I just wanted to go home.

The immigration authorities had said my crimes were deportable, but in 2007 someone in New York won a case similar to mine, so suddenly my case wasn't deportable anymore. Still, the authorities decided to keep me at Eloy. So in 2007, my lawyers filed a habeas petition arguing that they didn't have any reason for holding me, so I was being detained illegally. Which meant in order to keep holding me the immigration authorities had to prove I was a threat to society. The prosecutor argued that I was too dangerous to release based on the fights I'd got into at Eloy. I spoke direct-

ly to the judge about that and told him, "Look, in Eloy you're either a predator or you're the prey. If I didn't fight, I was going to be prey, everybody
and their mommas would be bullying me." I think that helped sway the
judge. He granted me bail for $5,000. I was freed September 27, 2007. I
was still under threat of deportation until 2010, but we fought and had my
convictions dropped. And after that, there was no threat of deportation.

DO YOU KNOW HOW HARD IT IS TO BE GOOD?

In 2007, I came from the SHU straight out to the street. The holding tank
at Eloy is where they process you to go out. It's crazy. It's the same place
they process you when you come into Eloy. People screaming and hollering
the whole time. They separate those going out into two groups: those going
back to the streets and those getting deported. There were five of us going
back to the streets that day. They let us out of Eloy at eleven at night and
dropped us off across the street from the Greyhound station in Tucson. But
the Greyhound station was closed. We couldn't get in until 6 a.m., so we
had to sleep on the sidewalk. In the morning I had to call my dad and have
him go to a Greyhound station and buy me a ticket from Tucson to Phoenix
to San Diego to LA to Fresno. That shit ride took more than a whole day.

At first it was a little trippy being out. I worked at the mall sweeping
up, but people putting me down got to me after a while. I prefer to be alone.

My son, he's gonna be twenty-two in May. He doesn't know me,
most of his life I was in jail. He never calls. I call him off and on. I would
love to have a great relationship with him, but he's definitely my son. He
has the same temperament as me. I've never been a father figure or role
model to him, so I don't blame him. I blame myself. I was never there for
him when he needed me. From 1992 to 2007, all I did was get locked up
or shot. I never had a real job or nothing. I have a good relationship with
his mom though.

My brother's locked up for life, right? Growing up, he didn't like me
and I didn't like him, but at end of the day we're brothers and family is

family. It's his fault he went away. He shouldn't have did what he did. But I still send him money because I know how it feels to be locked up and not have money in your books. I still talk to him too.

My dad and I got custody of his four kids. So now I have four teenagers on my hands. It's just me and my dad and my sister looking after them. My sister and her husband have five kids, so there's thirteen of us in my sister's four-bedroom house. We're making do, but sometimes I feel really, really lost.

At home I'm struggling. When you're in isolation, you get this peace of mind that you're safe because nobody can get to you, nobody can hurt you. I miss that shit. It's fucked up because I don't want to go back to jail, but my responsibilities are overwhelming. There's so much shit on my plate with the kids and work. Lately I'm trying to distance myself from the world. I don't know why. Usually I'm a really social guy, but lately I'm isolating myself. It's flashbacks from jail.

I got so used to being isolated from everything. So now I isolate myself from people. And it's fucked up. Sometimes I just want to be by myself in my room. Just like I was in solitary. Confined to my room, away from my family and friends.

When you're locked up your mind runs 150 miles per hour. You think of everything you ever did and how you could have done it different. You tend to overthink shit when you're not supposed to. When you're in the SHU you're safe, but you overthink. But mentally you're fucked in the head because you don't have nobody to talk to. Your best friend is you.

I want to get married. I want to get situated. But very few women will take a guy with four kids. I still want that companionship though. I miss that sometimes, I miss that a lot. I date, but I want a stable relationship. I lost my faith in a lot of things. I have a lot of heaviness in my heart. I've been going through girls like crazy, because as soon as something happens, I disappear for a few weeks. You get used to being by yourself in the SHU, so you want to get away from everybody. When I'm spending time with someone, I'll want to be by myself, and I just look for excuses to be alone. It causes problems. A lot. All I know is SHU. This shit is really getting to me, but I don't want to show my family because they're all depending on me. I don't want to snap, but I feel like I might sometimes.

In my room I'm just thinking most of the time. Thinking, like *Damn, I wasted most of my life doing stupid shit and getting locked up.* All I did was party and try to be a gangster. Try to live that American dream to be a fuckin' gangster. If I could change the past, I would do a lot of shit different. But you can't. You can't go back.

I want to move out, and my sister and her husband, they want us to move out because they want their house for their family, you know? But the rent down here is ridiculous. It's so hard to find a place. My dad helps out, but 99 percent it's my income supporting the family. It seems like nothing is fucking going my way. I'm trying, I don't do anything wrong. I don't drink, I don't get mad, but when I was bad everything was cool. But now I'm struggling. If you hustle, you make more money than working. Do you know how easy it is to be bad? Do you know how hard it is to be good? If I can't make it, I'm gonna have to go back to hustling or something because I got people who depend on me. I go to work every day and work overtime and I still barely get by. Being in jail was easier.

I work at Mills Peninsula hospital. I'm a housekeeper. I pick up linen and trash. I like my job, I get to meet people, and I actually feel like I make a difference because it's a hospital. There's a lot of positives, but some people won't talk to you because of your job. People look down on you when you pick up garbage, clean floors, toilets. And honestly, having a stable job like this sometimes feels like it's too good to be true. My whole life I'm a fuckup so when shit goes right I'm scared I'm going to fuck it up. It's a blessing to have a good job, but that work is tough to keep going back to.

I got a second chance, but it's a fucked-up second chance. I'm free from a cell, but I'm locked up with responsibilities and my job. The oldest of my brother's kids, he just started university. He wants to be a lawyer.

As far as them, I'm doing good by them, but I don't know how to raise kids, man.

I told my brother's kids, "You only get one chance in life. That's it. Don't be like me, starting life at thirty, still catching up on life." So I gave them a choice: either you're gonna be good or bad. Which one is it? You can't be in the middle. You can't do both. If you're bad, then go all out and be bad. And I can't do nothing but respect you because I did it. But if you wanna be good, go all out and be good. You can't do both. So they're good.

STEVE BLAKEMAN

AGE: 66

BORN IN: Des Moines, Iowa

INTERVIEWED IN: Port Angeles, Washington

Steve Blakeman got his start as a corrections officer late in life, but at age thirty-six he felt he had a calling. Before that he had been a marine serving in Vietnam (after enlisting at age sixteen), a postwar drifter with a motorcycle, a carpenter's assistant and homebuilder, and finally the owner of a construction company as well as a husband and father. We first speak with Steve in July 2016. Steve speaks in a direct, forceful manner—the way one might imagine someone who has spent decades as a corrections officer would talk—but he also has an easy laugh and often takes long pauses to gather his thoughts before speaking. During our long conversations, he tells us about his path to corrections, how he could easily have ended up on the other side of the prison bars, and his central role in helping to transform the use of solitary confinement in the Washington state prison system. Steve retired from corrections in November 2016, and ...d som...th him again in May 2017, when he reflects on his long career and wh... action... want his grandchildren to work in corrections.

I WA... ...BLE STUDENT AND JUST ...EEPLY REBELLIOUS

I had a triple hernia a... ...onia when I was born. Three months early— a six-month "preer... ...was October 1951, in Des Moines, Iowa. At one point the doctor ...mother that if anybody wanted to say good-bye to this baby that... ...better come in and do so. My grandmother brought her prayer group in. I survived, and the doctor declared it was a miracle.

My original dad wasn't around very long. He was gone by the time I was about four or five. He was an abusive drinker, I guess, which caused a divorce. But then when I was six, my mom met my stepdad, and he was a good guy, a real stable guy. He taught me right from wrong and a work ethic, and what it means to be a man in terms of responsibility.

Growing up, my stepdad was a delivery driver for Dolly Madison Bakery. My mom was a bank auditor. I had two younger brothers, Scott and Bobby, one two years younger and one six years younger. We were close and we had a good time. Iowa was a calm, consistent environment to grow up in. Winters, there was ice skating, tobogganing. Summers, we lived at the swimming pool. We had a lot of friends, a stable neighborhood.

Then when I was fourteen, my stepdad got a promotion and we relocated to Texas. That was very disruptive for me. We lived in Aldine, just a little north of Houston. Down there you could either be a surfer type or what they called a goat-roper—like a cowboy. I didn't fit into either side of that, and other kids saw me as a Yankee. I was a terrible student and just deeply, deeply rebellious.

I didn't get into serious trouble but just stayed on the edge of it. I felt like nobody was gonna tell me what to do. This was the late sixties though, during Vietnam, and a lot of young guys were going over there.

I had a grandfather—my stepdad's fathe[...]d been a marine and was in Iwo Jima, and that had always in[...]

So when I was sixteen, I decided I'[...]school and join the marines. It made a lot of sense at the ti[...]ly was all for it too. They probably thought it was a good idea. [...]ling in school, having a hard time. In those days you could h[...]ents sign off and go into the service. They signed a waiver, and [...] ble to go.

Boot camp was in San Diego. At that ti[...] guy in a Smokey the Bear hat slapping the shit out of me probably [...] my life. I didn't have that rebellious streak in the marines for very l[...]. Back in 1968, when you entered the marines you got with the program quickly.

MY CONFLICT-RESOLUTION SKILLS
WERE NOT HIGHLY DEVELOPED

The premise of marine boot camp at the time was, "If you're gonna give up, then do it now before it costs somebody their life." So that was the goal, to try to get you to fold out. I enjoyed the training. Yeah, it was a good challenge. It hit me at the right time. When I went in the marines, I weighed 135 pounds at five-eight. I came out of boot camp twelve weeks later at 160 pounds of muscle. I was seventeen. As soon as I turned eighteen, they sent me to Vietnam.

I was first sent to a landing zone in Danang as a rifleman, doing patrols, those types of things. Then after a few months, they put me in charge of distribution convoys north of Danang. In that position I had a lot more freedom than a lot of guys. I could go into town for purchases, talk to the people. It was interesting. Then, after a year, I came back to California.

After Vietnam, though, I was pretty messed up in terms of my attitude. I was doing too much drinking and too much partying and wasn't being very responsible. After Vietnam, my conflict-resolution skills were not highly developed. I'm not a big person, but I used to enjoy going into bars, getting into confrontations with guys who perceived themselves as tough guys, fighters, a███████e of those types.

My attitude and ██████s got me into situations with people that could've gone bad in a ██████ways a lot of times. I was never really drawn to crime per se or to be██████an to people. But you hear about adrenaline junkies coming out of V██nam, and I could be like that. Maybe 90 percent of the time I was running heads-up doing everything right, but the other 10 percent I was kind of unrecognizable.

After I was discharged, I just traveled around. I'd go to Houston and LA and Seattle and Chicago. I'd go set up, get a job and an apartment and get established, and then get bored and leave. There one day and gone the next. I would hitchhike to the next city and go do the same thing.

I met Pam in 1974. I was working at a boardinghouse in Seattle where she was living finishing her last year of nursing school at the University of Washington. She was this cute little guitar-playing hippie girl. I was taken by the fact that a nice girl would look at me, and she was kind of intrigued by this freewheeling renegade. We connected. It was very much an "opposites attract" thing. I was twenty-three and she was twenty-two. We were married in 1976.

Pam and I went down to Houston and got an apartment. I did construction down there. We wanted to get back up to Washington, so in 1978 we moved to Port Angeles in Washington.[1] I continued in construction for about ten years, and we had three kids during that time. I tried to make it work in construction, but the economy there was tough. During that time some other things happened as well that pushed me toward the work I'm in now. Sometime around 1986, I got a DWI. I was running around with a lot of bikers and crazies. At one point after a relatively bad night, a friend of mine pointed out that I was "typical PTSD." I didn't even know what he meant, but he gave me the number of a therapist to talk to.

So I did PTSD counseling. I'd go to this counseling for Vietnam vets and the counselor would drag it all out and have us roll around in it. You know—

---

1. Port Angeles is a coastal city of twenty thousand in the north of the Olympic Peninsula in Washington State.

"What did it taste like, what did it smell like"—and then when it was all out in the open, it would be, "Okay, time's up." Then I'd have to shove it all back inside and go out with my buddies, and we'd cry in our beers.

After a while it became obvious to me that *man* didn't have the answers I was looking for. I called out to the God of the Bible. There, I found peace and purpose and real direction for life. This really opened a new chapter in my life. Sometime in '87 or '88, I went with one of my Christian mentors to volunteer out at Clallam Bay Corrections Center, which had just been opened up a couple of years before.[2]

I don't remember that first visit clearly except that I was overwhelmed a little by the sensory details. The sounds of the steel slider doors opening and closing. I remember being struck by the cleanliness of it, the orderliness. I was surprised, and it wasn't the sort of impression I'd got about prisons from the movies.

Construction was just not supporting my family the way I wanted, so I'd gone back to school at Peninsula College, studying sociology under the GI Bill. I was thinking about corrections a little when I went to Clallam Bay. After visiting there a couple times I really had a sense of calling. So I pursued that path.

IT COULD'VE HAPPENED TO ME

In 1987, I went to work for the county sheriff's department and county corrections. The county system is ordinarily for people who are incarcerated for under a year or in pretrial detention. If you're doing time over a year, most people transition to a state prison. I found I had pretty good instincts for communication with the inmates. You know,

---

2. Clallam Bay Corrections Center (CBCC) was opened in 1985 as a 450-bed medium-security state prison. In 1991, it was converted to a close-custody facility, with additional restrictions on prisoner freedoms and privileges. After adding an additional four hundred beds, CBCC began housing maximum-security prisoners as well as medium- and close-custody prisoners. CBCC is located on the Olympic Peninsula fifty miles west of Port Angeles.

not being their buddy or anything, but just being able to communicate during stress. And not taking their verbal assaults personally, not becoming preoccupied with my personal pride.

The people who were coming to the jail, I felt like I knew them. I didn't know their names, but I knew what was in their heads. This is one of the reasons that I was good at it, I think, is I was able to connect with them. While I didn't spend time incarcerated or get into serious trouble, I was always on the edge of it. It could've happened to me.

Sometimes it felt like the whole place was a little on edge, and a confrontation with an inmate, like a murderer, could go really bad really fast. But being on edge was comfortable for me. Sometimes it almost felt like I was back home. Those things that I'd learned in confrontations in the bars and in Vietnam and those types of settings just kind of came back and became functional tools. A lot of times when everyone else was stressed and not thinking, I was able to think through things.

My work at county was a part-time, temporary position. Then to get more hours they started putting me in a juvenile detention center. Working with kids was weird. You start to have a sense of where these guys in the adult system came from. You have these kids come in to juvenile and they liked it better there than they did at home. They'd spend two or three weeks there and you get to know them a little bit, and then they'd get picked up by their drunk dads.

The County Sheriff's Office wanted me to stay there at juvenile and county jail, and get the hours in to full time, but I really felt a call to the state system and went to work for the Department of Corrections out in Clallam Bay.

"US AGAINST THEM"

I started at Clallam Bay in 1989 when I was thirty-seven. I was a little older, and a lot of the difficulties that young people have exercising authority over others had passed me a bit, so I think that helped me fit in quickly. When I got there, it had been open for a couple years and virtually every inmate there was pretty new, except for some people who'd transferred in.

Attitudes in corrections were changing as well at that time when I was just starting. In the late eighties, the attitude between corrections and offenders was very "us against them." Corrections in Washington, like other places, had gone through a cycle in the fifties and the sixties with a very punitive emphasis. For corrections staff, that meant not a lot of accountability and probably a lot of abuses.

Then in response to that the pendulum swung toward more of a psychology-based approach in the seventies. The emphasis was on "if you're nice to people, then they'll be nice"—that kind of mind-set. Psychologists were becoming superintendents and kind of setting the tone and climate for the facilities. They followed that strategy to the point where in the seventies, prisons might have a lifers club—an official committee of people with life sentences who interacted with prison management—who were allowed to speak to policies and procedures at prisons.

They had places in the prison called "free spaces" where corrections officers weren't supposed to go. People could volunteer to check lifers out of prison and take them to dinner. You know, the old adage of the inmates running the asylum really started to become more of a reality than a cliché.

Then in the late seventies, early eighties, there was a sense among corrections that things had gotten out of hand. When the department tightened up they had huge riots in Monroe, Shelton, and Walla Walla Prisons, and the corrections staff started undoing some of the psychology approaches of the seventies for more of a control-based approach again.

When I started at Clallam, we were swinging back to being definitively in control by virtue of force. It wasn't extreme in terms of emphasis on force, but it was moving that way. I think I got six days of training before my first day on the job. Then, "Here's the keys," and I got started.

It was an interesting first couple of months. At that time the laundry in the prison had been compromised, and there were drugs and weapons coming in through the laundry and being distributed to the prisoners in their laundry bags. We came to find out that all the workers there had been compromised and were bringing this stuff in, and the prison had to fire everybody in the laundry.

My first position was to step into this area where all the staff had been compromised and fired, and a lot of the inmates involved in the plan hadn't been removed. Those who were overtly involved, of course, had been moved out of there, but to a large extent, a lot of the issues around the problem were still intact.

I actually thought it was a great opportunity. I had a couple drug busts and found several shanks and had been in two or three one-on-one uses of force, where it was just me and the inmate. I had no backup. It was a good way to prove I could handle the job. At one point the sergeants and the lieutenant called me in. They told me they had gotten word that some inmates were planning to kill me that day. I didn't have a radio to check in with other guards or anything yet. I said, "Well, can I get a radio?" And they said, "No, don't have any extras."

So I asked for an extra staff member to help when the inmates came back to the work area, and I patted them all down and made sure nobody had anything coming into it, and apart from that there was nothing much I did. I was still in training, really. I hadn't even been to the Correctional Officer Academy at that point. I think I was good at defusing stressful situations, but that's not what my bosses noticed. I mean, it's hard to get accolades for what doesn't happen.

GLADIATOR SCHOOL

After a year they finally sent me over to the academy, and when I graduated I was top of my academy class. When I came back to Clallam, I started working the close-custody units.

It was during this period that Clallam Bay got a reputation statewide as being a gladiator school. In the general population units, we were fighting several times a week. That was just the way it was done. It was all physical combat. I was not always above the fray. I was as quick as anybody to use force. The rule of thumb was, you told 'em twice when they weren't complying. One of the standard phrases was, "Are you refusing a direct order?" And if the answer was yes or there was anything less than direct compliance, then that was justification for hands on.

The perspective of COs at that time was it was a slippery slope, and once inmates started disobeying anything, no matter how minor, it would spiral out of control. That is more or less the exact opposite way you should manage behavior, but that's the way it was done at the time.

Other than the general population units, we also had intensive management units, or IMUs. Those were the maximum-security segregation units in the state system. Inmates who were demoted to max custody were placed on an Intensive Management Status program.

On IMS an offender would have three primary expectations before going back into general population: Get no infractions, promote through the behavior levels, and complete an "Offender Change Program." So for example, an inmate might be assigned a program in an IMU for six months. He would have to have no behavioral infractions during that period. If he did have an infraction, he'd go back to the first stage of the process including starting the assigned time frame over again. Inmates could get stuck in IMUs for years if they didn't complete the program.

I remember my first time I had to escort a guy over to the segregation units. At the time it was single officer escort. I don't remember the circumstances for why. I put the cuffs up to the door window, and the prisoner steps back and gets cuffed up. The cells were single man, concrete, six feet by sixteen feet. They had a little partition wall between the bunk and the toilet, one window to see outside and one in the door looking inside. The windows were vertical, maybe four or five inches by twenty inches.

What really struck me about the units is that they seemed like a combat zone more than anything else. I did not really absorb the isolation and the numbness of the routine of solitary until much later, because there was always so much going on. At that time in the early and mid-nineties, the intensive management unit was very volatile. There was continual flooding of the cells, feces smearing, staff assaults, very definitively an "us against them" mentality. It was very noisy, and because of the feces smearing and stuff it really stank all the time.

Of course that makes for bad attitudes on both sides of the door. I'd hear stories from other officers about stuff they'd done like not feeding inmates. There was some instigation on both sides that kind of perpetuated conflict. It was assumed that when you had a use of force on one inmate that the other inmates were obligated to get in line for a cell extraction. The culture on both sides was to provoke each other.

This meant that inmates would cover their windows, soap the floors, tie the doors, block the cuff ports, prepare weapons, et cetera. You know, if you did one extraction, you did twelve. There was a lot of flooding. Sometimes the tiers looked like Niagara Falls. Sometimes I had to evacuate IMU over people setting their mattresses on fire by arcing their electrical systems. Now I look back at some of those things that inmates did at the time just to disrupt, and I go, *Damn.* At the time, that's just what I thought seg units were.

I was a corrections officer for three years before becoming a sergeant. From '90 to '94 I was involved in over fifty-one uses of force. What got you kudos as an officer was doing cell extractions, and there were corrections officers who liked doing it as well, liked the ongoing drama. I think nowadays an officer who had five years in might have twenty cell extractions on average. Then I was a sergeant from '92 to '96 and became an emergency response team leader in 1994, so I was the one called in to quell a lot of this stuff.

Back then, if a person refused to cuff up when he needed to be taken out of his cell, we'd come in and get him. Of course all of the other inmates would become involved with that process. Pretty soon they'd cover their windows and start making preparations for a cell entry, either by soaking their floor or blocking the door and setting up for flooding, or grabbing anything they can use for a weapon. We'd put a team together outside the door and we'd open the door and go in and get them.

It was a knock-down, drag-out fight and we'd haul 'em down and put 'em butt naked in an observation cell and have them eating Nutraloaf. Nutraloaf we haven't used in a long time. It was—how did they describe it—a "nutritionally balanced meat vegetable product." Yeah, it wasn't appetizing and was definitely meant to be punitive.

We went through a cycle, like all correctional systems, where there was a gross overuse of segregation. An individual could go to segregation without real cause. I think we had a program at one point where we could put an inmate in segregation for seventy-two days before we even had a disposition.

LIFT PEOPLE UP INSTEAD OF HOLDING THEM DOWN

In January 1996, Steve was made acting lieutenant and shift supervisor. That June he was selected to join a think tank attached to Peninsula College. Staff Training, Education, and Performance ("STEP") was a forward-thinking group of correctional professionals led by Dr. Cheryl Young. Starting in the mid-nineties, major riots were common in Washington's intensive management units, drawing media attention. Statewide legislation cut programs and resources for prisons and instituted further punitive measures, especially for those in IMUs, which led to more frequent protests. Even as the state legislature enacted these punitive, tough-on-crime measures, the state DOC was looking to develop standards that would lead to reduced conflict between incarcerated people and corrections officers. Over four years, from 1996 to 2000, Steve helped develop and implement new Emergency Response Team procedures that incorporated de-escalation techniques and innovative on-the-job training standards that incorporated nonphysical conflict-resolution training. In 2000, after a person escaped from CBCC, Steve returned to serve as training manager for implementation of the new procedures, and in 2003 he became supervisor of CBCC's intensive management unit.

I got back to Clallam Bay in 2000. It wasn't easy to get back at first. After four years of helping implement these training programs I'd become

kind of politically a persona non grata. Some of the officers at Clallam
had seen me as being part of this imposition of new ideas from academia
that really butted up against the longtime culture of corrections.

In 2000, they had a few openings for lieutenants, and I wanted to
come back as one. I'd left Clallam Bay as a lieutenant, but at first they
didn't select me, even though I was highly qualified. Then after an escape that year, they realized correctional officer training needed to be
redone, so they brought me back as a training manager.

Then after three years, I wanted to get back into the custody line of
things, and I ended up becoming IMU supervisor while the IMU was in
huge uproar. They'd been having hunger strikes and a lot of protests. There
was some resistance to me taking over among the officers because I was
seen as the "administration's boy," but it was a chance to put into practice
some of these ideas on how to lift people up instead of holding them down.

I was immediately overwhelmed. The conflicts, the grievances. . . .
You know, I just put one foot in front of the other every day. At first the
staff would hardly talk to me. But I had a couple key people in there.
Several of the instigators bid out.[3] Some good sergeants and classification
counselors eventually came in. These were staff members who were just
not interested in starting fights all the time.

My relationship on the tiers was that I knew the inmates and they
knew me. They knew my goal was not to hurt them. But they also recog-
nized that there were things that had to be done, like moving them out
of their cells to talk to a counselor, for instance. I tried to set an example
for the officers I was supervising. I always tried to be fair, patient, listen
to the inmates. Listening was not just important to the person you're
listening to——other inmates and officers see it too.

One of the things that happened early on in the unit was a lot of
cussing at inmates, and at each other, and just a lot of expletives happening throughout the unit. And then I'd see inmates getting infractions for
abusive language. I told the officers I didn't want to see any more of those

---

3. Put in a request to transfer to another position.

sorts of infractions or demotions until the staff learned how to talk without swearing. That's the kind of thing that wasn't received well at first. It was really kind of funny—when I'd be in the unit I'd hear some cussing being yelled down the corridor and next thing you know a head'd pop around the corner and say, "Oops, sorry, boss." They started to catch on.

But, you know, as they learned how to talk, that changed the tone and climate of the unit. I had a day-shift sergeant who was excellent at de-escalating conflict. I had counselors who were excellent at de-escalating circumstances. We still had conflicts of course. But after a while, when we'd have to do something like a cell extraction, we might only have to go in and get one guy instead of twelve guys at once. We had to do it sometimes because of safety/security issues, a guy cutting himself, or whatever the case may be.

But the uses of force significantly dropped. We went from two instances a week of use of force to months without uses of force. And then as infractions went down, it was easier for inmates to move through the system.

Everybody is affected though. Whether you're conscious of it or not. You're always fighting the "guard versus inmate" experience. You're always fighting that dynamic, a level of social entropy where things fall back into being a jungle. We've had a few staff who have actually gone out and entered into PTSD counseling. People who are emotionally precarious can fall off relatively quickly.

PARALLELS TO MY OWN PTSD

One problem was that some offenders would just get stuck in IMUs. The system was set up so that a person would be assigned to intensive management status, max custody.

Inmates sent to IMUs would come in on a level 2 status—that's where they'd start. If they didn't have any behavior infractions after thirty days, they'd get a radio, that's level 3. And sixty days later they'd get a television, that's level 4. If they didn't earn any infractions, eventually they'd be moved out of the IMU, maybe back to close custody.

But at any point in that process, if an individual would get an infraction, it would start the clock over again. So if he's five months into a six-month assignment, and for some reason or another he gets a serious infraction, then he starts over again—now he's got another six months. By the time he gets caught up in that cycle, one, two, three, four times, all of a sudden he's lived in a box for three years.

And that has a big effect. I've had a lot of opportunities to talk to these guys once they come out. I recognize some of the signs of how it's affected them, and there are definitely parallels to my own PTSD coming out of a war zone: the discomfort with physical proximity and sensory overload, the lack of confidence, being unsure about expectations or their capacity to meet them, the desire to go back into an environment that they're familiar with even though it's profoundly dysfunctional. A lot of times, that person becomes more comfortable in an IMU than in general population. And many times, the clock would run out on someone's sentence while they've been in an IMU for a long time, and then of course we'd open the door and drop him off on a street corner, and he'd be completely unprepared.

THE MISSION IS THE REDUCTION OF VICTIMS

From 2003 through 2013, Steve worked to revamp the Clallam Bay IMU system, including introducing new programming and more collaborative work with prison psychologists. In 2008, he began developing and implementing a transition program designed to help inmates in IMUs prepare for life in general population. From 2013 to 2016, Steve was coordinator of a nine-month intensive transition program, designed to help prepare people held in maximum-security for life after prison.

I retired in November 2016. It surprised me that I lived long enough for that. Now I've got grandkids, a big boat, a good wife. I still volunteer out at the prison, at Clallam Bay. I've been alternating with the chaplain on Sunday nights. I coordinate a Bible study on Tuesdays. It's something I've been doing ever since I first volunteered out at Clallam Bay in the 1980s.

One of the reasons I left the IMU and took over supervision of the intensive training program was that a few staff engaged in abuses and would lie about it, then cry to the union when it was addressed. It wears you down. Some people I worked with thought I was too much into giving classes and talking to inmates. But it was really about future victims. That's what I kept in mind. The changes in these men, when they got out and quit making victims, the good for them personally is almost a side thing.

You can punish people for what they did or work with them now and possibly eliminate or minimize the potential for victims in the future. We have virtually total control over someone's life while he's incarcerated, yet we often release him with less capacity to successfully interface with society than when we received him. That may be the greatest crime. It makes future victims. We have an ethical responsibility to do everything we can to minimize the potential danger to society when we drop these guys off on a street corner.

The punitive default is resilient. The punitive norm is self-perpetuating. We get fixated on making the pain so great that they'll move away from crime and not want to return to prison. But we aren't giving them something specific to move toward in terms of hope or a better vision. Or we'll give them things like janitorial certificates that don't make much of a difference in the real world.

I'm amazed at the resiliency of the human spirit in many ways, but you don't have to experience segregation for very long for it to affect you. I would go into a cell for inspections and sometimes it would even catch me in just the moment I was in there. I'd step into a cell and have the control booth close the door so that I could look at the back of the door, make sure nothing's in there, see what might be written on the back of the door, whatever the case may be.

I would tell the officer I'm with to close it, and I'd be in the cell and that door closes, and it would catch my breath. Just that confinement. I'm a scuba diver up here in the Northwest, and I'm used to diving at a hundred feet with little to no visibility. That's the same kind of feeling I had when a door closed in a cell.

As an adult, I think I could survive in segregation. The behavior performance bar is pretty low. I mean you stand on the line, you get your tray, you know, you cuff up when it's time to cuff up, you go to the shower, you go to the dayroom, make your phone call. I mean, it's not hard to stay out of trouble. But my eighteen-year-old self would have done absolutely terribly in that cell. I would've been one of these kids that got stuck in there.

In seg, you can create an environment where the expectations are that you are going to be trouble, or that you will try to get away with anything you absolutely can that disrupts or reflects some level of rebellion, and that's where a lot of these guys are. I can kind of understand that deep-seated rebellious attitude.

The Bible says, "The Lord has shown you, O man, what he requires of you and that's to do justice, love mercy, and walk humbly with your God." That's the balance: justice and mercy. Justice says that there are repercussions for actions, but mercy says there's that place and time, that when an individual is willing to learn and grow, that you introduce the space—psychologically, relationally—and the resources to allow them to move into doing and being a different person.

Would I want my grandchildren working in corrections? My answer to that is if you feel called to that, do it. If not, don't. A person who can enter that arena with vision, intention, and balance can do much good. There are many men and women doing great work in corrections. But there are many doing "eight and the gate." There are others who cause trouble on both sides of the cell door. One person with vision and balance can more than offset the trouble of the instigators. Corrections is not social work, nor is it police work, although it has components of both. Prison work is a unique profession that calls for unique people.

Right now, there are a lot of aspects about our system that hold people down, even to the exit point. I mean $40 and a bus ticket when people are released from prison? Not to mention the social stigma. It's incredible. It's amazing that our recidivism rate isn't higher than it is. But I think that mercy and justice in proper balance is the key. When that pendulum swings too far to either side, it does real damage. But when it's done right, it can make an incredible difference in peoples' lives, both in reconciling the past and giving hope for the future.

SHEAROD McFARLAND

AGE: 48

BORN IN: Detroit, Michigan

INTERVIEWED IN: G. Robert Cotton Correctional Facility, Jackson, Michigan

We corresponded with Shearod throughout 2016 and 2017 before visiting him at G. Robert Cotton Correctional Facility, where he is currently incarcerated. Because Shearod is in Michigan and we were not, interviewing him presented challenges. Interviews on the phone proved to be superficial. Prisons are crowded and loud, so our phone calls lacked intimacy, and because long-distance calls are prohibitively expensive, our calls didn't spontaneously meander the way good interviews do. So we wrote to each other. A lot. Shearod was able to acquire a tablet that works with the email system at Cotton CF. Though each page of an email costs five cents to send (and an additional five cents for each attachment) and emails can take a few days to arrive, this system allowed us to communicate more easily than we otherwise would have been able to.

When we visit Shearod, he's dressed in a blue prison-issue jumpsuit with or- *ange stripes on the shoulders and legs. He tells us he hasn't had a visitor in over two and a half years. Shearod's voice is gravelly and his face expressive, his brown irises ringed with dark blue. He's in good shape, especially considering he spent more than eleven years in administrative segregation, which Michigan prisoners simply call "the hole." Shearod began running away from home at a young age to escape his father's abuse, which led him to stealing (everything from food to cars), which led him to juvenile detention. In juvie, Shearod met friends who would introduce him to drug dealing and violent crime before his eighteenth birthday.*

Shearod was held in isolation at two different facilities in Michigan. His de- scription of the hole is brutal and unnerving, but he's honest about how his time in isolation gave him the opportunity to find an undiscovered part of himself.

I USED TO PRAY AND ASK GOD TO KILL MY DAD

Whenever I think of the year of my birth, the moon landing and Manson murders always come to mind. I was born in Detroit, Michigan, in September 1969. Back in those days Detroit was still one of America's great cities, but the next four decades would be filled with much struggle and disappointment. It's almost as if me and Detroit were bound by the same fates.

My father was a cement mason, and my mother worked for an insurance company. My earliest memories are of spending time with my mother. I loved her dearly. She was my world growing up—my everything.

My father was definitely a presence in my life from the very beginning, but I have no recollection of him until maybe around kindergarten or the year before. He was supposedly teaching me, a three- or four-year-old, the right way to put on my shoes and socks. Only if I didn't get the toes of my socks perfectly lined up with my toes, he would hit me with his belt a few times, threatening me, and calling me stupid. The same with the shoes: if I didn't get the bow on the knot perfectly symmetrical, he would hit me a few times with his belt. I don't know how long that so-called lesson lasted. To my child's mind it was forever, but in reality it may have only been an hour. What I do know is that the lessons I learned that day have lasted a lifetime. To this very day the line of my socks is always perfectly across my toes, my shoes are always tied with even bows, and violence has continued to shape my life in one way or another.

Outside of my home life I was a pretty normal kid. I enjoyed sports, especially football. I usually played running back. I was good too. I also had an intellectual side. Probably my oldest habit is books. I've been reading for my entire life. As nerdy as it sounds, me and my two main friends, Alex and Lamont, we loved *Star Wars*. Alex and I had all kinds of action figures and other toys. I was always Darth Vader, Lamont was Han Solo, and Alex was Luke Skywalker. I love *Star Wars* to this very day. Our same trio of friends also liked to imagine ourselves as X-Men. I was always Wolverine. Alex and I both had stacks and stacks of comics.

My mother was very popular, and a real go-getter, too. For instance, when I was eight I wanted to join the Cub Scouts. She volunteered to be a den mother, and before long, because of her personality and organizational skills, she became the head den mother. And not long after that she became the de facto pack leader. I didn't know it at the time, but my father was jealous of me and all the attention that I got from my mom. That may sound crazy to some, but parental jealousy actually exists. It's a real thing.

Both of my parents were from well-off families in a small town in Mississippi. I guess that also says something considering that both of my parents are Black and it was very difficult for African Americans to do well during that era in the South. Both my mom and dad went to college, too. My mother graduated from a small business college in Florida, and my father went to Tennessee State University in Nashville. He didn't graduate. Regardless of my dad's failure in this regard, I was still expected to get great grades.

The problem was not in my aptitude. Learning came easy to me, except for math. I was a high-energy child who was alone most of the time. So when I went to school I wanted to have fun, play with the other children, and just be a kid. Under those circumstances, academics didn't hold my attention. So for my very first report card I got bad grades, and my father made me strip completely naked and beat me mercilessly with a leather belt while reminding me of how dumb, stupid, and worthless I was. In his exact words, "You ain't shit and ain't never gonna be shit." Kids getting beatings with belts was nothing new to the Black community. That was and is an old tradition that we probably brought with us from slavery.

"Whoopings," as they were called, were already a part of my young experience. But school upped the ante. Oftentimes while my father was beating me for some minor mistake he would say things like, "Nigga, you lower than whale shit!" The physical abuse was often enough, but the emotional abuse happened almost daily. Eventually I began to believe the things that he said about me. I began to accept that I was just a bad child. I grew up in fear and even terror. It may sound totally warped and twisted, but when I was nine or ten years old, I used to pray and ask God to kill my dad.

A DIFFERENT PERSON

Sixth grade was probably the beginning of the end. I got bad grades for that year's final report card, which would mean a brutal beating and at least a monthlong punishment of no television, no going outside, no friends over, no telephone, no nothing. But this time, rather than waiting on my father to get home and give me the beating, I decided to run away from home. I went to family friends for refuge—who immediately called my parents and told them what I was trying to do. Both my mother and father came to get me that evening, and I could feel the violence emanating from my dad.

When we got to our house my father made me strip. This time instead of a belt he chose a thick green-and-red Christmas tree extension cord. Before I actually got my undershorts off he began to hit me with that extension cord, and the pain shot through me like bolts of lightning. After the first few minutes I knew that I couldn't take it and ran out of the house. The front door was open, but the screen was closed. My father caught me on the porch and was beating me in front of everyone in the neighborhood. I broke loose and ran down the street, but dressed only in my drawers, I had nowhere to go! After thinking on it by the curb around the corner, I decided to return home. For this second round, my dad took me to the basement and had me take off my last article of clothing, held me by my left wrist, and beat me mercilessly with that cord. The extension cord cut my skin like a knife. When it was over I had little horseshoe-shaped wounds all over my body. I was so terrified that long after my dad went back upstairs I just laid on this red-and-white-checkered couch, motionless and bleeding, scared to make a sound that might attract my father's attention. My mother didn't come to attend to me, and to make it even worse, I thought that I deserved this.

When it was over I think that I was a different person. Up until that point I had never been in any real trouble. No arrests, no suspensions from school, nothing that could be called serious. In seventh grade I began to get into fights and have all kinds of trouble in school. For the first time I was not only excluded but permanently suspended from my neighborhood middle school. I basically had given up even trying.

The first report card day of that school year was in a way the start of a new chapter in my life. That day my dad somehow knew that I'd be bringing home my school reports—and I was scared to death! So rather than go home, I didn't. I remember I had this burgundy and yellow Washington Redskins varsity jacket and I wandered the streets in that jacket for hours, cold, with nowhere to go. I guess being cold and homeless was a better option than that extension cord. Shoot, just about anything was. It eventually got dark, and I actually found an old, stained box spring on the side of a curb with someone's garbage waiting to be picked up the next day. I dragged that box spring to a nearby park and found a way to get some sleep that night. Just me, the cold, and an empty park, but no beating, no having to be afraid, and definitely no extension cord. I can't stress that enough—*no extension cord.*

At first when I would run away, I basically scavenged to survive. I slept in garages, snuck into friends' houses once their parents were asleep. I even lived in a vintage Jaguar E-Type for about a week. Once I was so hungry that I ate food out of a fast-food restaurant dumpster. Eventually though, when it started to get really tight, I began to turn to crime. Initially, I would steal food from stores, but then I got good at it and started stealing 40-ounce bottles of malt liquor from the local corner stores and would sell them for a dollar at this pool hall hangout in my neighborhood called D&N's. From there I graduated to stealing clothes and electronics from malls.

I BECAME A WARD OF THE STATE

At thirteen I was charged with grand theft auto and taken to Wayne County Youth Home. It was a huge, menacing complex with a prison wall around it and everything. I had never been locked up before and Wayne County Youth Home had a reputation for violence. I was processed, given a set of youth home clothes, which were jeans, a T-shirt, and a pair of cheap S. S. Kresge gym shoes. The next day I would wake up to what has ever since become my consistent reality of life in Michigan institutions.

I have spent thirty-two years in various Michigan facilities, and Wayne County Youth Home ranks in the top three most violent. Besides the wooden chairs that were everywhere, there were few weapons used, but young dudes went at it all day. One fight would lead to an entirely different fight for the most random reasons: changing the channel on the television, saying something to someone in the wrong tone, even winning a ping-pong game.

Legally I was in bad shape. The referee (that's what they called the judges) in juvenile court had found me guilty of being in possession of a stolen car. I was, but I was expecting probation because I had no prior felonies. Instead I was committed to the state. Which means my parents lost custody and I became a ward of the state who would be sent to either a private juvenile placement or a state training school. In other words, I would be locked up in kids' jail. I couldn't believe it!

I was placed in a halfway house for boys on the east side of Detroit. I stayed there for like a month. My mother came to visit me on a regular basis. In the beginning of November, I was sent eighty miles away to Starr Commonwealth School for Boys, in Albion, Michigan. This place was much more structured and supervised, with a program called PPC, or Positive Peer Culture, and it required the "students," as we were called, to cultivate and develop positive behavior and problem solving among ourselves. We had regular group therapy sessions. Being in Starr was a very positive experience. I grew and learned so much while I was there and made some lifelong friends. Starr also allowed us to go on home visits every major holiday. You had to be at Starr for at least one holiday before you could go home though. So I missed that Thanksgiving, but Christmas I was home and hanging out with my mom! We had fun together, but she was sick some of the time. In fact, one night we went to the movies, and she started throwing up in the parking lot. She thought that she was pregnant. I didn't know what to think. All I know is that I went back to Starr on January 2, and about three weeks later I found out that my beautiful mother was sick and had been in the hospital for a couple weeks. I was taken to go see her and she was really in bad shape. We barely spoke because she was only half conscious most of the time. I went back to Starr not realizing that that was the last time I would see my mother alive. She had just turned thirty-six. I was fourteen.

On the morning of February 2, 1984, my father called Starr and told them that they needed to get me to the hospital as soon as possible because my mother was in a bad way. So they immediately put me in a car with one of the head members of my group's staff. We arrived at the hospital an hour and a half later, where my dad was already waiting at the entrance. As we walked down a hallway, he leaned in and said, "Shearod, your mother passed away." His words landed on me like a mountain. My entire life with my mother passed through my mind in a matter of seconds, and then my knees gave in. I just collapsed in tears.

My very next thought was *Damn, now I have to be all alone with this dude.* They actually gave me the choice of returning to Starr or receiving an administrative release. I chose to return. We had the funeral and then I went back. I didn't want to be home with my dad.

I was released from Starr on May 5, 1985. I was fifteen years old. I was home alone with my bitter, angry father. And to make things worse, he was in the early stages of a crack cocaine addiction. The year my mother died, 1984, is the year that crack started really having a presence in the city of Detroit. And my father was among that first wave of addicts.

I RAN ALL THE WAY TO THE INTERVIEW

The last thing that my mother ever said to me was, "Shearod, be good." So when I got out of Starr I was determined to do the right thing. I had no criminal plans whatsoever. Coming out of Starr I was trying to prepare myself for success, so I went to school in the mornings and worked at Burger King in the afternoon. From the very beginning though I made two very serious mistakes. I started hanging out with the wrong people and I started smoking weed. Because I stayed high much of the time and had to catch the bus to work, I was chronically late. By the end of the summer my boss, Mr. Miles, finally became fed up. He demanded that I leave the premises and never come back.

While at Starr I had met and become very close with a boy I called "Black." This kid was the genuine article and was in Starr for getting caught with thousands of dollars' worth of heroin. He was the kind of young dude I admired. He was strong, intelligent, street smart, and a warrior. Plus, he had all kinds of style. I wanted to be like that.

When I came home Black was ready to celebrate, partner up, and become young drug lords. Black wanted me to sell drugs with him. For a sixteen-year-old boy, at least moneywise, he was doing well. He would flash large wads of cash and all kinds of expensive clothes and jewelry to try and convince me to get into the dope game. He and I had truly forged a family bond, and I was one of the only people that he really trusted. But I was committed to living a clean, crime-free life, until I got fired from Burger King. After that, something clicked in me, and I gave in to the weakness and temptation of fast money. I also had my first fistfight with my dad, which he won by punching me in the throat. That knocked all of the fight out of me.

As the final months of 1986 went by, I began to hang out with Black and started making more money. I continued to sell in my hood to my little rinky-dink clientele, which sometimes included my father and his circle of cracked-out associates. Getting money with Black, hustling out in the open, was probably the rawest level of street life that I had experienced. Until then, violence had barely been a factor in my drug-dealing history, but this was eighties Detroit, and everything was hyper-aggressive.

1987 came and my hope was that I would graduate and be in college or university within the next year. But at times it seemed like my problems only got bigger by the day. At the end of the school year, my guidance counselor told me that there was no way I would be graduating. I had done a terrible job of keeping track of where I was in the curriculum, and she told me that in order to graduate I would have to go to summer school and take the GED test. But there would be no walking across the stage with cap and gown. I was hurt. Part of the problem was that my school records from Starr had gotten lost in the move from school to school, so the time and grades from those classes were lost.

I was exhausted, frustrated with my life, using drugs more than ever, and becoming more and more disillusioned. Instead of the pipe I smoked coke rolled up in weed. In Detroit that's what we called a "51." I was also carrying a gun sometimes, which I had never done before. And then out of the blue, one of my stress-induced irrational decisions turned out to be one of the most rational things I could have possibly done: I said to hell with it all, sold my remaining product, and started looking for a job. I didn't want to live like that.

I ended up getting an interview with a company called Reymer & Gerser Associates, which was a telemarketing outfit. I still didn't have a car, which presented a problem. The day before the interview I asked my dad if he would take me to the Reymer & Gerser offices. He agreed, and I went to bed that night feeling good about the possibility of a new job. So the next day while I'm getting myself together, I notice that my dad isn't showing any sign of preparing to take me anywhere. So I go to his bedroom doorway and comment that he needs to get ready. His response was "I ain't takin' you nowhere." I ran all the way to the interview. All three and a half miles, almost nonstop. When I made it to their offices I was sweating and everything, but still made it on time. I gave a great interview and got the job! I feel good about that to this very day. I worked at Reymer & Gerser for what was probably less than two months and got fired for chronic tardiness. It was a combination of having no transportation and being high all the time.

I started selling again, this time "from the hip," meaning man to man, plus I opened up a "spot," which is Detroit slang for a drug house. I had a friend named Johnny, and his friend Clyde, who were both working for me, and I was doing pretty well.

On September 13, 1987, some friends and I went into this restaurant called Jeff's BBQ. While we were there some guys spotted us outside, and went and gathered a few more dudes who came into the eatery and started threatening us. They either didn't know or didn't care that I was a ticking time bomb. Out of pure rage I shot a boy named Robert Woods, and I chased down another dude with every intent of killing him, too.

Shearod was convicted of second-degree murder and a felony firearms charge and sentenced to twenty-five to forty years in Michigan state prisons. He spent his first two years in prison in segregation. After eight years, he was transferred to Carson City Correctional Facility, in Montcalm County. While at Carson, Shearod stabbed two inmates. When guards came to break up the fight, Shearod and other inmates began stabbing officers, and a riot broke out.

I-MAX TORTURED YOUR SOUL

For the incident at the Carson City facility, I ended up getting sixteen to forty years. So instead of getting out in 2009, my first possible out date is 2023.

Ionia Maximum was the state's only level 6 facility. That means every cell is an isolation cell. The entire facility was long-term segregation. I-Max was supposedly a facility for the system's "worst of the worst." Most dudes who got into serious trouble like murders, serious staff assaults, escape, et cetera were sent to ICF, which is the acronym for Ionia Correctional Facility. I used to say that "ICF" stood for "Insane Criminal Facility" 'cause a significant number of its population was mentally ill in some way. Some were like that when they got there, and others were made that way by the prison. I-Max tortured your soul.

Those I-Max doors were super-oppressive. The cells were probably eight by seven. Like being locked in a closet or bathroom. I-Max had these colorful cells with tile floors, a brick-red desk mounted to the wall with an attached swinging stool, yellow heat registers, and a green window frame with a shuttered window that you could open by turning a knob at the bottom. The window was right above one end of the bunk. The toilet was at the other.

Inside, the walls were made of cinderblocks, which means they were hollow on the inside. Guys would tear off the metal stools attached to the desks and use them as sledgehammers to break through the walls to go at their enemies. The officers were major players in this as well. Many of them were like cruel children torturing fenced-in dogs. They would emotionally torture the inmates, assault them, starve them, throw away their mail, tamper with the food of prisoners they didn't like, all kinds of craziness.

Dudes would wage noise warfare on each other with nonstop banging and biological warfare with urine and feces. When you entered some units you were immediately struck by the pungent smell of human excrement. There literally were shit wars.

I had a neighbor in detention who used to routinely yell, scream, and bang his metal cell foot locker lid all night. He would also smear feces all over his door and the heat register, which was almost the same as him smearing it in my cell. Nothing smells worse than human feces.

Plus, I-Max was infested with mice. In maximum-security facilities the power goes out at 12 a.m. From midnight until six in the morning, the lights are automatically turned off, which means for six hours your cell is in almost complete darkness. You would barely notice the mice during the day, but at night they would come alive. The sound of rodents romping through the heat registers was loud enough to wake you up. It may sound weak, but being awakened by the sounds of mice in the middle of the night is extremely traumatizing. That along with everything else was a form of psychological terror. It either brought the aggression out of you or drove you crazy. I feel blessed to have survived it with my faculties intact. Many men didn't.

The yard cages are how we got yard in the hole. For one hour, five days a week, each man is put in a separate cage. They look like kennel cages. There are seven cages in total, all of them attached to the other. At most Michigan max joints the yard cages are made of heavy-duty steel, but at I-Max the cages were just made of plain old fencing. Because of that, dudes would tear the cages apart and have actual cage fights.

Because I had come for something considered super serious, I was automatically put on suicide watch, which is MDOC policy.[1] The hostility began from the very beginning. Officers refused to feed me and threatened to assault me if I came out for showers. I-Max had an in-cell

---

1. MDOC is Michigan Department of Corrections.

intercom system and they would give me my food trays and then get on the intercom and say things like, "How did you like that ball sweat on your tater tots?" Officers were known to break into an inmate's cell at unexpected times and kick his ass, so to protect myself and be prepared for late-night combat, I slept fully clothed on top of my sheets and blankets for two months straight.

In Michigan they have two levels of segregation, punitive seg and administrative seg. They both are the hole, but one doesn't allow you to have any property and the other does. I-Max had five units. All segregation. You could call units one and two "the hole inside the hole." Those two units were nonstop bedlam and also where officers kicked the most ass.

I was in unit two. The officers were seriously whooping ass over there on a daily basis. Fear was a constant. Eventually I was released from detention and put in an administrative segregation cell in another unit.

I BEGAN TO REMEMBER WHO I REALLY WAS

I once heard a guy say, "If you are Black and you do a substantial amount of time in prison, it's going to have one of two effects on you: make you hate white people or make you want to kiss their feet." I believe that there is some truth in there somewhere. The MDOC is almost completely run and staffed by white people. The majority of the prison population is Black.[2] It begs the question, why does crime in urban Black areas translate into jobs for rural or mostly white areas? There are white-majority towns in the state where the main industry seems to be corrections.

The cell I was placed in had such a drafty window that ice would accumulate all over the frame and surrounding walls. It was winter by the time I was moved there so I had to sleep under two blankets with a hat and towel over my head, plus socks, thermals, and coat. I brought the problem to the attention of staff many times, but they didn't care. I don't know if

---

2. According to the Prison Policy Initiative, in 2010, Michigan incarcerated Blacks at nearly six times the rate of whites, and nearly four times the rate of Latinos.

I was put there by design or not. But again, as a kid I'd slept in abandoned garages in the dead of Detroit winters. So I could deal with all of this.

It seemed like once you were in I-Max, it was impossible to get out. There were different levels to the place, but no hope of leaving. Two positive things happened while I was there though: around '96, my father started trying to reach out and support me. Up until then I barely heard from him. The other thing was I had a spiritual epiphany.

At I-Max, once you were released from detention, if you could afford it, they would let you listen to music in your cell. Throughout my life music has always been a source of comfort. That has not changed in prison. Besides music and books, my major focus was analyzing my existence. I would constantly ask, *How did my life come to this?* I investigated my every thought, memory, and emotion. The primary question was always, why?

One day I was listening to a Jimi Hendrix song, "Straight Ahead," that I'd never heard before. In the song, Jimi sings: "The best love to have is the love of life." This small statement hit a massive switch in my mind. I rewound the tape to that lyric three, four times, and the tears began to flow. I felt different. I was different. From that moment on I had a feeling of rediscovering myself. I began to remember who I really was: not this hateful, bitter, violent, racist predator but a lover of people, and music, and art, and kindness.

MORE HOLE TIME

I was seeing the SCC (Security Classification Committee) one evening in January 2000 when the resident unit manager asked me, "Are you ready to get out of here?" I paused in surprise and said, "Yeah, I would love that." She replied, "Okay, I'm putting in a transfer for you." I couldn't believe it. After four and a half years I was leaving this insane asylum!

My heart did a little dance. I was told the night before I left that I was going up to "Marquette." Marquette was Marquette Branch Prison in the Upper Peninsula of Michigan, the second-oldest prison in the state, and the oldest max joint. All maximum-security facilities are filled with the most aggressive prisoners. My main concern was the staff though. Serious assaults on officers were not easily forgotten by MDOC staff. The department holds grudges like no other. But at least I might be getting out of the hole! And Marquette was known for giving the worst of the worst a shot in general population, or GP.

I faced SCC at Marquette wearing an all-white jumpsuit. I tried to say what I thought they wanted to hear to be persuaded to release me to GP. Then I heard the words that made my heart stop: "Maybe one day someone will give you a chance in population. Put him in D block." I was drained and dejected. More hole time, with nothing definite to look forward to. I was escorted, cuffed up and on a human leash, to D block. These blocks were old, dirty-looking, dark on the sunniest of days, stank like a sewage treatment plant, and LOUD!

PART OF THE AD-SEG MADNESS

Marquette had three tiers of barred cells, not doors. That was the reason it was so goddamned loud. Dudes screaming down the rock all day and night. I preferred the bars to the doors, just not the nerve-racking constant noise. The bars created a greater sense of freedom. I know that sounds super ironic—being behind bars giving a deeper sense of freedom—but it's true. There was more openness.

It's actually difficult to describe the insanity of "the hole." It's like the third panel of the painting *Garden of Earthly Delights* by Hieronymus Bosch. Surreal and grotesque. The blocks in Marquette were basically big, hollow, rectangular structures with three rows of cells stacked on top of each other back to back. Sound just bounced off the walls. When one prisoner got gassed on your side, we all got gassed. And people getting gassed is an everyday possibility in segregation.

I used to sell cigarettes in the hole. Dudes in GP would send me tobacco, candy, tape players, tapes, batteries, all kinds of stuff. Around

2002 they took all tape players and battery-operated appliances out of segregation in Michigan facilities.

In the hole is where I learned just how powerful cigarettes were. Dudes would go crazy over them. Give up their food, money, whatever. I never used to power trip over it though. I would make some fun out of it to break the monotony. At the time the game show *Who Wants to Be a Millionaire?* was still kind of popular, so I used to run a game show in the hole called *Who Wants to Smoke?*, where I would pose questions and whoever answered it first would win a cigarette. I would try and make it so that everyone in the area won at least one smoke.

MY ALONENESS WAS COMPLETE

In April 2000 my dad came to visit me with his soon-to-be wife, Kathryn. It was a decent visit. Three months later he was married to Kathryn, and three months after that doctors discovered a massive tumor on his brain.

My father died in March 2002. I shed a tear, but truthfully I didn't feel anywhere near what I should've felt had I had a normal, healthy relationship with the man. The tear I shed was more for myself than my father. Now my aloneness was complete. Because I was in maximum security there was no consideration of going to the funeral.

The days became weeks, the weeks months, and the months years. I worked out, read, studied, thought, and dreamed. As a child and young man I used to dream of academic achievement, financial and career success, and the blessing of family. I was always a relationship dude who wanted a wife and four or five children. Now here I was nearly twenty years later fantasizing about going to a maximum-security prison's general population yard. Prison had become the limit of my dreams.

I didn't even think about being free anymore. Around 2005 I had begun to fall into serious despair. I started to envision myself hanging from beams and having other suicidal visions. In a strange, perverted way they used to give me comfort. I guess it was just the thought of my pain finally being over. In another way though, I felt that I deserved my hurt. I had taken someone's life and nearly taken another one at Carson City. How could I expect sympathy or mercy? Just as my circumstances were the exact opposite of all that I'd planned for, I became the exact opposite of the kind of man that I ever wanted to be.

In either late July or early August, some staff at the facility ran a sting operation and broke my little smuggling ring. They thoroughly searched my cell and found food that I'd saved from a previous meal, which caused me to be placed on seven days of Nutraloaf. Nutraloaf is this horrible concoction of all the food from each meal cooked into one solid block. This was a punishment specifically for dudes in the hole who had food violations or used food containers to throw feces and the like. I never ate a bite of it though. The men in my area made sure that I never went hungry or had to eat that slop.

THE THOUGHT OF GETTING OUT OF THE HOLE!

On the afternoon of Friday, September 2, 2006, an officer came to my cell and told me to back up to the bars and cuff up. I immediately thought they wanted to shake my cell down again because of the smuggling sting. I asked the officer, "What's this all about?" He said, "The deputy wants to talk to you." I got to the office and Assistant Deputy Alexander was waiting for me. He said, "Someone is thinking about releasing you to population and I'm here to talk to you about it." My heart started doing double time.

He asked what I would do if released to population. I had to wing it 'cause I really didn't know other than the basic stuff like use the phone, eat, go to yard. He made it his business to tell me that if I attempt to do harm to any of their staff, I would be shot and killed. Marquette has gun towers everywhere. He then tells me that since it was the Friday before Labor Day he would think about it over the weekend and make the decision Tuesday. I was so wound up and excited that I literally couldn't sleep for two days. The thought of getting out of the hole!

Tuesday came, and I didn't hear anything. Wednesday, nothing. Thursday, I had to visit the in-unit nurse's station for my annual birthday check-up. That afternoon me and maybe five other guys were in the yard cages when the big, heavy metal door that led to the yard area begins to open up. As soon as I heard the keys against it I had a feeling. One of the officers opens the door, steps just outside of the doorframe and said, "McFarland, Happy Birthday." And closed the door. I literally jumped for joy. And then dropped to my knees right there in the middle of my cage. What I felt in that moment is indescribable. It was pure exhilaration. A rush of pure happiness! I didn't know what to do with all that joy. I was bursting at the seams with it. The ironic thing is that once I got back in the block they actually rushed me out. They needed me out before count time. I obliged them. After six and a half years in D block, and eleven years, one month, and eighteen days in the hole they were letting me out and I couldn't have been more pleased. It had been a long journey through the hole, but I was coming out strong and intact. I thank the love that my mother gave me for keeping me strong and helping me grow.

SONYA CALICO

AGE: 33
BORN IN: McAllen, Texas
INTERVIEWED IN: Dallas, Texas

We begin talking with Sonya in 2017, shortly after she was released from her final two-month stint in a Dallas men's prison. When we meet Sonya near her home in Dallas, she's wearing a long black dress with a neckline that reveals a "trust no man" tattoo on her chest and her long nails are freshly done in various colorful designs. A tattoo on her neck reads "Mercedes," an homage to her mother. She speaks quietly, smiling a bit when she talks about her business acumen. Though reserved, Sonya talks openly and honestly about her life, which has taken her from small-town Texas to migrant communities in Idaho and into the depths of American jails.

After being found guilty of fraud, Sonya landed in solitary in both Oklahoma and Texas. Because Sonya is transgender, she was placed in single-cell isolation, supposedly for her own protection. After being released, she got involved with the

Trans Pride Initiative, a Dallas nonprofit that works to empower the trans commu-
nity. With Sonya's help, TPI was able to reform the way trans women are housed
in Dallas county jail. It's progress Sonya is proud to have been a part of. Countless
trans prisoners remain in long-term isolation throughout the United States under
the guise of "protective custody."

MY PARENTS WANTED TO LIVE BETTER

When I was little, I would wanna play with girls in school. I used to hate
PE class, I wouldn't want to play nothing. I was always real feminine even
when I was in elementary school. I'm not going to say that I got bullied
because I wasn't, but people used to make fun of me because they knew
I was gay.

It was just something I couldn't help. It was something I was born
with. Growing up with my girl cousins, we played dolls and I was never
outside playing with the boys, none of that. I always thought I was a girl.
And sometimes I would cry because I'd be like, *Why do I have to live this*
life every day, worry about people laughing at me, making fun of me, saying I'm
gay and this and that. Why me? Why me?

I was born in 1985, and I have one older brother named Louis and
one younger sister, Lyzette. I'm originally from the valley, from McAllen
in south Texas.[1] It's a very small border town. McAllen is a place that
nobody would want to go back to. It being a border town, the population was like 95 percent Hispanic. Even the teachers would talk to us in
Spanish most of the time. I didn't learn how to speak English until I was
in third grade.

I grew up seeing my parents struggle. I was born in the United
States and I'm a US citizen, but both my parents are Mexican. Their
names are Mercedes and Edward. They didn't get US citizenship until I
was about eighteen. When I was growing up in McAllen, they were able

---

1. McAllen, Texas, is a city of 140,000 that is part of the Reynosa-McAllen metropol-
itan area of 1.5 million on the Texas-Mexico border at Texas's southern tip.

to find work, but always for just a little pay. Most of it was agricultural work—cabbages and fruit and stuff grew around McAllen. My parents would work in the fields for a few dollars an hour, but it was worse down in Mexico, so they didn't really mind doing it. But I remember them coming home with their fingers all busted up and things like that.

I have some fond memories of family, especially my mom's big family who also lived around McAllen. She has ten sisters and three brothers, and they all had a lot of kids. So I had lots of aunties and cousins. We had lots of parties, get-togethers, things like that. But my parents wanted to live better and decided to move.

First we moved to Idaho, around when I was in second grade. One of my mom's sisters, Aunt Laura, was up there, and they paid more for agricultural work up north. What we didn't know was that it would be so cold and snowy. I'm not going to lie, the year we stayed up in Idaho made me feel like an immigrant, or the child of immigrants, because of the living situation we had. We stayed in a camp. It was kind of like the projects for agricultural working people. We stayed in a tiny two-bedroom cabin in the fields surrounded by mountains with my aunt Laura's family, so six kids and four adults in a little two-bedroom. And in the winter it snowed all day, every day. My parents and siblings and I would sleep on the floor with just a space heater that was mounted in the wall. We'd have to keep the stove on just to get enough heat to stay warm.

And then when we had school, we had to walk a mile through two or three feet of snow to get to the bus stop. In Idaho, unlike in McAllen, none of the teachers spoke Spanish. My teacher brought in a translator for me, but I could tell it was hard for her, and I felt really out of place. All the other kids in the class would look at me like, *Where's this person from?*

I remember seeing my mom coming home from work and crying because that life was not what she wanted for us. She got in contact with another sister, Deralez, who lived in Dallas. Aunt Deralez was basically like, "I don't know why you're up there. Why are you even going through all that when you could come down here and start working with our family here?" My cousin used to own a warehouse back in the day where they made all kinds of plastic molds and stuff.

So we moved to Dallas when I was in third grade, when I was about ten years old. My parents both worked at the factory packing up molded plastics, things like makeup cases. It was much better money.

I remember Dallas being different, in a good way. We lived with my auntie Maria. Her apartment was much bigger than the place we'd had in Idaho. Three bedrooms, two bathrooms. The one thing, though, was that Auntie Maria was the one sibling that all the others had problems with. She was just a difficult person about every little thing.

I WANTED TO LIVE LIKE A GIRL

I had a cousin named Cassandra who lived in the next building over from us. She lived with two brothers. She was transsexual, and my auntie Maria didn't like her because of her lifestyle. One of my aunt's friends lied to my aunt and told her my mom was trying to move in with Cassandra behind her back. Really my mom had asked Cassandra if she could do laundry at her apartment because Cassandra had a washer and dryer.

I remember that this was Christmas Eve. We had come back from washing clothes at Cassandra's house and Aunt Maria was waiting for us. When we got there, she said, "I was waiting on you to get back, bitch. How you gonna dare move outta my house behind my back after I moved y'all from over there! As a matter of fact you didn't even have to take this long to move the fuck out." My auntie started grabbing all our stuff and she's throwing it out the front door, and then she threw us out the house.

I was crying and crying. We didn't have anywhere to go, so Cassandra was like, "Well, come on, I'm not gonna let y'all out like this. Why don't you come stay over here until you figure out what you wanna do." So Cassandra allowed us to move in with her, and then she helped my parents find their own apartment.

Cassandra was someone I always looked up to. And I had another cousin—the son of my aunt Maria, actually—who never transitioned but who dressed up as a girl every weekend. I'd be around him and Cassandra a lot when they were getting dressed up and putting makeup on and stuff. It was so interesting to me, and I just wanted to be around them.

I didn't have any friends in middle school or high school—or only like three or four friends, and they were female. My parents were strict. They expected a lot from us kids, and I always felt like the black sheep. But by fifteen, I'd realized that I was not only gay but that I wanted to live like a girl. I wasn't getting much out of school, and I just stopped going most of the time. I even got picked up for truancy, and my mom refused to pay the fine. I had to work it off myself. I felt like my parents wouldn't accept who I was—I feared rejection. So I moved out when I was fifteen. I moved in with another cousin named Rosa who lived half an hour away. That's when I got my first job, at a Sonic Drive-In. Rosa was the manager there, and she hired me to take the orders out to customers. Rosa was also someone I felt like I could tell everything to, and she and I became closer than I was with even my siblings.

It was actually just supposed to be a summer job, but I wound up liking it, so I took it upon myself to learn how to do every job there. I ended up becoming a manager at the restaurant by the time I was seventeen years old. It was just hard because I was going to school *and* working. That's when I left school. I was like, *You know what, I don't even need school, I'm doing good.* I was an independent person. Now, being older and looking back, I really wish that I had never left school.

When I was eighteen, I went to a gay club in Dallas for the first time, and I met my first group of friends who are still my friends to this day. I was able to go out with these friends and be so comfortable with them because they're all gay. I decided to stay away from my family. I'd decided to transition, and I didn't want to see them until I had. I didn't want anyone to argue with me or try to talk me out of it. I didn't want to see them until there was no going back.

I started getting hormone treatments from my auntie when I was eighteen. She showed me how to do it, and then eventually I started giving myself the injections. That was also around the time I first went to jail.

THEY'D LAUGH AT YOU

My first arrest was for possession of marijuana. I was driving with a friend through Farmers Branch, which is a suburb of Dallas that's known for racial profiling. It's real racist there. I'm Hispanic and my friend is African American, and we got pulled over. When I asked the cops why they pulled me over, they didn't give me a reason. But they asked to search the car.

We were coming home from picking up some Chinese food and we had two little dime bags of marijuana we'd just picked up. The bags were closed, we hadn't even smoked. My friend put them under some lo mein noodles in the food. But the cops searched so deep they even dug in the food boxes and found the weed, and I was arrested.

I had no idea what to expect. I'd never been to jail. Even though I'd just started transitioning, I was most scared about what might happen to me because I'm trans. When I got to Lew Sterrett jail, the officers at the jail asked me if I was gay.[2] They had a "homosexual tank," and that's where they put me.[3] I was in jail for about ten or fifteen days. I was lucky to be in the homosexual tank with a girl who'd transitioned. She'd been arrested for prostitution, and she kind of took me under her wing and showed me how to be in there, what to do and what not to do. So my first time in jail wasn't so bad, but it was still kind of scary just not knowing what to expect.

In my late teens, early twenties, I continued to transition. Other than hormones, I started getting body modifications at twenty, twen-

---

2. Lew Sterrett Justice Center is one of five detention facilities within the Dallas County Sheriff's Office. The facility houses more than 3,200 maximum-security inmates.

3. Because gay, lesbian, and transgender people may face specific challenges while incarcerated, some facilities house these populations separately.

ty-one. When I was out at clubs I was meeting older transsexual people, and that's where I met my godmother, Nikki Calico. She looked at me and was like, "There's something about you that I like, and I've always wanted a daughter." We were compatible—I could tell she was someone like me who just didn't have many friends growing up. And she helped me with body modifications, how to feminize my face with fillers, that sort of thing. I took her name, Calico, in remembrance of her and in appreciation for everything she taught me and did for me. You know gay people, we consider our friends to be our family. I took her name just to continue it.

One thing about transitioning is that back in the day, if you were a transsexual and went to apply for a regular job and they knew who you were, they'd laugh at you. So there was a lot of pressure to turn to escorting. It was just something that was in the lifestyle. So I turned to that, and I was making a living at it. I'd kept in contact with the girl I'd met in jail, and she showed me how it worked.

Around that time, in 2005, Hurricane Katrina hit. Then in 2006 the apartment complex where I was staying was used as a home for a lot of people who were pushed out by Katrina. I met a man who was a victim of the hurricane. I started dating him, actually. And he was like, "You know, we could make some money because I know all the answers to the questions they ask you when you call to apply for FEMA benefits."

He showed me how to do it, and I started getting benefits, like $2,500. I linked up with one of my friends and I told him about it. At first it was just supposed to be like, "We gonna get a certain amount of money," but my friend got greedy and he kept going and going and he got caught. When he got caught he snitched on me. I was the one who showed him how to get those benefits, and I ended up going to jail for it.

The police actually arrested me at my parents' house, when I was with my mom. It was right after Thanksgiving. The officer was a woman in plainclothes who had an old photo of me and didn't know I'd transitioned by then. She told my mom that I'd given her my contact info at a bar! She said, "I've been trying to call him, but no answer," and my mom's like, *Uh, that doesn't make any sense.* But she called me to the door, and that's when all these other officers came in and arrested me.

So I got arrested and I ended up bonding out and then getting five years' probation. But I kept smoking marijuana, and my tests were coming back dirty. My probation officer warned me that the next dirty test, I'd go back to jail. So I decided to run. I stayed in Dallas and just stopped reporting to my parole officer, which meant I had a warrant for my arrest. I figured they'd catch me eventually, but I ran for three years, and I really turned to escorting again then to support myself.

"I'LL BEAT THE FUCK OUT OF YOU"

I ended up finally getting picked up in Oklahoma City in a sting around the end of 2011. I was arrested for prostitution. The jail in Oklahoma City was different than county jail in Dallas. They didn't know where to put me—they didn't have anything like the homosexual tank. It took them six hours to figure out whether to put me on the male side or female side. I was brought in at 2 a.m. and they had to wait for the sergeant to come in at 8, 9 a.m. He asked, "Did you have the full surgery yet?" And to make a long story short, they eventually decided to put me in single cell, in segregation. On the men's side.

The way the segregation cells are set up in Oklahoma City, the pods have two floors of cells and then at the ground floor is a kind of central area with tables and chairs for the eating area. I was on the top floor, behind a solid door with a little window. I could look out the window and see the other cells and the eating area, but I'd only get one hour a day that I could be out. I'd use that time to shower. Some people would go watch other people's cells through their windows and just talk to them and stuff like that. I had a lot of guys who would come to my window just because they were so curious. They would come and say, "Show me your titties." Just all that stuff. There were a lot of guys who would come to my window and be like, "You fucking faggot bitch. If you get out the same time when I'm out, I'll beat the fuck out of you."

But at least in Oklahoma City, you could see other people through your cell window, so you weren't completely alone. You could talk to people, and they weren't all scary. I even had a cool guard. He used to come to my window. He was a younger guard. I guess he was a new employee. He used to come to my window and actually talk to me. He didn't care that I was a transsexual. Maybe he had transsexual relatives or maybe he was attracted to transsexuals. I don't know. He never came at me like that, but he was always real cool. He would make sure that every time he was on shift, he would come talk to me for thirty, forty-five minutes.

I would read books. That's my main thing. But I would read, and it wouldn't stick in my head. I would just read whatever I could get and I would read just to be doing something. I would read the newspaper beginning to end, do the crosswords, and even read all the inserts. The inserts were how I would take myself out into the world. That's how I would keep my mind sane because I was really going crazy in there. The Bible was offered to me in there too. I didn't have nothing but time to sit there and get into the Bible. When I would go into the Bible and read though, I was like, *No, this is not me.* I believe in God, but I don't believe in the Bible.

I was by myself in single cell for six weeks before the court date. I was actually able to get out of that prostitution charge because the arresting officer did things he shouldn't have—played with my breasts, put my hand on his private parts. I told the judge I could describe his privates. He was supposed to show up in court, but with everything going on, he didn't show, so the charges were dropped.

ALL YOU CAN HAVE ON IS YOUR BOXERS AND YOUR SOCKS

After my charges in Oklahoma were dropped, I still had a warrant out in Dallas. Authorities from Texas came up and put me in chains to take

me back to Dallas to serve time for my fraud arrest. I was sent to Lew
Sterrett to serve my time.

I was in the "homosexual tank" for the first three months. Then they
had a shakedown. That's where they come in and order everyone to take
their uniforms off, to strip down to their boxers. All you can have on is
your boxers and your socks.

But me having breasts and all that, I asked one of the sergeants, "Sir,
can I keep my shirt on?" Because after they make you take everything off,
they make you walk out of your tank and walk into the hall where the
men in all the other tanks are. I'm not going to be coming out, walking
out with my breasts out and all that. The sergeant told me, "Yeah, you
can keep your shirt on."

When we were walking out in line out of the tank, the main sergeant was a female, an African American lady. She was waiting, inspect-
ing everybody as we came out of the tank. When I came out, she was
like, "Why do you have a shirt on?" I said, "Ma'am, I already talked to the
other sergeant. I have breasts." She was like, "Step out of line and stand
right here by the wall." She waited until everybody got out. She said,
"Come here." She put me in a room with just her. She said, "Take your
shirt off." I was like, "Okay, but I want to still be able to keep my shirt
on after you make sure that I don't have nothing on me, right?" She said,
"Let me tell you something, bitch." She put her finger on my forehead. "If
you don't take your motherfucking shirt off . . . you're still a man. You're
going to forever be a man. Everyone else has to pass through without a
shirt, it ain't any different for you." I told her I just wanted to put my shirt
back on before passing the other tanks, and she said, "Take it off before
I mace you." I took off my shirt. I wasn't trying to get maced. Then she
said, "Okay. Put your shirt back on. You need to go in there, grab your
shit, and get the fuck out there."

I asked, "Ma'am, where am I going?" She said, "Don't worry about
that." I said, "Ma'am, if you don't tell me where I'm going, then I'm not going to do nothing because I have a right to know what the hell is going on."

She grabbed me and threw me against the wall. She said, "Bitch, I told your faggot ass, you're going to follow my rules." Then she slammed me against the wall, and I blanked out. My first reaction was to push her back. I pushed her back, and she fell back and slid across the floor. That's when the guards came and grabbed me and threw me on the floor. Then they picked me up, made me go get my stuff, and then they put me in solitary confinement.

RED KEPT ME SANE

They put me in solitary confinement because I pushed her, but she made it seem like it was protective custody. She felt that since I looked like a girl and I had breasts that I didn't belong in the tank. Mind you, the tank is a homosexual tank. The floor sergeant said, "It's for your protection," but she was just saying that to give a reason for putting me in lockup. When I tried to appeal it, it was denied because she said the reason was "protective custody." What about my protection the three months I've already been in there? I didn't have no issues for three months, so why should I have an issue now? That's the whole point of the homosexual tank.

They wouldn't let me come out of solitary confinement. I was in there going crazy. Solitary at Lew Sterrett was different than Oklahoma City. In Oklahoma City, at least when you looked out your window you could see other people, talk to them. But in Dallas, the view out the window in my door was nothing but a white wall.

In solitary confinement in Lew Sterrett, you have your own shower. It's your bunk bed, your shower, your little table. They bring you a tray of food to your door. So you're completely isolated from other people. The only thing that kept me sane was that every cell has a vent that the A/C comes out through. Every vent is connected to all the other cells. The inmate who was in the cell next to me, he basically had a crush on me because he had seen me being put in there. He was like, "Baby, I know what you are. I know you're transsexual, but I'll help your stay here be better, and I'm sure that you talking to me will make mine better."

All I knew was his nickname, Red. He was in solitary because he had a lot of tattoos, some with supposed gang affiliations, and so he kept getting into fistfights and stuff. He voluntarily went to solitary so he wouldn't get in fights. So he was in protective custody too.

I would move my bed, my mat by the vent, and we would talk through the vent. We would pretend that we were out in the free world. Red was like, "Okay, this is what we're going to do. Just put in your mind that we're actually out there, and this is our cell phone." He would be like, "Ring ring ring." I was like, "Hello," like I'm actually answering my phone because I started talking to myself being in there.

Twenty-three hours or whatever, I was in there questioning even me living my life the way I'm living, like I really started doubting that. *When I get out, should I try to be a man? Why do I have to go through this? Why? Why am I going through this? I didn't do nothing to deserve this kind of treatment. I know I did something illegal, but I'm already in jail. Why am I getting treated even worse?* It was just that one guy. If it weren't for him, I would have gone completely crazy.

I asked for a psychiatrist. The only thing the psychiatrists did when they came and talked to me was put me on Celexa for depression and another pill that I forget the name of. I didn't want to be taking that medication every day because I didn't want my body to get used to it and then when I got out, I would have to take it every day too.

I was in that solitary cell for the rest of my year at Lew Sterrett, so nine months of solitary. I kept appealing, but they wouldn't let me out. I was talking to myself a lot. I didn't hallucinate, but I'd have conversations with myself. I'd ask myself questions and answer them. Then I'd go back and be like, *No.* Red would hear me talking to myself. He'd be like, "Sonya, who are you over there talking to?" On the other side there's another guy, but I'd never talk to the other guy. The other guy actually, his mind was gone. He thought he was a person from the Bible. Every day I would wake up, and he would say scriptures of the Bible. Yeah. He knew that I was a transsexual, so sometimes he would take it upon himself to be like, "You're going to hell. You're going to burn in hell." I'd be having to deal with that every day. I thought, *Oh god.* That's when Red would say, "Don't listen. Come here. Come talk to me."

I had a routine already. I would exercise before I would shower because by the time I got through exercising I'd be sweating, so okay, shower time. I'd hear the nurse coming through to bring people's pills. I'd take my pills. Fifteen minutes later, I'm knocked out. I wake up at four o'clock in the morning. There's breakfast. Get my breakfast tray. Eat my breakfast. Go back to sleep. Wake up. I'll be in my deep sleep from four all the way until 11, 11:30. Then they'd bring lunch. Lunchtime I eat my sandwich. They called it a cold tray. Every day you'd eat bologna, bread, cheese, Jell-O, and sometimes pasta salad. That's every day. The only time that it changes is dinner. You get a hot meal. Everything in there is made out of soybeans, so it's fake stuff. You look at it, and you'd think, *Oh, this is dog food.*

It was loud. People would be yelling, kicking doors all the time. And I remember feeling scared when it was time to sleep, worried that anyone could open my door and come at me anytime. They could open the door and call me out for a nurse and then an inmate could be walking by and try to hurt me or something. I felt like I basically slept with one eye open and one eye closed.

I read the *Dallas Morning News* every day from front to back. Did the crosswords. That was my only entertainment. I could also go to a gym by myself for an hour a day. I remember being let out and walking down the hall, and people would be spitting out their windows, smearing their own shit on themselves. They'd see me and it might be like, "Fucking faggot." These people had lost their minds. I remember looking into the windows and seeing them in there, and maybe they'd have made a swing out of their sheets and were just wrapped up in them swinging. I was afraid I'd become like that. That's what I was scared of, that eventually I would turn into that.

But Red kept me sane. He'd read restaurant listings in the paper. Then he'd call me through the vent. He was like, "Baby, where are we going to go? We're going to go check the place out. What you want to eat? Get dressed. I'm going to come pick you up at seven o'clock." Then at seven, I'd call him—"Hey. It's seven o'clock. Are you coming?" He'd be like, "Yeah, I'm on my way."

Meanwhile, the guy in the cell on the other side of him could hear us and would make fun of Red. "You're a faggot ass nigger. You're talking to that bitch." Red would be like, "I don't care what y'all say. I don't care." And he'd tell me, "Don't listen to them. Just blank them out." Then the guy who would do the whole Bible thing, he would be like, "Oh God this and God that." We had to blank them out and just keep on with it.

IT WAS DISCRIMINATION

My mother came to get me out when I was released in 2012, and I went to live with her for a while. I was overwhelmed when I first got out. It took a month for me to be able to break off the thinking that people were staring at me or that they were going to attack me. Then I'd start feeling nauseated like I want to throw up. One day my godmother Nikki took me to a place called Traders Village, which is like a flea market, where they have vendors outside in the open. On Sundays it gets really super packed to a point where you can't turn around or move.

I got there, and as soon as I got there I felt like something broke inside me. Nikki asked, "What's wrong?" I was feeling really dizzy. I was like, "Mama, I don't feel good," and I started throwing up. She said, "What's wrong?" I said, "Mama, you know I can't be around a lot of people like this." I said, "Give me your keys." I had to go to the car and lay back in the front seat and just sit because I couldn't be around people. It took me a long time to break off that.

When I was living with my mother, I'd spend all my time in my room, just watching TV. My mom would have come up there and be like, "You need to come downstairs to eat." I'd say, "Okay, I'll be there." Even then I would wait until everybody left the table. Then I would go eat by myself and hurry up and go back upstairs. I was like that for a while. And ever since I left jail I never read the newspaper now because it reminds me too much of being in there.

I met Miss Nell through my best friend, Pocahontas.[4] Pocahontas, she's a transsexual advocate in Dallas. She had me come to a chat they held once a month, and Miss Nell was the guest speaker. Pocahontas had me come to the chat because I didn't want to be around people. After I got out of prison we had been hanging out with some friends at her apartment and I couldn't be around them. I had bad anxiety. I started throwing up because I wasn't used to being around people yet because I had just got out.

Miss Nell runs the Trans Pride Initiative. After the meeting Miss Nell was there and Pocahontas said, "Miss Nell, this is my friend, Sonya, who I told you went through the whole solitary confinement. She just coming out her little shell." Miss Nell said, "Baby, I've been wanting to meet you." She said, "I got this thing going on." Miss Nell told me she works a lot with incarcerated transgender people and their rights. That she fights for people who are in there, people who have been discriminated against in prison. They write her letters, and she fights for them. Miss Nell said, "I have this meeting coming up with the head of the jailhouse. Do you want to talk in front of them?" I said, "Yeah," When the meeting happened though, I actually didn't make it there, but she told them my whole story.

In jail, it seemed like they had a rule that every time someone who's transgender goes in, if they have body work, they automatically go straight to solitary. It was discrimination. People don't understand that solitary confinement really messes people's heads up. It really does. I was just lucky enough to snap out of it when I got out, but some people don't snap out of it. They stay stuck in la la land.

Apparently the heads of the Dallas prisons didn't know really what

---

4. "Miss Nell" is Nell Gaither, director of the Trans Pride Initiative, a Dallas nonprofit that works to empower the trans community.

was going on. But Miss Nell took my story to them and it played a part in getting things changed. Miss Nell is someone who gets things done. They were able to come up with a solution. Now as a transgender woman in a men's prison you have an option: you can go to the homosexual tank or go to solitary confinement. It's your choice now. You don't have to be treated like an animal.

In March 2018, we speak to Sonya to catch up.

These days I don't have no worries. I'm very happy with myself. I finished my probation, and I'm completely stress free. I don't go to sleep at night worried about going back to jail. I'm traveling a lot. It's a blessing. No matter what obstacles I went through as a transgender person I still pushed through. I'm no longer feeling doubts about my lifestyle. Because of the legal issues I was going through I felt like I failed my family. But now that the legal troubles are behind me I feel like they look at me as a different person. I'm very happy with my family, and I'm even closer with them, especially my mom. I really love Mercedes.

TRAVIS TRANI

AGE: 46

BORN IN: Pueblo, Colorado

INTERVIEWED IN: Colorado Springs, Colorado

Travis Trani grew up in a family of corrections officers—his dad and his uncle both worked in prisons in Colorado. When he was in high school, Travis had already made up his mind that he would join them. Travis started working in Colorado's prisons at the age of twenty-one and has been working in them ever since.

Travis first saw solitary confinement up close as a new corrections officer working in a medium-security prison. In the mid-1990s, the maximum time in solitary confinement for prisoners was sixty days. By the late 2000s, the Colorado Department of Corrections (CDOC) had more than 1,500 people being held in long-term administrative segregation, many of whom had been there for years with no hope of release. In 2011, then executive director Tom Clements initiated a top-to-bottom review of Colorado's solitary confinement practices.

In 2012, Travis was put in charge of Colorado's harshest prison, the Colorado State Penitentiary (CSP), and tasked with implementing what would eventually be among the most high-profile and successful efforts to reduce solitary confinement in the United States. In October 2017, CDOC announced that it had eliminated long-term solitary confinement: confinement in a cell for twenty-three hours a day is limited to no more than fifteen days (consistent with recommendations from the United Nations). Anyone confined longer than fifteen days will receive a minimum of four "out of cell" hours each day to interact with others and cannot be held in those conditions longer than twelve months.

Travis now works at the CDOC headquarters. We interviewed him from a tidy office with large windows offering views of the Rocky Mountains. Travis's suit and tie, along with his youthful features and quiet—almost deferential—manner of speaking, seems incongruous with the authority he wields within CDOC. During our conversations he explains why, after these reforms, he does not believe that Colorado can ever return to the old ways of solitary confinement.

I WANTED TO DO SOME TYPE OF PUBLIC SERVICE

I was born in 1972 in Pueblo, Colorado, and grew up east of Pueblo.[1] My dad was a Vietnam veteran. He kinda bounced around jobs when I was younger. But when I was in middle school, he started working in corrections. I think his military background drew him to it. And my uncle also worked in corrections, so there was that connection. My father was hired on at Fremont Correctional Facility, at Cañon City, and then the CDOC opened Arkansas Valley Correctional Facility, and he actually went there.[2] He liked what he did, the challenges that he faced every day. It seems like there's something new always coming

---

1. Pueblo is a city of around one hundred thousand located in southern Colorado.

2. Fremont Correctional Facility is a medium- and close-custody prison that's part of a large correctional complex and was opened in 1962. Other facilities that are part of the same complex in Fremont County include the Colorado State Penitentiary and the Centennial Correctional Facility, a level 5 maximum-security facility.

up. And then there's the camaraderie with the staff. Yeah, he enjoyed what he did.

I would hear my dad talk about work—how prisons operated and things that he saw. You know how intriguing that can be, especially when you're a child, to hear what it's like inside a prison. So that really sparked my interest. Growing up, I always knew I wanted to do some type of public service, and law enforcement kind of interested me. It seemed like it could be a challenge—to give to your community, I guess, and do something bigger than you.

My mom was pretty much a stay-at-home mom until around the time I was in high school, and then she started working in daycare and then had home daycare for a while. I have an older sister who's a teacher at South High in Pueblo. I don't know her exact title, but she's something like the chair of special education for the high school. So she also had a calling to public service.

I was very quiet, very shy as a kid. I remember as a young child, I'd get in trouble with my parents because I was so shy I wouldn't want to say hi to people—just manners, you know, to acknowledge someone and say hi. I'm pretty introverted.

Pueblo was fairly middle class. They had the steel mill there. I can't remember what year the steel mill went down, but a lot of people were laid off. There was a lot of unemployment in Pueblo when I was younger, but it was fairly middle class and it was fairly safe. I grew up east of Pueblo, which was more of a farming community. Immigrants would come in to work on the farms. They would come in the summertime and then be gone, and I don't remember a lot of them going to school with us. In the summers, I mowed lawns for people. I worked at the Pueblo Trap and Skeet Club setting skeet machines. I worked at the supermarket. I worked at Little Caesar's Pizza. I worked at a service station, a gas station.

Growing up, I had one experience with crime. My cousin, who lived on the north side of Pueblo, had a paper route. I was helping him with his route one morning, and I remember we were talking, and I said, "Okay,

I'll go get this house," and I rolled up the newspaper. I heard somebody say, "You're not going to get any house," and this guy came out of his house and actually shot a shotgun above us. I was scared to death. Yeah! So basically, we got the police involved. There was a whole criminal investigation. The man thought we were breaking into cars, and he was defending his property. That's what he claimed. I still don't know why he did it. We were in the middle of the road, not even near a car, on our bikes, with bags full of newspapers on us. Who knows why he did what he did.

By high school, I pretty much knew I wanted to get into corrections or maybe on the federal side, like the marshals. I graduated from high school in '91, and right away after high school, I went to get an associate's degree in criminal justice because you had to have an associate's degree to work corrections.

I think my first impression during my internship was how confining that would be, to be an offender, to lose your rights and then be told when you eat, when you shower, when you can go recreate. I think that was kind of an eye-opener for me, to see that these are adults, older than me, and the staff are telling them what they can do. And the other thing I remember from that internship is some inmates were playing games with me because I was so young, trying to intimidate me.

I turned twenty-one in November 1993, and then I was hired on in April 1994 and went into the academy. You had to be twenty-one. There were, I'd say, between thirty and forty in our class. I think everybody made it through.

I WAS PRETTY GREEN

I started work in Colorado Territorial Correctional Facility in Cañon City. Territorial is medium custody. They have close to nine hundred inmates, right around there.

My first day on the job, I remember the staff didn't know we were coming that night, and there were quite a few of us who went to Territorial from that academy. They weren't really prepared for us all to be there. But I remember being assigned to the infirmary. They gave me a group of offenders to take down to the basement and supervise while they cleaned. And I didn't know what I was doing; I was pretty green. So I remember the offenders, they pretty much wore me out that night, trying to get over on me, asking to go in different areas. And I wouldn't let 'em go. I said no a lot that night. I didn't really know what I was doing, so I just said no.

I started on night shift. It was a sort of training shift. People wanted to get off the night shift as quickly as they could. I remember thinking there was a lot to learn. But it was difficult to learn things on night shift because there wasn't a lot going on. So that was kind of a challenge, depending on where you worked. They had a lot of towers at that facility—they still do—and tower duty is boring. You just sit in the tower eight hours a night and watch. That was torture for me.

At Territorial they had a punitive segregation unit, and I remember working that unit, feeding 'em in the mornings. Punitive seg's different from administrative seg. It was an old cell house, and there was just the old jail steel, where the offenders could reach out and grab you, just the bars. And I remember feeding 'em in the morning. You'd line up a cart with trays on it, and they'd just open the door. And they'd come out and you'd get the trays. It was old school.

We'd move around quite a bit on night shifts, so I don't remember how long they would stay in punitive seg in those days. I want to say the maximum time in punitive segregation was sixty days for a murder. I don't remember anybody being there for murder, but a lot would just go back to the general population at Territorial. They'd do their punitive seg time and go back.

I was probably at Territorial a little over a year, and then San Carlos Correctional Facility was opening, and I put in a transfer to go there for two reasons: one, to come off night shifts; two, to experience something different. It was a new facility. I thought it was a good opportunity to go and experience opening the facility, just to see something different.

PRISONS WEREN'T BUILT TO HOUSE MENTALLY ILL PEOPLE

San Carlos was a mental health facility, so there was learning that balance between the clinical side and the security side. We didn't have anything like it in the state, really. There were some units that were focused on mental health, but at San Carlos, the whole facility was dedicated to dealing with mentally ill offenders, so there was a strong presence of nursing staff in the units. There were nurses who actually worked in the units with the officers. It was blending that treatment side with the security side to make sure everybody stayed safe. There were some clinical staff who had never worked in a prison. They came from a therapeutic environment to an environment where you have offenders who are dangerous—some *very* dangerous there, some not so much. Trying to strike that balance and make sure everybody stays safe while we're still meeting the needs of the offenders—that was always kind of a fine line.

In the academy, I remember some training in mental health issues. And when I went to San Carlos, there was an orientation phase, and there was mental health training as part of that forty-hour orientation. The training prepares you; it gives you a good idea. But until you're face to face with it? I mean, there's nothing like the experience. And there were some sick people there, very sick people.

San Carlos is situated on the state hospital grounds in Pueblo. So we would take a lot of offenders to the hospital there, the state hospital, or have 'em in the forensic unit, have to send them over there for treatment. And through school I knew about deinstitutionalization of the mental health hospitals. Yeah, there were a lot of times you would look at some of the offenders who were *seriously* mentally ill and wonder why they were here. Obviously, they committed a very heinous crime—that's why they're in prison—but is there another alternative? Because prisons weren't built to house mentally ill people. There were the state hospitals, and then you had the prisons. But there was that shift over time. People were moved out of the state hospitals and were on the streets and committed crimes—they had to go somewhere, so they were sent to prisons.

HE CUSSED ME UP ONE SIDE, DOWN THE OTHER

I was at San Carlos about a year and a half, I would say. From San Carlos, I went to the state penitentiary as a sergeant, first on night shift and then on swing shift. Then I'd been an officer for about three years when I went to CSP, which was a 100 percent ad-seg facility.[3] I was probably twenty-four, twenty-five years old. It was an eye-opener for me because I was used to communicating with offenders face to face and resolving issues.

I remember, probably the first night on the job, an inmate just started banging on his door. Now, this is the graveyard shift. And I remember walking up to the cell just to talk to him, like I'd approach any other offender, and saying, "Hey, man, what's going on?" And he cussed me up one side, down the other, and threatened me. I thought, *Wow, what's going on here?* So it was definitely a different culture, to the point where it was very difficult to communicate through a door. At CSP, there were up to sixteen offenders in a day hall, so anytime you talked to somebody, you had an audience. They're standing at the door watching you, listening. It's very difficult to communicate with somebody and gain compliance through a door with an audience watching—next to impossible.

At that point, I don't know what the average length of stay in there was, but that was back in the heyday of administrative segregation. CSP was kind of at the forefront. We had lots of states coming in on tours to see ad seg and how it was run in Colorado. Colorado was seen as a model for how to do it.

When you walk in a unit, there are eight pods, what we call "day halls," so there are eight day halls, 126 offenders total, all single cell. Day halls 1 and 8 hold fifteen offenders, day halls 2 through 6 hold sixteen. And there's an upper tier where you can walk around, with a small exercise room and a shower on each tier. The cells each had a stainless steel toilet/seat combination unit, a shelf, a light, and there was an outlet. Offenders could earn the privilege of having a TV at that time. And the TV was a management tool for the staff. If the offender acted out, staff

---

3. The current Colorado State Penitentiary facility was opened in 1993 and can house approximately 750 individuals, all in administrative segregation.

could take the television away from the offender, have an immediate con-
sequence for behavior, so that was a big tool back then.

At that time, it was kind of a level system at ad seg. The offenders
would come in at level 1, and they wouldn't get a TV. They would have
to go thirty days without any incidents, and then they could go to level 2
and get their television. That was kind of a long stretch for some of them
to go, locked up twenty-three hours a day, to not get in trouble and get
that TV. Laundry, mail—everything was delivered to the cells.

The way the offenders communicated with the staff—that made an
impression on me. Staff didn't do a lot of communicating with the offenders because it didn't get them anywhere. Once in a while, as the sergeant, I
would see a staff member start to argue with an offender, and I'd intervene
because that would set the offender off. Then the offender would cover the
window, and you'd have to suit up a team to go get him or create unnecessary conflict. If I'm the corrections officer and you're the offender, and
I make you mad, maybe you assault the next person who comes through,
throw feces on 'em. That was a huge problem back there, offenders throwing feces on staff. So what I saw was we tried to treat 'em with respect and
not engage with them verbally, not spar with them, not threaten them, not
send 'em off, not give 'em a reason, because they would assault the staff.

It could be hard. I once had urine thrown in my face. I was upset. I
was definitely upset. I walked away. Yeah, there's nothing you can do. The
offender got a write-up for that, of course. It set him back in his levels.

I thought the door between officers and offenders with every interaction was a big contributor to that type of behavior. I'd worked general
population and been able to talk to some of these guys, communicate
face to face, gain their compliance. So from day one, I always thought
that that door was a huge contributor. And you'd see it on the staff side
too; some of the staff who would posture or talk down to the offenders.
A lot of them were new staff and had never worked in a general population setting, so that was all they knew. Because that door's between
you the whole time, you really don't learn how to communicate in an

environment like that. There were some bad people there—don't get me wrong, some very dangerous people—but you would see guys get caught in a cycle; they would act out and lose something, and then they had nothing to lose, so they would just continue to act out and spiral.

Lengths of stay in the seg units at CSP could be years at that point. And looking back on it now, we expected the offenders to be angelic, to move up the levels and then move out to other facilities. They'd have one bad day and cuss someone out, and they'd completely regress to a level where there was no realistic hope of getting out of solitary anytime soon. I mean, hindsight is always 20/20, but that was the way it was set up. You're dealing with felons you're putting in the cell twenty-three hours a day, and you expect them not to have a bad day, not to cuss and get frustrated. It is not realistic. And if they did, then they were regressed for that type of behavior.

After two years of being sergeant at CSP, I was promoted to lieutenant and stayed there for two more years. I made captain at the Cañon Facility for Women. I was ready for a change, to go experience something different. The women's facility was different. The women communicate a lot more. They're more animated, I would say. So it's just totally different. You go from an ad seg where they're locked up to a facility where there are all these women offenders who want to talk. And that's what they did. So it was completely different. And it was mixed classification—we had minimum custody up to close custody. I went to Women's in 2001, and then I left there in 2004 and went to Fremont Correctional Facility as a programs manager. I was there for probably just over two years. Fremont's population is around 1,700. As programs manager, I was responsible for education—academic, vocational education, library—recreation, food service, laundry, and volunteer programs.

That was the first time I had significant responsibility outside of being a custody officer. So it was the first time I really saw the complexity of a prison. It broadened my perspective about how you can effect change through education. It really opened my eyes. Everything I'd known before, that was just from a custody side, controlling people and punishment. This was the first time I'd seen offenders engaged with positive efforts for their betterment.

WHEN WILL IT STOP?

In 2003, there were big budget cuts in the state, actual layoffs of employ-ees. It was a significant impact for our agency, and it set us back, as far as programming, 'cause we had a *lot* of educational programs back then, in the 1990s, early 2000s, especially at the female facility. There were different philosophies, different governor, different executive director of the Depart-ment of Corrections at the time. So it kinda shifted more to the warehous-ing-of-offenders mentality—just lock 'em up and keep 'em out of society.

A lot of the staff was upset—I mean, the teachers, obviously, and even the line staff. Especially at the female facility, the staff bought into the programming and opportunities for the offenders, so it was difficult for a lot of the staff and made it more difficult to manage the offenders too. They have fewer opportunities and less to do, fewer positive things to engage in. I've heard this and I've always believed this: programs make good security for offenders 'cause programs keep them engaged and give them something to work toward, something positive. If you take that away, then what do we have?

The overall offender population in the 2000s was still going up. I remember thinking, when will it stop? I'm trying to think of all the fa-cilities that were opened, 'cause there were a lot of new facilities. Limon was opened in the early '90s, CSP was opened in the early '90s, Denver Women's Correctional Facility was opened in 1998, Sterling Correc-tional Facility was opened. And then Trinidad Correctional Facility. So you wonder, *How much can you grow, and when will it stop?*

Next I went to Limon, which is a close-custody facility, level 4, the highest level under CSP, hard custody. So it was fairly violent, lots of fights, lots of assaults back then, gang activity.

The seg unit at Limon was disciplinary, punitive segregation. But I remember we were still growing ad seg then, and we didn't have enough beds in ad seg. So a lot of guys were wait-listed for ad seg. They were classified ad seg, but there were no beds for 'em. They'd be at punitive seg, wait for a bed to come open, and then move. So you'd have an assault and need to remove that person from the population to keep everybody safe, and you'd be struggling to find a bed for him.

EVERYBODY KINDA KNEW THERE WAS AN ISSUE

After Limon, I moved around a lot for a few years. Then in 2012, I went back to CSP and Centennial as a warden. Tom Clements had been named executive director in 2011 and seg reform was one of the initiatives he brought. And they'd actually consulted with the National Institute of Corrections to come in and review what we were doing in Colorado. So by the time I got to CSP, that review had already been completed and NIC had given the state the recommendations.[4]

I think everybody kinda knew there was an issue, because ad seg had stalled. There weren't enough spots for people who needed programs, and there were waitlists. But inmates were required to complete a program to get out, so we had unrealistic expectations and the whole thing was bottlenecked. One thing Mr. Clements asked to be done was to have the deputy directors go in and review everybody who had been in ad seg a year or longer. They started pulling wardens to go in and conduct those reviews. We would bring line staff with us to the reviews as well, and a lot of them would tell us, "We don't know why he's here. You know, he never causes issues." That was *really* an eye-opener, 'cause I hadn't been in that environment for a while, and the line staff were telling us that there was no reason to keep them here.

There's one case that sticks out in my mind. There was a guy that

---

4. The National Institute of Corrections is a federally funded agency within the Department of Justice that provides policy guidance and other technical assistance to prisons and jails.

was placed in ad seg because he shook some female volunteers' hands too long and made them feel uncomfortable. That's how he ended up in ad seg originally. When I talked to him, he'd been there two years because he'd acted out and wasn't progressing through the steps. He was pretty upset about it. It was almost like he'd given up. He was very bitter. He point-blank told me he didn't want to progress through the stages. He didn't want to leave. He didn't want to go back to general population because he was afraid something minor would happen again and he'd just get sent back to ad seg.

When that review started, probably around 1,500 people were in ad seg, I would say. Our total prison system at the time had an inmate population of 20,000, right around there, maybe a little less. With 1,500 in ad seg, we had probably close to 8 percent in seg units, and that was relatively high.

We got a lot of good input from the offenders during the ad-seg reviews. We had such unrealistic expectations of asking an offender to not cuss someone out ever in those conditions, or demanding they complete a program when we didn't have enough teachers to deliver the programs so that the offenders could get out. And then we would hear some of the reasons they were placed in ad seg. And it was kind of a surprise. Talking to the offenders really lined up with what NIC had recommended.

I think in some cases, the stay in ad seg was definitely too long. They were in there much too long. They were in there for the wrong reasons. And it was apparent we were releasing people from ad seg to the streets, which was a problem.

When I was in Denver, a lot of offenders were released from the reception and diagnostic center, and there was a bus station across the street. I'll never forget one time when one of my deputy directors and I were out driving in front of the reception center. We'd seen guys released to the bus stop, and we stopped to talk to 'em. There was one guy who was released from ad seg and you could tell there was a lot of anxiety. You could tell he hadn't seen sunlight in a long time. We were thinking, *How safe is that, really? To take somebody from twenty-three-hour-a-day lockdown, and now he's on the street corner in Denver, catching a bus with civilians?*

I think the staff understood why reforms were needed. They understood it was partly a public safety issue. You know, it's going to create a safer community, since we're not keeping 'em locked up twenty-three hours a day and then pushing 'em out on the streets. We're giving 'em opportunities to make positive change. So you always try to tie it back to safety, and it makes sense at the end of the day. For some of the staff, it made sense too because I'd say, "Do you really want somebody locked up twenty-three hours a day for years on end to go and live next to your children or your grandfather or your mom and dad?" And obviously, the answer should be no.

That initial move, based on the NIC recommendations, dropped the ad-seg population down from around 1,500 to around 700 offenders.

In March 2013, Tom Clements, then executive director of the CDOC, was murdered at his home, and the prime suspect was Evan Ebel, who had recently been released from administrative segregation at Sterling Correctional Facility. During the eight years that Ebel was incarcerated, he spent most of his time in solitary confinement. Shortly after taking office, Clements had launched a study of solitary confinement and decided to close Colorado State Penitentiary II, the state's brand-new prison built entirely for isolation. At the time of his murder, Clements reported making significant progress in reducing the number of people released directly from solitary confinement to the streets. Clements's successor, Rick Raemisch, continued his work of expanding solitary confinement reforms. In the fall of 2017, Raemisch announced that the CDOC had abolished long-term solitary confinement.

DO AWAY WITH AD SEG ENTIRELY

Mr. Clements was murdered after we started the NIC recommendations, and then the reforms kind of stagnated. At that time, we were looking at ways to provide outdoor recreation at CSP. Our director of prisons, who had been planning on retiring around April, continued with his plans 'cause he had other job offers. So we lost Mr. Clements and we lost our director of prisons. There was a big lull when we didn't have leadership in our agency. By no means did we slip back, but we were waiting for some leadership, some new direction.

I don't know that slipping back to the old ways of doing ad seg was a concern. It really didn't cross my mind to worry that Mr. Clements's murder would prompt a public backlash and halt the reforms. I think my bigger concern was how to continue to move forward because under Mr. Clements, we'd also started a residential treatment program at Centennial. That was just getting started, and we knew we needed some additional resources there.

I don't remember the exact date Mr. Raemisch came onboard, but the interval between Mr. Clements's murder and Mr. Raemisch's appointment seemed like an eternity—to me it did. I'm sure it was several months.

When he came in, it wasn't full steam ahead. He kind of assessed where we were and then where he wanted to take us, his vision. I'll never forget the first time I heard it. We were at an international conference here in Colorado Springs. He basically said he wanted to do away with ad seg entirely. I think the first time I heard him say that I thought, *Well, that's an interesting concept.* How are we going to do that and keep the facility safe? You have to have some method of keeping things safe 'cause there are dangerous people in prisons. But now I understand that his vision is to not lock offenders up twenty-three hours a day, to give them more out-of-cell opportunities, to set time frames on how long they can be in an extended restricted-housing environment. And ultimately, his goal is to get the offenders out of their cells up to four hours a day.

We now have strict criteria for somebody to be placed in disciplinary restrictive housing, which is twenty-three hours a day and capped at fifteen days. We reduced it from a population of 750-some inmates in ad seg to a population of around 160 to 170 in extended restrictive housing—that's at least four hours out of cell per day and a maximum of twelve months.

We focus on creative management control of units, such as a progression from restrictive housing to letting eight offenders come out at a time for up to four hours a day.

In theory, it's a step down to general population because they're out among each other, participating in recreation, watching television, some programming. And then from there, they progress to a transitional unit. In the transitional unit, sixteen at a time come out six hours a day. They go to classes together. So that's how it evolved.

In restrictive housing, disruptive behavior and use of force have decreased. You don't see the number of events in extended restrictive housing that we did in ad seg. You don't see the forced cell entries or the uses of force or the feces throwing. There are still dangerous offenders, but you don't see that constant disruption in that population. You can walk in the units and you don't hear the screaming and yelling.

That change is probably due to a lot of factors. It's a shorter stay, so they're not at the end of the road with no way out, so to speak. There is a way out. There is a progression. So I think it's changed the offenders' mind-set. Like I said before, some of them would dig themselves a hole, and then they wouldn't see a way out. It's like, "game on" at that point. They'd just be as disruptive as they possibly could. We don't see that anymore 'cause they know they're gonna come out.

It was evident that some of the guys were afraid to be in the general population, and that's why they were in ad seg; that's why they wanted to stay there, that's why they would act out. Under Mr. Clements, and continuing under Mr. Raemisch, we created protective custody for that population, so they didn't have to act out to get protection. The conditions in the PC unit mirror those for the general population now. They have programs in the PC unit. They're out of their cells; they go to recreation. It's just compartmentalized.

It's evolved. Now they're coming out around two hours a day. They have restraint tables, and they'll bring out up to four offenders at a time to play games at the table. At a restraint table, four offenders can be seated there together, and they are restrained to the table in a way that still allows them to play cards or dominoes, to still interact with one another.[5] And then they get some additional recreation time. So it's evolved even just from the twenty-three-hour-a-day lockdown.

I don't ever see us going back to where we were with ad seg. I really don't see it slipping back. We will be continuing with that effort, continuing to refine the residential treatment programs for the mentally ill, trying to be kinda outside the box and creative in general population facilities and how we manage the offenders and give them opportunities to make change. Trying not to make the environment so austere—that's one of Mr. Raemisch's things too. Does the environment make them more violent, make them act out more? Being in this job, I get to go out and visit the facilities. A lot of wardens have had wildlife murals painted in the dining halls and have retiled the dining halls so they look like a cafeteria, not like a prison dining hall. They've tiled the showers with nice tile, put murals in the hallways, inspirational sayings in day halls. I don't think our wardens want to make the environment austere 'cause this is punishment. In our organization, talking to our staff now, I don't think anybody thinks our job is to punish these guys.

IN A PERFECT WORLD, WE'D START
BEFORE THEY COME TO PRISON

I think society really does need to look at what it expects corrections to do at the end of the day. And then, whatever society expects us to do, we need the support and not just have unrealistic expectations and forget about it. I would hope that society expects us to make these offenders

---

5. Restraint tables are a common feature of many jails and prisons. The tables and chairs are bolted to the floor, and the person seated at the table is generally wearing a waist chain that can be attached by handcuffs to the underside of the table, preventing the person from leaving the table but leaving one or both hands free.

better 'cause in Colorado about 97 percent of them are coming back to the community.

I think in a perfect world, we would start before they come to prison, and have more programs in the community, especially for at-risk children. I would love to see more missions on the front end to keep them from coming in. I've seen some offenders change behaviors that were very difficult to manage. You don't hear a lot of success stories about offenders leaving and not coming back. I mean, we don't get a lot of that feedback from the public, but we know there are guys who leave and are successful, and we do hear some of those stories. So that reinforces what I wanted to do when I came into this career. I've seen that throughout my career and more so the higher up I've gone.

I'd like to see the media be more balanced in what they report, instead of always focusing on the negative. Because there is a lot that's positive, and it can be disheartening to staff, just to see themselves in the media always portrayed in a negative light, having that battle just to say they do positive things.

It is quite an accomplishment by our staff to go from 1,500 in ad seg about four or five years ago to now having eliminated solitary confinement as we knew it. People said it couldn't be done. I personally thought it couldn't be done. But these reforms have proven that we can safely manage this population and effect change in behavior. For someone in corrections who doesn't believe it, who does not think they can do it in their jail or prison, I would say: come here and see it for yourself. Until you see it, until you talk to the offenders and staff, you can't understand how you can eliminate solitary. You have to put your eyes on it. And it's all for the better, for public safety, for staff and for offenders.

I don't know if ad seg will ever go back to the way it was. There's nothing to hang our hat on; we could never say, "Yeah, we changed offender behavior for the better by locking them up twenty-three hours a day." The studies say the opposite—we did more harm than good. The majority of our offenders are going to be back on the street. Our job is to balance prison safety and public safety. Our job is to protect the public and try to effect change when people come back into society. Our job is rehabilitation. It has to be.

TONJA FENTON

AGE: 44

BORN IN: Starkville, Mississippi

INTERVIEWED IN: New York, New York

Tonja Fenton is a songwriter and mother of two boys, who spent almost all of her life in New York City. Impeccably dressed, Tonja speaks in measured tones in a deep baritone voice, often with a sly smile at the corner of her mouth. Tonja primarily worked in the restaurant industry to support herself and her family, and for much of her life had little personal contact with the criminal justice system. She was living a stable if financially difficult life with her then-wife and sons when, in 2011, she was sentenced to three years in New York prisons for allegedly failing to return deposit money to renters who were going to sublet part of her Queens home.

In 2012, lawyers from the New York Civil Liberties Union (including editor Taylor Pendergrass) received a letter from Tonja describing what it was like to live in one of New York's "Special Housing Units," or SHUs, where Tonja was sent to

173

live for a year as punishment for a nonviolent rule violation. Tonja had already independently filed a lawsuit challenging her placement in solitary confinement. She later became a lead plaintiff, and the only woman, in a class-action lawsuit alleging that New York's solitary confinement practices were unconstitutionally cruel and unusual. In April 2016, a five-year settlement was approved that would overhaul solitary confinement practices across the New York State prison system by focusing on reducing the use of solitary and improving the conditions in SHUs. By May 2017, in just one year's time, the population of people held in solitary confinement in New York prisons had dropped by almost 25 percent.

Tonja was released from prison in March 2014. The marriage she had successfully maintained while incarcerated fell apart, and she spent much of her time over the next two years on the streets of New York City looking for work and housing. She eventually got into another relationship and found some stability, but after that relationship ended she returned to the streets.

MY REPORT CARD ALWAYS SAID, "TONJA TALKS EXCESSIVELY"

My dad was just sixteen when I was born, and he worked at the Ford plant, though I didn't know him because he died when he was young. I was born in Starkville in 1974, which is in north Mississippi.[1] It's the home of Mississippi State University.

I grew up in Brooklyn, New York, and then my family moved to Queens when I was older. In New York I had an average childhood. I had two older brothers, an older sister, and two younger brothers. Dan was born in 1968, Pete in 1969, Donna in 1970, Chance in 1978, and Norris in 1980.

And we also sort of adopted other kids. I have a Jewish brother, a Korean brother, a Trinidadian brother, a Guyanese brother. Seriously. What would happen was, if one of us siblings knew a kid who was having trouble with their family or not eating right, we'd bring them home and my mom would let them stay. But it's just like an extended family. I say my family is like the Rainbow Coalition. My mother is from Mississippi, she's

---

1. Starkville is a town of twenty-five thousand people.

biracial. Her father was a sharecropper. So, her thing is, you should at least feel accepted, wherever you are. She never made anyone feel not accepted, you know?

My mom worked first as a lunch lady, and then later she worked nights cleaning office buildings. By the time we were getting in from school my mom was leaving to go out. By the time we were ready to leave in the morning, she was coming back in. When she was working, we were latchkey kids. When I got to be twelve or thirteen years old, my mom was basically disabled—she had a heart condition, I never really knew exactly what—and stayed at home all day.

But my mom taught me how to cook. Every southern dish you could imagine. A lot of vegetables and breads. In southern cooking, the vegetables tend to be more of a statement than the meat. For instance, in the South, getting the cornbread stuffing right makes all the difference. Good soul food, I guess it was.

When I was in elementary school, I was a good student. I was a great student. My report card always said, "Tonja talks excessively. If she could just not talk so much." But I never got in trouble.

I was probably closest to my oldest brother, Dan. We shared a lot of interests, including basketball, and he always encouraged me to try out for the team. But I spent a lot of time with all my brothers. We'd do some of everything—sports, play games, music. I've always been creative musically. Music speaks to me.

When I was about twelve, my two younger brothers and I were determined to write this great song. I can even remember some of the lyrics to this day. It was the worst song ever. Literally, the worst song ever. I remember the lyrics, but I won't tell them to anybody. No way. But I loved music.

I went to Thomas Jefferson for high school. I made the basketball team my freshman year, but I found out I enjoyed watching it more than I enjoyed playing. I was still a good student in high school, and the school offered me a job as a tutor.

Around 1989, my mother, after she had taken sick, she decided that she wanted to move back home to Mississippi before she died. I was around fifteen. We understood, we said, "Okay, fine." However, once we get down there, it's crazy. Mississippi is the only Confederate state we got left, you know? We were kids raised in New York. Now we had to go back down to this Mississippi life.

Pete and Dan were constantly back and forth from New York. Dan is Black, but he makes a lot of white people look like they've been out in the sun too long. And he's not albino! This is just his look. But in Mississippi that doesn't fit too well; he looks like a Black man trying to be white. His trips back to New York City made people suspicious. The next thing we know, there's the sheriff's department, with their pump-action shotguns, and they took my brother out in his underwear. They claimed he was doing all this drug trafficking.

Now, my mother wanted to take the charge for him. My mother was like, "If this took place, it was not him. I did it. This is my child." My mother's logic was, "If they get a hold of him, they'll kill him. You know, with me, it'll be a little different." And we're all like, "Mom, you can't do this." But my mother took the charge for him and did six years and one day in federal penitentiary.

So we came back up to New York, and we were in the foster care system. The two boys, my younger brothers, got to stay together. They went into a foster home with a woman who is still a part of our lives today. But I went into a group home. They split us up. Well, I immediately left. Just walked away one day and went AWOL. For a few years I was just off the grid.

YOU NAME IT, I DID IT

I tried to go on to college, but it was short-lived. I had this idea that I wanted to own a funeral home, so I studied mortuary science and business management. I also worked as a cook. I figured people always have to eat and they have to die, so I'd never run out of money. Pretty soon, though, I realized I was scared of dead people. I took as many classes as I could tolerate, but then I'd had enough.

After I left school, I did a lot of cooking. I was a professional chef in every facet of the culinary world. I was the head cook of a senior citizen's center. You name it, I did it.

But I was also concentrating on music. I did a lot of studio work, a lot of production work. I submitted lyrics for a TV show. I'd make music that might sit on the shelf for years not getting used, and then it gets put into something.

I started dating Lakeesha around 1994. She was younger, and we met on the pier one night in New York. I was actually pregnant at the time with my first son, Taylor. His father was gay. So was I, but I hadn't come out yet to my family.

I came out to my mother a while later, when I was twenty-two, and she was out of prison. I'll never forget, because it took me two tries to tell her. I started to tell her the first time, and was like, okay hold on. I went and got a beer, like a ridiculously huge Colt malt liquor, then came back and told her. She was doing a puzzle book and just looked up at me and said, "Tell me something I don't know, Tonja." And then she went back to her puzzle book.

Within about three, four days of meeting Lakeesha, I was in love. We moved in together the following year. Taylor was born the same year. Then we decided to have another baby, and the father was the same as with Taylor. We had Tyler in 1999. I was writing music and cooking, Lakeesha was going to school for early childhood education and working two jobs, always. We were doing okay, but just trying to keep the boys healthy and in school.

STRAIGHT TO THE AUTHORITIES

By 2009, we were all living together in a house out in Queens. I wouldn't say we had a financial situation, but things were tight in our household, which is what prompted me to sublet part of the house we were renting.

We were renting the whole house, and the basement was set up like a full apartment. I'd been using it as an office and studio, and my kids played video games down there. But we decided we'd sublet part of the house—the basement and the top floor, so we'd be living on the ground floor. I took security deposits from two separate couples that applied to move in to the two floors I was trying to sublet.

Then we had an issue with pipes in the house so I had to back out of both agreements. At this point, the couples were like, "Oh no, something doesn't sound right." So I'm like, "Okay, here's your rent back. Give me a couple of days, I'll give you the deposit back, too." I had already spent part of their deposit money on fixing the pipes. One of the tenants went straight to the authorities and filed a complaint that just sat there apparently.

Then at the end of 2010, we were having a New Year's Eve party. There was a group of guys that was stopped for casing some of the houses on the block, and the police were making a report. They took our information, our neighbors' information, on both sides of us. They're returning everyone's ID—they returned Keesha's ID; she went inside. They returned my neighbor's ID; she went inside. And they looked at me, and it was like, "Oh, we actually have an open complaint on you, so you're going to have to come down to the station." I said I'd come in the following morning. It's New Year's night! I have a drink in hand. I'm in my socks. And he's like, "No, we're going to have to take you in now." And that's when it really started, from that point on.

And when they asked me, "Did you accept this deposit money from the tenants?" I'm like, *Yeah, I did.* When the police asked me if I still had part of the funds and I said yes, they decided to arrest me and charge me with grand larceny and scheming to defraud.

GOING OVER THIS BRIDGE TO NOWHERE

I was sent to Rikers Island the next day. This was the first time I'd ever been incarcerated. I remember the bus ride over to Rikers, sitting in this moving cage and going over this bridge to nowhere. The first thing

I remember about Rikers was the smell. It was like every kind of waste you can imagine—bad food, bad body odor. I was at Rikers only maybe twenty days. Then I was bailed out and given probation.

Part of the stipulation of the probation was to make restitution payments to the rent applicants or face incarceration. However, I couldn't make the payments, so I violated my probation and I was back at Rikers. At that point I spent maybe about six and a half months on Rikers Island going back and forth to court with the probation violation. I pleaded guilty to the probation violation, and though I didn't understand it at the time, that meant they found me guilty of the grand larceny and fraud charges. The judge had no leniency. He was just like, "Okay, you were supposed to pay it, you didn't, that's it, violation." I was sentenced to three years in prison.

There was absolutely nothing to do day to day on Rikers. In the dorms, I was stuck on my bunk with a person on either side of me less than three feet away. Dorms had maybe fifty to eighty women total. We had one hour of rec time outside every day, but the space outside was surrounded by four brick walls that went all the way up. So you just sit. Literally, you just sit there. There's nothing else to do.

We had jobs that we were sent to do, and I worked all the time—by choice, because I couldn't sleep—in the mess hall, in the laundry, all sorts of things to keep the jail running. We did jobs seven days a week, but we weren't being paid for them.

We were allowed a maximum of three visits a week. I made sure I had all three visits every week. Taylor was about sixteen, Tyler was about twelve when I was first incarcerated. Rikers visits were one hour of no contact. I could hug my sons, but that was it.

After about eight months at Rikers, I was scheduled to be transferred to Bedford.[2] A few days before I was supposed to be transferred, I refused to go to work. I didn't want to do my job, since I wasn't getting

---

2. Bedford Hills Correctional Facility for Women is a maximum-security prison in Westchester County, New York, fifty miles north of New York City. It's the only women's maximum-security prison in New York State.

paid, and it wasn't supposed to be mandated if you hadn't been sentenced yet, which I hadn't. I was written a ticket for that. Ten days bing time—my first brush with solitary.[3] But I never had to serve any of those days in the bing. I was moved to Bedford first. If I'm not mistaken, to this day, I have those ten days of bing time over my head if I ever go back to Rikers.[4]

IT'S JUST SO SAD IN HERE

When I stepped into Bedford, in August 2011, I was first put in reception, where I was treated like scum that had to be cleaned off. Everything I was wearing was thrown in the garbage. Period. No exceptions. Then I was deloused, forced to have these chemicals sprayed on me. Until I completed medical testing, I was supposed to stay in the medical unit. But they found something in the exam, so I ended up staying in the medical unit longer than normal.

They diagnosed me with cervical cancer. Then later they changed the diagnosis to uterine cancer. I was actually supposed to pass from Bedford immediately to a prison upstate called Albion.[5] But because of my medical condition, they wouldn't release me from the medical unit at Bedford. The problem with the medical unit, though, is you are much more limited there in what you can do—you can't move around much, you don't interact with other prisoners as much, you can't go to the yard. I ended up spending months in the medical unit.

They wanted to give me chemo, but I refused because I really didn't

---

3. The "bing" is slang for a solitary confinement cell in Rikers.

4. In 2015, New York City ended this practice, known as the "old time policy," where anyone who left Rikers prior to serving their complete solitary confinement sentence would be forced to serve the remainder if they were ever returned to Rikers. In December 2017, the city agreed to pay $5 million to individuals held in solitary confinement under the policy.

5. Albion Correctional Facility is a women's prison in Albion, New York, approximately 350 miles northwest of New York City and 35 miles west of Rochester.

believe they were going to give me the right treatment. It's hard to explain why, but it's like the same with the food in prison. The prison is required by law to provide me with three meals. You're not going to give me one meal a day and expect me to account for you giving me three meals. Either give me what you're supposed to give me, or nothing at all. So that was just how I felt with the medical treatment. I really didn't believe they were going to give me the right treatment. The doctors would hit you with, "This is an experimental drug we want to try." I'm like, *No, I don't want to be a guinea pig.* So I just refused.

Fortunately, we were able to have a lot of visits at Bedford—up to six a week. I had a minimum of two a week from my family, but sometimes more. The visits meant everything to me. It's not even just the contact with the outside world. Those visits were my contact with life. Because my kids were under eighteen, we could be in an outside area together. We'd play basketball together, me and my two boys. Believe it or not, the majority of the time we'd sit at the table and just talk, and the crazy thing was I'd pretty much always say the same thing to them. We all knew that there was just a sadness to the place where we were. My youngest son would always say, "This is the saddest place I've ever been. It's just so sad in here." He'd say that no matter what, if I was smiling or not. Our conversation would just be like, "Make me laugh." That's all we did. That became our weekly thing. They had some really good jokes to tell me when they came up for our visits. That was our thing, telling jokes.

But when I wasn't having visits, I was stuck in the medical unit. Because I was refusing medical treatment, they lifted my medical hold and sent me upstate. I was transferred to Albion in January 2012.

GET DOWN WITH THE PROGRAM
OR YOU BECOME A PROBLEM

Albion is far upstate, near the Canada border. It's about twelve hours by bus from New York City. The rules at Albion were like rules at a gated

community. Seriously. You either get down with the program or you
become a problem. I saw other women punished for all kinds of reasons.
I saw one woman get forty-five days in the SHU for feeding a bird a piece
of bread. Soon I became a problem.

A few months after I arrived at Albion, I got in trouble with a friend.
My friend was someone I'd met back at Rikers Island. Back at Rikers,
this friend had shared things like snacks with me, and at one point, we'd
been intimate. But at Albion, we were strictly friends. Still, there was
this rule that when you come to a facility, there's a thirty-day waiting
period before you can get anything sent to you through the mail. She arrived and wanted some things, so I ordered them for her. Now there was
another rule that you couldn't have credit cards on the prison grounds. I
didn't. But I knew my credit card number from before my incarceration.
So I gave it to my friend so she could order some basic things she needed
like commissary food items and toiletries.

She also ordered some additional things that I never told her she
could order—sneakers and a curling iron. When my partner Keesha saw
that on the credit card bill, she called and told me. I reported that to the
guards at Albion, thinking they would intervene.

That was a mistake. Instead of resolving the situation, they charged
me with violating the prison's correspondence policy, the phone policy,
and mailing rules. They tried to charge me and my friend with stealing
the credit card information. I told them it wasn't stolen. They didn't
want to hear that. I had Keesha call in as a telephone witness stating that,
yes, those were my card numbers. It didn't matter.

I knew going into the hearing that I was probably going to be found
guilty. Of course I hoped there would be a different outcome, but when
women have to spend time in the SHU for feeding birds, I knew I wasn't
going to get out of it. I don't remember my state of mind when I heard
the sentence. I knew it was going to happen and had tried to keep my
family abreast of what was going on. I just remember asking the hearing
officer if I could have time to call my kids to let them know I won't be

available for visits. But she refused the request. I received a year in the SHU for my violations in June 2012.

THE OBJECTIVE WAS TO KEEP YOU IN NOTHINGNESS

Going into the SHU, I just remember these hallways full of walls. Then the slamming of the door after I went into my cell. Those first few hours in the SHU still haunt me to this very day. You hope that something can be done. You don't want to admit defeat, but you have no choice. The cell is barren, just a metal slab for a bed, and a combined toilet and sink contraption. The way it was set up, there were three corridors in the SHU unit with sixteen cells in each corridor, eight cells on a side. It's just cell after cell. In my first cell, I was in a corridor with other people so we could talk. The first thing everyone talks about is why they're there in the SHU. We all couldn't believe what we'd done that got us put in the SHU. Some were there for physical altercations. But a lot were not—just petty stuff.

After a little while, they moved me to a corridor where there was nobody else in any of the cells, and so there was no one to talk to. Someone would come by to do the count. A guard would check to make sure we were alive in the morning, and to feed me. They'd slip a tray in a slot under the door, and sometimes they'd push it so hard the food would spill all over the place. The SHU diet is the ultimate diet. There were people who went in for a week and come out and it's like, *Whoa!* It's a drastic difference. Granted, it's prison food. It's the same food that you'd get with the general population, but the condition of the food when it gets to the SHU—it's been sitting longer and handled by so many people. The main thing that anyone in SHU would eat was bread.

It's very easy to get dehydrated in the SHU. They have this toilet and sink combination in the cell. One big metal thing. It deters you from drinking the water from the sink since it's like it's coming out of the toilet. And you don't have lotion or anything, so your skin gets dry. It's almost like being out in the wilderness, in the elements with nothing.

My time in the cell was supposed to be twenty-three hours a day. But I did a lot of twenty-four-hour days. Rec for people in the SHU is in a big steel cage. You're cuffed, taken out, and walked to this twenty-by-thirty-foot outdoor cage. There's nothing in it like a table to sit at or a ball to play with or anything. But I didn't go every day. The guards would do little spiteful things, like, it's fourteen degrees, but they'll say, "Oh, we don't have coats today." You can go, but you'll just be in your standard-issue short-sleeve shirt. One time they took me out in the morning when it was raining freezing rain. And they didn't give me a coat or anything. I was in my short-sleeve prison greens.

I passed the time by reading a lot of law books. A guard would come by sometimes with a book cart, but they didn't have much besides law books. When you have nothing but time, you can go through a book pretty fast. So I started filing a lot of lawsuits! There's really nothing else to do.

Other than reading, I was sleeping. The more you sleep, the more you want to sleep. You don't know if it's day or night. In the SHU, hygiene is on the back burner. You might shower three times a week, but that's only if they decide to let you.

I saw my family on visit days. At first, I wrote them a lot, but after a while, there was nothing else to say. How many times can I tell you that I'm doing nothing? Mentally, nothing happens in the SHU. That's the problem. You can entertain yourself for a little while. And when you run out of things to make up—there's no stimulation. None. Time stands still in there. Everything just stops. I created dreams in my head. I don't know. You run out of ideas, and that's when you start questioning your sanity.

I made a couple of games. I was allowed to have manila envelopes and folders and a pen. So I tore them up to make a deck of cards. But once I altered the envelopes, they were contraband. I wasn't allowed to have those cards, so the guards took them. I also made a little peg-jump game out of one of my legal folders. They took that, too. I played tic-tac-toe with myself for a couple of days. I don't remember who won. I got beat a lot! I *could* write piano and keyboard songs on the paper. That was okay. They never took that.

The guards did random cell searches. Their system was that every day they picked two cells in every corridor to randomly search. But I was on a corridor where there was only one occupied cell—mine. So I got "random-ly" searched twice a day. The objective was to keep you in nothingness.

TO THEM I WAS ON HUNGER STRIKE

Then I stopped eating. One day I got my food and my rice was green. I didn't trust it at that point. When I stopped eating, I was still taking the tray of food. One day, I was out on a visit when my food came, and when I got back the meal was just sitting in my cell. I think it was supposed to be waffles, but it was mashed up into this mountain of I don't know what. I told the guards, "It would be really fucked up if I actually wanted to eat this, right?"

I started refusing the tray of food altogether. And when I started refusing the tray, then to them I was on hunger strike. They'd have a nurse in my cell five times a day taking my urine and checking my blood pressure. I went months eating very little food. When I had my visit on that Saturday or Sunday, I would eat all I could eat from the vending machines on the visiting floor. Every now and then, if there was bread that came in that was untainted, I would take the meal and maybe I'd eat the bread. They told me they'd get a court order to force-feed me, but they never did it. I started eating again when I got transferred out of Albion.

In October 2012, four months after she began her first yearlong sentence in the SHU, Tonja was given two additional 180-day sentences. The first sentence was for allegedly falsely reporting a sexual assault by one of the guards outside her SHU cell. The second was for an incident two weeks later in which Tonja mailed a sample of her food to the US District Court in Buffalo as evidence in support of a lawsuit she had filed.

They transferred me down to the Bedford SHU from Albion. I was never told why, but it happened soon after I went for a medical check and they found that I'd lost over eighty pounds. Then I was in the Bedford SHU for almost seven months. It was better than Albion. Even down to the rec. When I did get to go to rec I had at least some interaction with other inmates, some human contact. Back at Albion I'd been in an isolated cage.

At Bedford, sometimes there'd be another three or four people. There was a basketball, a table. At Bedford the contact with the officer was more frequent. Every now and then an officer would actually come to the door and have a conversation. Some were genuinely concerned—"You alright?" Any conversation makes a huge difference. I don't know if it keeps you sane, but it helps. My family would visit once a week, and that helped.

Mentally and physically I was a lot better at Bedford. It's still a SHU, and SHU is a world of its own. You just sit idle. That's just pretty much it. Being in SHU at Albion had even affected my eyesight. My depth perception was gone. I couldn't make things out more than six feet in front of me.

In other ways, Bedford lagged. Bedford was notorious for turning away visitors. I'd talk to my family on the phone after they missed a visit, and I'd say, "I was told you didn't come." And they'd tell me, "Oh, really? Because they refused to let us in."

I got out of SHU with about a year left on my sentence. Going back to the regular prison population was a trip. I wanted out of that SHU cell so, so badly, but then when I was out I almost couldn't deal with it. If all I can drink is water and then you give me the opportunity to drink something else—I'm like, yeah, I could, but I think I'll just settle on the water. I didn't know how to act at all, it's like, *Damn I'm dealing with people now.* Really delicate. The normal everyday feelings that people have, you don't have that.

So even though I was out of SHU, I kept getting tickets and they'd give me "keep lock"—where they lock you in your regular cell for twenty-three hours a day. It's better than SHU in some ways, like you have your stuff and see people moving about, but worse in other ways because you are so close to other activity but have to just sit in your cell. I guess that creates more of a yearning to participate in whatever is going on around you. I think I spent about eight months of my last year in prison in keep lock for various lengths of time, a month here, two months there.

THE EFFECT OF RELEASE WAS IMMEDIATE

I got out March 28, 2014. The effect of release was immediate. You're used to being in a cell by yourself, and that's what your brain has accepted, that's what you're conditioned to. And you'll also feel like anyone else that's in that cell is a threat to you. I was fine coming home, until we hit Grand Central station. I couldn't deal with the people, there were too many people. I was like, *Okay, I really can't do this.* I spent the first night at home. I reacted poorly to the presence or attention of another person. I didn't know I'd react that way. You can't go to that from not being around anyone. It was an issue with everything, including my marriage.

To this day, there are a lot of things that I'm still dealing with. I have developed zero tolerance for anything. I wasn't like this before. And there have been certain times when my sons are like *All right, calm down.* I'll explain my logic and it makes sense to me, but they say, "Really?" They don't know what I've been through. There's a way that I react to things because I've been subjected to this for so long. There are times when I'm living and I'm like, *Damn, do I really want this?*

I often say to anyone who offends me: you know something? Swing on me and hit me. It may hurt, but that wound will heal, and I'll get over it. But if you say something to me, it's going to resonate in my mind forever. I'm never going to get over it. And solitary, the effect is like those words that resonate forever. No matter what, I can still remember the first day they put me in, the first hours of that feeling. That feeling is probably stronger than any other, and that's the smallest part of my solitary stint.

When it comes to solitary, I don't think anyone is thinking about the consequences. If someone is a menace to society, and you isolate them, yes, you are going to make it safer for everyone else, but eventually you've got to let them out. Yes, the public is safe for that time, but now you have this menace who is developing a shitload of other problems. It's like taking a dog, putting it in a cage and mistreating it for years, and then letting it loose in a playground with children. It's going to act exactly how you'd expect it to act.

WHAT WAS THE POINT OF THIS WHOLE DAMN LAWSUIT?

In August 2017, Tonja was rearrested on new charges stemming from allegations made by her former girlfriend and reincarcerated with a new four-year prison sentence. We spoke with Tonja shortly after she arrived at Bedford Hills Correctional Facility, where she had been placed back in solitary confinement pending the outcome of a disciplinary hearing.

I'm bugging right now. On the outside, I was making progress—I got into a relationship, I had somewhere to live. When I ended the relationship, allegations were made, and the court told me I couldn't go back there anymore. Then I got another case. I had all the odds stacked against me. I already have a criminal record, you know? The judge told me she was going to give me the max, like fifteen years or something. So now I have four years, but I'm fighting from the inside to overturn this conviction.

I just got served with a ticket and they put me in SHU. This ticket does not warrant me being in SHU. Even if I am found guilty of all three of these charges, the maximum I can get is thirty days in keep lock. So why do they have me in SHU? Isn't that what we fought against? What was the point of this whole damn lawsuit? The system has the upper hand.

LEVI STUEY

AGE: 35

BORN IN: Vallejo, California

INTERVIEWED IN: Stockton and Vallejo, California

Levi Stuey is built like an armored vehicle—tough and compact. He has light, short-cropped hair, plenty of scars, and his nose has been broken at least once.[1] A front tooth is chipped, giving his frequent smile the look of a kid who just started losing teeth. He's covered in tattoos, including white power symbols on his arms and neck.

When we first meet, Levi is wrapping up a year spent living in a halfway house in Stockton, California. Levi grew up in the Bay Area city of Vallejo, California.[2] After getting introduced to drugs at a young age, Levi became accustomed to juvenile detention and the California state prison system, often spending months in solitary

---

1. Narrator's name and certain details have been changed at his request.

2. Vallejo is a city of 121,000 in Solano County, thirty miles northeast of San Francisco.

for various offenses. During our conversations, Levi discusses the politics in California prisons and the reasons it's better for many to be placed in solitary for committing an assault on another prisoner than to be in protective custody for having been assaulted.

THEY WOKE ME UP OUT OF BED, GUNS DRAWN

I was born in 1983, in Vallejo, California. I didn't know my dad—I was with my mom at first. I grew up with a big family around me when I was young, and we all lived within a few-block radius of each other. My grandma's house was like the main hub, and then a block north up the street was my cousin's and my uncle's house, and then maybe another two blocks to the east was my aunt's house. Growing up in Vallejo was alright. I mean, it wasn't completely harsh when I was in grade school. I had a lot of friends. I was popular.

When I was with my mom, I was a single child, and I had everything I wanted—toys, food, clothing. But when she got pissed off, then it was a whole different story. She could get violent. I don't know if it was toward everyone. I know it was toward me. Like if I had toys lying around or something, she'd get mean and say, "I'll beat your fucking ass. Pick your shit up."

I was hit, that's for sure. I wasn't spanked. I was hit. Sometimes it might be a kick. Sometimes it might be getting hit with a toy. I remember one time, we were supposed to go somewhere and I was just shoving my toys out of the way, getting the floor cleared, and she came in out of nowhere and was screaming at me to clean up my mess. And as she's telling me to clean it, she's throwing shit all over the place, throwing shit toward me, and trying to smack me. And I'm crying and trying to pick everything up while she's tearing my room apart and telling me to clean it up. But she'd always be nice in front of other people.

Then one night when I was in second or third grade, the cops came in. They busted down the door. They completely tore the house apart. They woke me up out of bed, guns drawn.

I'm a baby still, you know what I mean? And I get woken up by a police officer. I'm told to get dressed. I get dressed. I'm like, "Where's my mom?" I remember walking through the house and it looking like if you were to take a dollhouse and shake it with everything in it, and then see where everything lands.

My aunt—my mom's sister—came and picked me up. I'm asking, "What's going on? Is Mom okay?" And my aunt told me it was all a misunderstanding. Everything was going to be okay. It was kind of pushed under the rug, and I'm a kid so I wasn't really asking a lot of questions.

My mom didn't go to jail, but after that, I went and lived with my grandma. My mom had an apartment down the way, too, but I was never really there. I was mainly living with my grandma and going to school, which I didn't like. I just didn't want to be there, you know? I'd wait for the day to go by and then go home and play. I'd want to go to the creek and jump around in the water and crawl around and fish and shit like that. Have fun.

I LEARNED HOW TO BLEND IN

I was nine years old when I took my first hit of meth. It was at a friend's house, on Christmas. My grandma was in the hospital. My uncles and aunts and everybody were there with my grandma. So I went and stayed the night at my friend's house, and in the middle of the night, his older brother was like, "Hey, you want to smoke some shit?" And I was like, "Alright. What's it going to do?" So me and my friend's mom and his brother got high. This was in their apartment in downtown Vallejo, in the mom's room. It was weird. I mean, here I am hanging out with somebody much older than me, doing something I'm not supposed to do. But I felt cool. I still didn't even know my own body yet. I just knew whatever was going on, I liked it.

It fucked me up. I don't remember much, but I know it kept me up—I don't know—five days or something like that. After being up for five days, my friend was like, "You look like shit." With the amount that we smoked that night, if I were to smoke that today, I'd be able to go to sleep. But being so young and having such an underdeveloped body, it had ten times the effect then than it would have on me now.

I wanted to smoke meth again. But even though I'd smoked it, I didn't really know what meth was or how to get it, so I didn't have access. That was about it. I don't think anybody really noticed. It wasn't like I was smoking and smoking and smoking. In a way I was still innocent because I was really into sports. I was a star football player. I played football, boxed, raced BMX bikes, all nine yards. So I still did all that. But smoking that first time definitely changed me.

I'd say one thing was that experience opened my eyes to what was going on within my own family. I got curious about my own realm. I already thought my mom was weird. As a kid I was always wondering, *Why's she acting like that?* But after hanging out with my friend and seeing how his mom was, things started clicking. I mean, not everybody in my family was using meth, but there were people close to me using. I understood right away that my mom was using. It was like, *Oh, okay. I get it. She's one of them. That's why she's acting the way she's acting.*

The end of grade school, around fifth grade, is when it started getting a little rough. I had a bunch of older cousins, and they just really weren't the best influences in my life. I started drinking, smoking cigarettes. Then one uncle had this little lawn chair that he always sat in outside, and the lawn chair had a cup holder in the armrest, and I'd find doobies in the cup holder. I'd take them and I'd smoke what was left. I met some older kids who would sell me a little. My cousins would catch me smoking, and then instead of saying, "What are you doing?" it was like, "Why are you smoking that shit? Try this instead." So it just progressed, and I got used to better weed.

Around that time, I was with some kids from the neighborhood, and one of them had a neighbor across the street who had this gold model plane that we could see through the window of the house. The kids I was with dared me to go through the window and grab the plane, so I did. I took it, then I went home. Hours later, the Vallejo police were at the door. They took me to the police station, booked me, and then my uncle had to come get me. I ended up in juvenile hall for breaking and entering.

It was scary going in there the first time. I wanted my mom. They've got hall units for different age groups, and hall units for kids who have mental issues and a hall unit for kids on trial for murder and other major crimes. During the day, they'd make us go to school. After school, we'd go to our rooms for a couple of hours and then have dinner. After dinner, we'd go back to our rooms. Then at night, I think it's for an hour, an hour and a half, we get to have free time and can play ping-pong, basketball, watch TV, take a shower, things like that. Then go to our rooms and go to bed. I was in juvenile hall for about a week and then out with an ankle monitor for another week.

I was still in fifth grade when I got arrested again for assault with a deadly weapon. I was with my buddy Eric at his apartment complex. I can't remember how it started, but we were hanging out on his balcony and ended up talking shit with this fat older dude and his buddy down below us. A teenager, I think. This guy said to come down to where he was. My friend and I ran down there, and on the way, I grabbed a bat. I got down there and smashed the guy with the bat in his side. I didn't really do anything to him—it didn't knock him down. But then I pulled out a big-ass knife that I got at the flea market and said, "Come on then." The guy's friend just said more shit and then they walked off.

My friend and I were walking down the street back to my house when the police pulled us over and found the knife on me. I got booked for assault with a deadly weapon and for brandishing a deadly weapon. It turns out the guy I'd hit with the bat was actually a woman. I thought she was a dude!

So I was in juvenile hall for a couple more months. I was eleven. The first time I went into juvenile hall, I was scared, and it sucked. The second time, I knew more what to expect, and it still sucked. I was too young to understand where I was really. But I don't believe that institutions like that help in any way, shape, or form, other than to hone your criminal skills if you want to be a criminal. I'd say the main thing that juvenile hall taught me was how to keep my mouth closed. It taught me how to blend in.

YOU GET USED TO IT

I made it to high school but got kicked out freshman year for fighting. I was a hothead. Right before I was going into high school, I had football coaches coming to my games watching me and talking to my coaches, telling them that they want me to come to their high school to play ball. I had a good opportunity with football, but my anger got in the way.

I spent some more time in juvenile hall. I was going back and forth through middle school and all my high school years. I'd go in for things like theft, more breaking and entering, assaults, numerous parole violations. One of the little counselor dudes at juvenile hall told me, "We should give you a key you're here so much."

In juvenile hall, I was constantly in trouble. They got this shit called "risk" and then "maximum risk." You get put in max risk if you're a violent threat. But you know how kids are. One thing I'd learned is to get off first. That means, if you're in a hostile situation with someone, you punch them in the mouth before they punch you in the mouth because that's what's coming. I was constantly hitting other kids, so I was always in risk or max risk.

When you get into a fight, three or four counselors with names like Dion and Mondo, a goon squad, would come and fuck your ass up. They were breaking kids' arms, pulling them behind their backs. You'd fight back, they'd pepper spray you. They'd tell you to stop, and if you didn't, they'd spray you again. If you didn't stop *then*, they'd slam you to the ground, cuff you, and take you to your room. The first couple of times I got sprayed, I stopped right away. It burned like hell. But just like anything, after you've been through it a couple of times, you get used to it.

I'M IN JAIL WHILE I'M IN JAIL

Levi continued to move in and out of the prison system after turning eighteen, typically with sentences of a few months to a few years. In his early twenties, Levi's girlfriend, Maddie, became pregnant, and they married. They had four daughters together, even as Levi continued to return to prison for various lengths of time.

His longest sentence was for four years on burglary charges, of which he served
two. It was while he was serving time for that burglary conviction that Levi first
experienced solitary confinement.

The first time I was in solitary was when I was in San Quentin. I went
in on a four-year sentence for burglary, breaking into houses, and just a
bunch of stolen shit.

A regular cell at San Quentin still has bars. In the cellblock area,
there's five tiers. Each cell is about big enough to stretch your arms and
touch both walls. Each cell has a bunk for two people. You sit on the bunk
against one wall, and the wall across from you is like a foot away. In the
back of the cell is a sink and a toilet, which are together in one little unit.
Then you've got a shelf in back. I remember first getting to the cell and
being like, *How are we living in this shit?* And you're in there with your cellie,
another guy in the same small space. We all spent a lot of time working
out. There's enough room for someone to be doing pushups and then a bird
bath.[3] Other times we'd spend reading, talking, writing. Where I was in
the H unit, the yard was open from 8 a.m. to 3:30 p.m. Then we'd go back
to our cell for the count and to eat. After that, the yard would open back up
until 10 p.m. So at least we were free all day running around.

I was sent to ad seg for a week, week and a half, for supposedly helping to plan a riot that hadn't happened yet. Ad seg is the hole, solitary
confinement. When you go to the hole, everything is done by committee. You don't just go straight to the hole. You got to go to classification
first. That's where you go in a room that's got the warden, the captain,
all the bigwigs, and a classification sergeant. They go over your file and
what you're back there for. They don't want to put you in a unit where
you're going to get stabbed or beat up because you're a rat or whatever
the reason, so they go over your file and classify you. The whole process
of getting the paperwork together and reviewing it can take maybe two
weeks and during that time you're just in the hole with no yard time at all.

---

3. A "bird bath" refers to a quick body wash using the sink in a standard prison cell.

At San Quentin, the ad seg cells are exactly the same as the regular cells, only in a different cellblock, and you're there by yourself. When I was by myself that first time, it was like, *Fuck, man*. If you're in ad seg, at first you only get out of your cell every other day to shower. The only contact you have with another person is when the guard comes to escort you to the shower for five minutes.

Once you've been classified, then you get time in the yard every other day. Depending on what you're in for, when you get yard time you might go to a dog cage. A dog cage is a kennel for a person—just a metal cage that's like eight by twelve feet. But you're outside. You don't have anything with you in the dog cage, there's no weights or anything like that in California prisons. So you work out by doing pushups, burpees, squats.

That first time I was in solitary, I felt like, *I'm in jail while I'm in jail*.

PRISON POLITICS TO THE FULLEST

Levi was released from San Quentin in 2008 but was back in prison twenty days later. He was sent to California State Prison in Solano for a year on an assault charge. Levi says he assaulted his mom's boyfriend because he was beating her up.

I'd only been in Solano a week, and I wanted to earn a name, a reputation.[4] After a week, a child molester showed up on the yard. I'm not going to live with a child molester and nobody else who's on the yard's going to live with a child molester, just like they wouldn't live with a rapist, a rat, or somebody who hits old people. People like that have got to go. That's just what it is. A child molester is going to get smashed on. Of course, I can only speak for myself. I've got issues around child molestation. That touches a personal note for me, and I'm not going to be around a chil' mo'.

---

4. California State Prison, Solano is located in Vacaville, California, approximately thirty miles northeast of Vallejo. Though it was built for a capacity of 2,600 inmates, its actual inmate population has been more than a thousand greater than that through much of the past two decades.

Me and this other dude got him in the chow hall. We just started punching and kicking him, whatever we could do, until the guards shot us with block guns. That's a gun that shoots a nonlethal projectile, something like a wooden block. So a guard shot me with a block gun, and it completely knocked the wind out of me and knocked me to the ground. I was doing no more fighting after that. I was done.

First, they took the guy we smashed out on a stretcher. Wherever he went, he went. I don't know. Most likely he was taken to a SNY, which is protective custody.[5] I wound up with twelve months in SHU for causing grave bodily injury.

Unlike at San Quentin, the SHU cells at Solano had doors that electronically opened and closed. The cell has a window slit in the door that's maybe three inches high by a foot, and that's all there is to look out into the building. The rest is all enclosed, and it's quiet.

When I got to the SHU, the first thing I did is something called "fishing." That's where you make a "car," which could be a piece of soap or an envelope or anything you can find, and you spin line with any thread you have and tie it someway to the car. Then you can take your car and slide it out the slit under your door, then yank the line so it'll go to the cell next door to yours. That way you can pass notes or whatever it is you need to pass.

Then there's also COs. There's COs who are there to be assholes, and then there's COs who are there to get a paycheck and mind their own business. The COs who are there to get a paycheck, it's probably one of the best jobs for guys out there, literally. Unless you're in a really high-level prison, you don't do anything but babysit a bunch of dudes. Depending on where you're from and how long you've been in, you might have a CO who's willing to do shit for you.

---

5. In the California state prison system, SNY stands for "Sensitive Needs Yards." SNY units were established starting in the early 2000s to protect certain people, including ex-gang members, informants, sex offenders, and others, from others in "mainline" units. Protective custody can be requested by incarcerated individuals who fear for their own safety and can often, but not always, be a form of solitary confinement. For more on protective custody and other forms of solitary confinement, see glossary, page 262.

Not long after I went into the SHU at Solano, a CO showed up at my door and was like, "You got paperwork?" I showed him my paperwork. Paperwork is the incident report that explains why I got a lockup order in the SHU. Now, the paperwork will either say you're an aggressor or a victim. If you're the aggressor, then you need to produce that paperwork so you can say that you're "good." Your paperwork might say "assault on an inmate," and that actually looks good. It means you're active, you took care of a problem. It might also say "mutual combat" and that's okay, cause it just means two guys got into a fight. But if it says "victim," you don't want to show anyone your paperwork. Because that means you got attacked for a reason. In the prison system, if you're a victim, it's probably for a reason like you're a child molester, rapist, rat, abusing elderly people. A jailhouse thief. Those would be the reasons you'd get attacked. There's also a section on the paperwork that says "Statement." That needs to be blank. If you make a statement about the incident that got you locked up, you fucked up; something's going to happen to you.

It's all prison politics to the fullest.[6] However your race runs things inside is how it is, and how you're expected to act. And every race is different—white race, Black race. For me and my kind, if you're white and you're active, you're going to act a certain way and you're *not* going to act a certain way. We're too good to lose our shit. We're expected to be better than that.

I think it's like that because you got guys in prison who are still holding on to them old days when things were more racially divided. In prison you're racially separated because that African is not going to help you if you're getting whooped by a Mexican. And that Mexican sure the fuck ain't going to help you if you're getting whooped on by a Black man or even a white man. So who do you have? You have your own people because your people are going to have your back. It's just the way it is.

---

6. "Prison politics" generally refers to racial segregation in California men's prisons. Those housed in the California prison system are classified as a certain "race" and are generally housed and treated as a bloc in their movement and behavior with members of the same "race." For more, see glossary, page 261.

I didn't have any white power tattoos before prison. I got the swastika tattoo on my stomach after a riot at Solano State Prison against the Blacks. The other tattoos I didn't give a fuck. When I was in prison and following the politics, I could see the hatred from the Black men. You can see the animosity, you can feel it from them. You know they don't like you and you know they want to hurt you—it's all bad. Even when shit's not happening you can tell that they want to hurt you. So, I was in there and that opened my eyes. These swastikas that I have on me, to an older generation's Black man, it's an eyesore, it's blatant disrespect. Well, when I was in there I was all about disrespect to those mutherfuckers because I know they don't like me. I didn't put the swastikas on my body because I'm racist.

This is the thing—when I was in prison, I was a full-blown convict. It's what I believed in. I wasn't going to do anything or act any way other than the way I was supposed to be acting, which was as a strong white man. Hold my mud or hold my ground, or hold onto my character until it was over. I did what I had to do. It didn't matter how long it was going to be. I knew the moment I did what I did that I wasn't going to the hole for a short amount of time. I knew that. I was prepared for that. I knew that was coming. I actually expected to catch more time.

I'D HEAR OTHER PEOPLE LOSING IT

It's hard to explain what it was like in solitary, but I can say that being in the SHU made me feel like an animal. Made me feel like a dangerous person. Made me feel in a sense like a badass, because you're in a place where the cops won't even have any interaction with you unless you're cuffed up.

I tell you this much—being in the SHU in Solano was the most I ever thought. That was the most that my mind fucked with me and played with me. What went through my head most was, *What are people outside thinking of me? What's my wife doing? Where's she at? Who's she with? Is she fucking somebody? Is she thinking about me right now? Who's around my kids? What are they doing right now?*

Maddie, my wife, would come visit every weekend. Even when you're in ad seg, you can still get visits. They're behind glass when you're in ad seg, but you can still get visits. After my wife's visits, I'd get back to my cell and I can remember thinking, *Somebody's in the car waiting for her.* Or maybe I'd get a letter from her, and I'd start thinking, *Her handwriting looks different. She's doing something.*

Sometimes you'd get to the point where you'd just yell, "Fuck!" All the time I'd hear other people losing it. There'd be other guys in the hole who'd cause scenes and just do shit to get cops at the door.

One time this guy smeared shit all over himself and laid on the ground. The cops walked by and checked on him, and he didn't respond. They had to get medical tech out there, and he still didn't respond. They opened up the door, he's still unresponsive. They get him out the door and they get him on the stretcher, and then he's fine. He'd just been in there too long. He was just bored.

It's hard to explain because nobody can really grasp and understand the feeling of being so alone unless they're there. When you've been alone and you've been in jail, and you've been by yourself for so long, going to a place where you're really cut off, it's easier. I'm not saying that it didn't get to me. I'm not saying that at some times it didn't drive me nuts. I'm not saying that at times it didn't break me down to where I cried by myself. I'm not saying that. But I can't sit here and say it drove me absolutely insane because I was used to the shit. It was just another experience in prison. It was just another section to be in.

Is it torture? I'd say yes because we crave human contact. After you've been in for a while by yourself and you get to go to the yard, you're like, *Yes.* I remember going to the yard after being alone and the first thing everybody asked was, "You all right? Are you okay? How you doing?" We need that shit. The SHU is its own prison within a prison. You're in your cell all day. The light's on 24/7. No darkness. It's always lit up. It drives people crazy. Of course it does.

The last prison I was at was Salinas Valley State Prison, level 4, a max prison.[7] When I left there I knew how to make a paperclip into a knife, I'd learned how to fucking make a saw with thread that cuts for real, I learned how to make actual 100-proof whiskey, and numerous other things that I'm not going to put out there. But the point is I'd learned how to be more crime efficient than I did how to be a good citizen of the public.

PUTTING A ROOF OVER MY FAMILY'S HEAD

When we meet Levi in 2015, he's been living in a Salvation Army halfway house for nearly a year as part of a twelve-month, court-ordered treatment program. He's split with his first wife, Maddie, and has a baby daughter with his soon-to-be second wife, Brooke, who has been with him through the halfway house program once already.

Where I'm living is a house. It's got a rec room, a little gym, TV area. It's got a bowling alley up there. Two lanes. Then there's a dormitory. There's four-man dorms and there's a third level, which is more rooms, more dorms, and then it's got a hall of single rooms for guys who are in phase two of the program. Right now I'm at eleven months and in phase two. I have my own room.

There are two phases of the AA program I'm in. Phase one is mainly all program—you work your steps with your sponsor. You got classes, rehab, relapse prevention, anger management, family workshop. You're also working forty hours a week in the home. They call it "work therapy." You might work janitorial, or in the kitchen, or nights at the front desk. When I started, I'd work the desk from 10 at night to 6:30 in the morning. There's a curfew. The doors lock at 10:30. If you're not in, you're locked out and you're discharged from the program. There's no second chance. One strike and you're out. That's it. Phase one all together is a busy schedule, and it goes for your

---

7. Salinas Valley State Prison is a maximum-security facility located near Soledad, California, in Monterey County. Built for a capacity of 2,400, the prison houses more than 3,300 people.

first six months. Phase two, you do less meetings, but you also get to run them at the house. Also, you get to go out and look for work.

I didn't have a choice in being here. I'm court committed. It's actually the second time I've been in the program. The problem is, when I get high, I only stop when I'm in handcuffs and back in jail. That's what happened the first time.

That first time, I was here for a year, I graduated. I got high the next day. My fifth daughter was almost due. I got out on May 7 and she was coming June 7. I didn't want to be high when we had her, so I stopped. I was there at the delivery. Then after she had been home for three or four days, I started getting high again.

I hid it from my girlfriend, Brooke. She found out, but at first she didn't know. My woman ain't never smoked dope in her life. She ain't never been around a tweaker. She don't know what to look for. She knew I got high in the past. She knew what I did, but as far as being around it and really knowing what to look for and knowing what's up, she had no clue. She had never experienced it.

I was getting high every day. All the time. I knew it was wrong, but once that beast is unleashed, there ain't no stopping it. I justified it in my head with, *I ain't getting high with the fellas. I'm not committing any crimes. I'm working every day and not only am I working, but I'm supporting my girlfriend and I'm taking care of my child and on top of that my four other daughters. I'm supporting them and I'm giving money to their mama to help out.* I justified it as, *Hey, as long as I'm doing that, handling my responsibilities, why can't I get high?*

The difference between this time in the program and that last time is that I'm committed. I want to be clean because I've got five daughters, and I haven't had a relationship with them. My oldest daughter is ten. I didn't come into her life until she was four years old. All the other ones, they know me, but they don't know me. They know me as Daddy. I've been there, but I've always been in and out of their lives. This one, my youngest daughter, the relationship that I have with her is amazing. I'm experiencing what it's like to be a father. I don't want to give that shit up.

I'm excited. Brooke and I are going to get our own apartment. The program here advocates for you with housing if you finish the program. And then we're getting married.

When we meet with Levi again in the spring of 2017, he's selling meth from his garage. He and Brooke are married, living in an apartment with their young daughter in a rundown section of Vallejo. During our conversation Levi shows us a loaded AR-15 rifle he bought illegally to protect himself.

I left the program and as soon as I turned the corner I was blazing a blunt. I got home and the little monkey in my head that wanted to get high was scratching at me. And you know I know where to get it. So *boom*. I got it. Now I'm getting high. I smoke a lot. I smoke all day. I want to get high. I don't want to quit right now.

It was great working. I had the pipe going and the money fueling my habit. I was making good money, man. I was working over a hundred hours each two-week pay period. And I was getting high the whole time. I wasn't out robbing nobody, I was doing no crime.

I lost my job though. One of my coworkers decided to get something out of my truck, and he found my pipe. I was working, painting at this job site and wanted to go take a puff. I went to go get my pipe, and it wasn't there. Later the boss calls me in and says, "We hear you're getting high." And I'm like, "Yup, I ain't going to lie to you." He said, "We can't have that," and let me go. I was hella bummed out and feeling down, and it just fueled the old me to come out.

I didn't have no income and that made me scheme and plot. My buddy was selling crystal so he helped me get it going. And I started doing whatever I could to get money. Stealing from houses, stores, getting stuff out the back of trucks. Getting money or getting things I could sell for money. Anything. When I had my job I was at home. I was getting high, but I wasn't getting into no trouble. I ain't got no job now so I'm out here wheeling and dealing.

After I lost my job Brooke was pissed off. She was bugging me about why I can't stop, why I won't stop. Why this is so worth losing everything to me. She said she was going to try it with or without me. I was like, "You're joking, right?" And she's like, "No. I want to know what all the hype is about. I want to try it." I told her to swear on our daughter that if I didn't give it to her she was going to go get it herself. And she did. I couldn't have her going and getting it from some predator motherfuckers, because she don't know nothing about the dope world. She's naïve to the game.

So I gave her some shit. I mixed it in some juice and made sure to give her enough to make her sick. I gave her hella that shit. She was throwing up all night. She got sick as hell, but the next morning she wanted to try smoking it to see if she'd feel better, and she instantly liked it. I mean instantly. For the last five months she's just been smoked out nonstop. I don't know if I blame myself. I mean I gave it to her, but I gave it to her to avoid her putting herself in a real dangerous and dumb situation. She's good though, she's still going to work and taking care of our daughter and things.

Being in prison, being in the SHU was hard, but hell, I hear voices to begin with. The voices, sometimes it's whispering, sometimes it's yelling. Sometimes it's like an echo. It all depends on what I'm going through. It stems from depression, but also, the meth don't help, that's for damn sure because my mind's already going.

I've calmed down hella much. But if I get caught, especially with what I'm working with now, I'm either going back for life or the cops are going to kill me because I'm shooting it out with them. I got a trigger lock, which means it's basically twenty-five to life if you're caught with a firearm. I'm not going back. If it comes to that, I'm shooting it out.

HEATHER CHAPMAN

AGE: 47

BORN IN: Nyack, New York

INTERVIEWED IN: Fort Lauderdale, Florida

*Heather Chapman lives in a small two-bedroom house in Fort Lauderdale, Florida,
with her husband of fourteen years, their two young daughters, her nephew, and a
rotating cast of animals—some the family owns, and some she rescues and fosters
until they're rehabilitated enough to go to a forever home. Their house can be
loud and chaotic. When we visit, a ferret and three dogs run around our feet while
Heather recounts the struggles her family is facing.*

*Her first child, Nikko Albanese, was arrested in 2011 for armed robbery and
sentenced in 2012 to ten years in prison. Nikko began medication at age ten for a
range of mental and emotional challenges, and Heather says that life in prison—
especially in isolation—is deteriorating his mental and physical health. She says
he's twice been found unresponsive in his cell, and she fears he could die before his*

release. Heather is animated and emotive when we talk, and though she's lived in
Florida for twenty years, she speaks with a heavy New York accent. Over the course
of dozens of conversations, Heather describes the brutality of solitary confinement
on her son as well as the impact on her and her family.

I HOLD NIKKO'S SHOES

My son Nikko Albanese has been incarcerated for the past six years. And
he's been in solitary confinement for that entire time. They're torturing
him. They're torturing me. They're torturing my daughters. They're
torturing my husband. They're destroying our family.

When I hold Nikko's shoes, I mean, it's all I have. It's all I have of my
son. Nikko would have the worst-smelling feet. He'd take off his shoes
and the whole room would smell terrible. I used to yell at him all the
time. I would make him spray his shoes with Lysol and put them outside.
And now I smell his shoes because I'm so desperate for him. Every time
I get a letter I put it in a ziplock bag just in case I can smell him because
I know he touched it.

I ache for my son. I ache for him and I won't clean his shoes. I keep
them in plastic bags and when things get bad I take them to bed with me
and I hold them. I won't let anyone else touch them.

NIKKO WAS THE ONE WHO GAVE ME THE STRENGTH

I always wanted children, but Nikko wasn't planned. I would have preferred
to start having children when I was financially in a better position. I was
waitressing at a Denny's, and that's how I met Nikko's father, Glen. He was
one of the waitresses' sons. She kept trying to set me up with him. Something about him scared me, and I didn't want to meet him. I'll never forget
she literally dragged me to him one time, and everything about him just
frightened me. But I ended up going out with him and it went from there.

I worked up until I was eight months pregnant. Glen and I were engaged when I got pregnant, and I kept making excuses to push the wedding date back. He just was not a nice person.

Nikko was born in September 1992. He was my first baby. He was born in the same hospital as I was, in Nyack, New York. Before Nikko was born it had been gray and raining for six weeks straight. It was September in upstate New York so there were no leaves on the trees. I woke up and I knew it was time to go to the hospital. I was in hard labor for thirteen hours. I was twenty-two, and I wanted to deliver Nikko naturally, and I did. The nurses handed him right to me and it was the greatest moment of my life. I still remember the way he looked at me and the way he smelled. He smelled like Nikko.

Glen was there at the hospital. At that time we were living in a duplex in Valley Cottage, New York. When I brought Nikko home it felt like a dream. It felt like a miracle. I was in disbelief that this beautiful little creature was mine. And like every parent, I thought he was so perfect and so beautiful and I was—and still am—so in love with him. He was my world; he was my everything. And I brought him into a miserable environment.

Glen had the neighbors watching the house. If I even stepped outside, he would get a phone call at work. Glen had them all convinced that I was crazy and trying to steal his child. I wasn't allowed to speak to anyone. Nikko's father seemed like such a great guy and everyone liked him, but they just didn't know who he was.

I left Glen when Nikko was eleven months old. Actually Nikko was the one who gave me the strength to leave. I would never have been able to do it without Nikko. I'd been with Glen for three years, and it was something out of a horror movie.

He would take me to the supermarket and give me only enough money for the groceries. I would save like a nickel here, you know, twenty cents there, and I eventually saved up seven dollars. And when I saved up the seven dollars, I made arrangements for a women's shelter to meet me at the local supermarket. The only things I took with us were Nikko's pictures. I put them in a blue garbage bag. And I knew that when I left the house in a cab that Nikko's father was going to get phone calls and that's exactly what happened. One of the neighbors was a state trooper and was able to get information from the cab company so they found out where the driver had dropped me off. I'm holding Nikko's pictures and I'm holding Nikko and the woman from the shelter is late picking me up. Every minute felt like an hour. I'm standing out in front of that supermarket holding Nikko so tight. I was literally fearing for my life.

I went to a shelter because of Glen. I was very scared of him. So Nikko spent his first birthday in a battered women's shelter in Walden, New York.

NIKKO COULD DO ANYTHING

I moved to Boca Raton, Florida, where I got my license to do nails. I worked around Nikko's schedule. I got Nikko into Catholic school, and how I paid for it was I would do the nuns' nails two or three times a week.

When he was in kindergarten, I remember walking into the school to pick him up and one of the teacher's assistants came running up to me and she said, "Nikko was on the roof!" And I said, "What? What was Nikko doing on the roof?" And she goes, "I don't know . . ." so I hurried to his classroom and there he is drawing a picture like nothing was happening. And I said, "Hi, Nikko," and he gives me a hug. I said, "Nikko, were you on the roof?" And he said, "Yeah." I said, "Well, why? Why were you on the roof?" And he just kinda looked at me said, "'Cause my ball went up there." To him it was a crazy question to ask. His ball went up there so he needed to solve the problem. He had found a way to get up on the roof of the school to retrieve his ball and didn't see anything wrong with it. That was Nikko. If there was a problem, he'd just solve it. Nikko could do anything. He was very determined. One time he saw some man on TV do a backflip. Well, Nikko decided that he wanted to do that. And he taught himself to do it. I don't know how long it took, weeks maybe, but it didn't matter. If he jumped up and landed on his head a hundred times, he would just continue to do it until he mastered it.

Nikko didn't have much of a relationship with Glen, though he'd wanted one. Nikko loved his father. Glen would come maybe twice a year to visit Nikko, and Nikko lived with Glen for a little while in White Plains, New York, while I took care of my mother, whose cancer had come back.

But when Nikko was ten, we were in church and Nikko grabbed my cell phone, and he said, "I'm going to call my father and wish him a Merry Christmas." That was fine with me. So he walked out of church and when he walked back in, he was completely white and he kind of sat back in the pew and was just staring down. And I whispered, "Nikko! What happened? What's wrong?" And he looked at me and said, "My dad said he wants nothing to do with me. That I'm more trouble than I'm worth."

It was traumatizing. And the whole thing happened because Glen was with a very nice woman for six or seven years, but the whole time he had a girlfriend on the side. Nikko didn't think it was right so he told Glen's main girlfriend. And then Glen severed the relationship with Nikko. After that Nikko would call his father probably once a week asking, "Will you see me now?" And the answer was always no.

I DIDN'T REALLY UNDERSTAND THE DIAGNOSIS

I didn't have the energy for Nikko. By the time I would finally get him in bed I felt like my brain was oatmeal. Like I was just sitting there with drool coming out of my mouth. I mean, I could barely get myself into bed. Nikko was my first, so at first I thought it was me. I didn't understand it. But then I started to realize there were some other issues going on.

Nikko would always handle a situation the way he saw fit and would never think anything through, he would just react. He got into fights, but he wasn't some violent kid. At the time I didn't fully understand what was happening. And then he got labeled. And that was that.

I was having a lot of behavioral problems with Nikko, and I knew it wasn't a disciplinary thing. So I took him to a hospital and the psychiatrist there gave us the initial diagnosis. I don't like to use this term because it's horrible, but it was "severely emotionally disturbed." It doesn't really mean anything, and I didn't know enough to dive into that and ask what that meant. I had no idea. But really it was multiple disorders. Bipolar and attention deficit and compulsive disorder and separation anxiety and, you know, he just wouldn't think before he would react.

Nikko at the age of ten was diagnosed with bipolar disorder. That's when we began medication. Nikko would never go out and be a bully or be mean to a kid. He has compulsive behavior where he would ask the same question repeatedly and he may annoy another child, and so that kid would say, "Get the hell away from me," and would hurt Nikko's feelings and then Nikko would react. Not even in a physical way, but maybe say something. He wouldn't say it quietly like the kid said it to him, but so the teacher would hear it. It was considered bad behavior.

I didn't really understand the diagnosis, and it's not like anyone explained it to me, or how the process works. That was something that I had to learn. And when you're in the middle of something like that, there's so much going on. Okay, so he's got a diagnosis, but there was always that underlying thing of, well, if you were a better mother, this wouldn't be happening. There was always that judgment there, even from within the medical profession. And I would say to myself, these are medical people, and I must be a bad mother and I need to do better.

It's a very difficult system to navigate. So if you don't know the right questions, you're not going to get the right answers. I was confused. I didn't really understand what was happening, and things weren't really getting better. Especially for an adolescent that young, you know you have a medication cocktail and you're constantly adjusting levels until you find one that works and then that's only going to work for a short time because the chemicals within the brain are continually changing. And I didn't know any of this. So I thought it was my fault, I thought it was Nikko's fault. I didn't know the right questions to ask and I just didn't have enough information.

I remember once waking up at four or five in the morning and Nikko had been up all night. He had taken apart all these electronic devices. He was twelve or thirteen and he had this crazed look on his face. Very driv-en, very focused. I asked, "Nikko, what are you doing?" and he said, "I'm taking these apart and then I'm going to put them back together," and he had like five different devices taken apart. Everything had changed, like his facial expression, and that was a clear indication that the medication was not working properly and I should have done something right then, but I didn't.

There wasn't a light switch that went on and off. He would be on different medications and his body chemistry was constantly changing, so it wasn't always the same symptoms. It was a slow process. By the time I realized that he was in crisis, and he realized that he was in crisis, it would *definitely* be a crisis.

After the diagnosis he kind of felt that he was defective, I guess. That he was broken and he was carrying around a big shame and a big embar-rassment. He didn't want anyone to know. He was treated as damaged goods by the medical staff, by the school, by everybody.

HIS INNOCENCE WAS GONE

I was fighting to keep him out of the special ed school. The school board was pushing and pushing to put him in. I felt his behavior would escalate if he went into that type of environment. He finally went in there in fifth grade, and he was there until he went to the first juvenile detention cen-ter. Then they wouldn't take him back.

He would get suspended all the time. At thirteen or fourteen he would fight with the bus driver. I think the bus driver just didn't like him and would single him out and embarrass him in front of the other kids, and Nikko would just react. I couldn't get him stable for a long period of time. The doctors that we were dealing with told me to get him in the court system and once I got him before a judge, a judge could order him into a facility, the best that money could buy. And the only way he could get there was if a judge ordered him. But getting him in the system was the worst thing you could possibly do.

My husband, Freddy, and I kept calling the police anytime anything would happen. Looking back, Nikko was hitting puberty, and I had just given birth to Nicole and was pregnant with Jackie, so, you know, there was a lot going on. One night Nikko and I got in an argument over the remote control, and it just spiraled. And it got physical. I was as much to blame as Nikko.

Nikko would decide he didn't want to take his medication, and so I would call the police. And we got him into the system. But once Nikko was in the system, it felt like he was taken out of our hands. I tried to stop it, but there was no stopping it. Nikko had to go to court regularly because he was in trouble for school truancy and domestic violence.

We went to court for over a year because the judge was monitoring Nikko's progress. He put all these crap programs into our home that weren't doing anything. These people would come to meet with Nikko at home, and I felt they weren't qualified for anything. I wanted to get him into a program called the Sheriffs Youth Ranch. It's a very long process, but the program is supposed to be very good. I was on the last step of getting Nikko in that program. We were in court and before the judge sentenced Nikko, I said, "Please don't sentence him. I almost have him in the youth ranch. I've been working on this for the past eight months." The judge took a recess and called the youth ranch, and no one answered. He came back and said, "I don't believe you, I think you're lying to me," and sentenced Nikko to the juvenile detention center.

There's not just one thing that happened. We got Nikko into the system, and then it just took on a life of its own. The judge wanted to see progress. I don't know what kind of progress they were expecting. I was confused. Nikko was confused. We couldn't all get on the same page, and it went downhill from there.

It was a nightmare. The first time Nikko was supposed to spend six months, he was there for eight. He was one of the youngest kids and the only white kid, and it was a horror. He was sent to Thompson Academy, and there was a lot of abuse.[1] Later there was a lawsuit. It's all documented. Nikko has never been the same since. Never. I didn't know who he was. I lost Nikko then. His innocence was gone. You could see that he'd been through something horrific. He was just . . . different. He was sad and angry.

The years after were difficult. He went to another facility. In and out of other institutions. They were basically preparing him for prison. And it's not like he did anything really terrible, it was more just that he was in the system. I was looking for help and doing it wrong. The system absolutely made him worse. The system failed him time and time and time again.

Nikko's medical costs were covered by social security as a child. But when he turned eighteen the social security stopped because he became an adult. We had to start the process of getting him covered all over again. He lost access to his medication and doctors, and he started to self-medicate with oxycodone. He became addicted to it.

Nikko was desperate to stop. But we were turned away from every detox rehab there was—from West Palm Beach to Miami. We even tried to get him into a mental health facility, into a crisis unit, and we couldn't even do that. We were literally turned away. There were no beds. We were in the middle of an epidemic of oxycodone. At that time Broward County was the only county in the United States that didn't have a cap on how many pills you could get in a month, so there were people coming from all across the country into Broward County to all the pill mills.[2] There was a pill mill on every corner. It was a huge epidemic—between Broward and Palm Beach County eight people were dying every day due to oxycodone.

---

1. Thompson Academy was a privately run juvenile detention facility, located in Broward County. Owned and operated by Youth Services International (YSI), Thompson was shut down in 2013 following allegations of rampant physical and sexual abuse and neglect of minors at the facility. In 2016, the state of Florida cut all ties with YSI.

2. "Pill mills" are pain clinics that recklessly prescribe opioids. In 2011, NPR called Florida the "epicenter of a prescription drug abuse epidemic," citing that "doctors in Florida prescribe ten times more oxycodone pills than every other state in the country combined" ("The 'Oxy Express': Florida's Drug Abuse Epidemic," March 2, 2011).

Nikko needed a lot of money to support his habit. He would want to take the family car to go and pick up drugs, and I wouldn't let him. So there was a lot of turmoil in the house and that's what the girls remember. Mommy and Daddy fighting with Nikko. I didn't know who he was. Nikko didn't know who he was. His addiction had control and it came to the point where I sat Nikko down one day and I told him that he had to leave. We both started crying. It's one of the hardest things that I ever had to do. I have two younger children, and Nikko's addiction was in control—Nikko wasn't.

The robberies happened right around Nikko's birthday. He had just turned nineteen. It happened at the end of November 2011. Nikko robbed a Pizza Hut and a CVS. They were armed robberies, but there were no bullets in the gun. At CVS he waited in line and when it was his turn he robbed the store. I don't know what he got. Whatever it was, it was under a hundred dollars. I believe the Pizza Hut robbery was in the early afternoon, when it had just opened. There was no one in the store, and it was pretty pathetic the way the whole thing went down, but that too was under a hundred dollars. His codefendant was the getaway driver. He was older, and his family had some money, and so as soon as they were arrested his family was able to obtain a lawyer. Shortly after that the prosecution made a deal and I think the codefendant did two or three years. Then he got out and ended up fatally overdosing.

Nikko called from jail and the first thing I asked him was, "Did you do it?" He said yes and that was it. Nikko has always been that honest. If he did it, he'll absolutely tell me that he did it. And he's prepared to take the consequences.

NOBODY ACKNOWLEDGED WHAT HE SAID

Nikko was in jail for a year, basically awaiting trial, and he had a public defender. The lawyer brought him into court a week early and was forcing him to plead guilty. By this time Nikko had been in jail a year with no medication, and he wasn't doing well. He was getting very sick. I walked into court and that lawyer was standing over Nikko, sticking his finger in his face. When I realized what was happening I just looked at Nikko, I shook my head, and I put my hands out, saying, "No, don't plead guilty." And the public defender looked at the bailiff and gestured, and the bailiff took me out of the courtroom. And Nikko pleaded guilty. The lawyer's reasoning was, "You don't want to piss this judge off." He said, "You have to plead guilty."

When Nikko was arrested, Glen wrote Nikko a letter in prison apologizing for rejecting him. And Nikko ended up reading that letter to the judge in court. Nikko hadn't been sentenced yet. While reading that letter, Nikko said that he suffered with bipolar disorder. It was the first time that he ever said it out loud. And it went completely unnoticed. I remember looking at Nikko when he said that, feeling two different emotions so strongly. The first emotion was pride—that he was able to stand up and hold his head up high and say in public, "Yes, I do suffer with bipolar." And the second emotion was empathy. It was such a hard thing for Nikko to do and so painful for him to say, and the fact that it wasn't acknowledged broke my heart. Nobody acknowledged what he said—not his lawyer, not the judge, nobody. And I remember looking around and thinking, "Maybe they didn't hear him." But it was such a huge moment, and I just looked at Nikko and mouthed the words "I love you. I'm proud of you."

Nikko was sentenced to ten years mandatory minimum sentence in August 2012. His public defender did absolutely nothing to prevent this. It felt as though he was working for the prosecution. I walked out of the courtroom and said a few words to the attorney. They were not kind. And I grabbed Nicole's and Jackie's hands and walked down what felt like the longest hall in my life, and as soon as we turned the corner I dropped to my knees. They just gave out and I started crying.

NIKKO JUST SHUT DOWN

As soon as Nikko went to prison I filled out paperwork for visitation for me, Freddy, and our two girls. So I was awaiting this paperwork to come back clear—they do a background check. I hadn't heard from Nikko for a month, so I ended up calling the prison and found out that Nikko was in administrative confinement. So that means that something happened. I found out that he had gotten a tattoo, and because of that he was put on a disciplinary squad. Something happened on the disciplinary squad with an officer. To this day I don't know what it was, but I know Nikko.

In February 2014, he was found in the solitary confinement cell unresponsive. Nikko just shut down, stopped eating, stopped talking, stopped moving. He was just lying there waiting to die. There was an advisor at the National Alliance on Mental Illness that I would call obsessively, like a lunatic. He made a phone call to check on Nikko. And that's how I found out that Nikko was in the crisis unit and had been there for several months, and that he had been found in a catatonic state in solitary confinement. That day was horrific. I thought a catatonic state was something from the fifties. I didn't even realize that a human being could go into a catatonic state these days.

The prison doctors diagnosed him with schizophrenia. Now I know that Nikko doesn't have schizophrenia because this is something that the doctors and I were looking for when he was younger. I've read everything there is to read on solitary confinement and what happens to the brain, how it will shut down, and how you'll start hallucinating. The human brain is just not designed for this type of isolation. So it will mimic the same effects as schizophrenia, but that doesn't mean you have schizophrenia. It means that you're basically being tortured. Really, the prison doctors were seeing Nikko react to isolation. He's not schizophrenic, but they're medicating him like he is. And these are serious medications. They're not medicating him for the conditions he has, they've misdiagnosed him and are torturing him even more with the wrong medications. It's like they're punishing him for having symptoms of isolation.

A VERY, VERY SHORT TIME TO GET NIKKO BACK

The first time I was allowed to visit was 2015, and that was because he was found to be forty pounds underweight and near death. The first visit was horrible. Nikko had already been in solitary for two and a half years. He spent sixteen days in general population, and the rest of the time he'd been in isolation. He was at Union Correctional, which is about six hours from where I live.

I remember being nervous, thinking that Nikko was going to be horrified, that I looked so stupid, that I looked so old. I was worried that I was going to upset him. I'm shaking. I'm scared. The visit happened to be on death row, which was, in itself, very upsetting. I didn't know why I was visiting my son on death row.

So the guards walked me in and told me that I could buy Nikko food. All I brought was $25, and I spent every cent of it on anything they had. They filled this box with the food and then they put it into a phone booth type of thing. I guess they opened the door to this phone booth thing, and there was an inmate standing there. They started to remove his shackles. I thought to myself for a split second, *Oh, they're putting the wrong inmate in the room. Nikko is supposed to go there. Should I say something?* And then I realized that it was Nikko.

Nikko—he didn't know who I was. His bones were protruding. He could barely stand up. Three guards had escorted him from his cellblock to the visiting area in death row. He could barely walk. And they're having a hard time getting the shackles off him because he's having a hard time keeping his balance. He's blinking his eyes like the light's affecting them. He looked like a Holocaust victim. That's all I thought, that he looked like a Holocaust victim. It looked like rigor mortis had started to set in around his eyes, his cheekbones—everything was set back. And he had that daunted look, like a beaten dog. He's blinking and looking around. I stand up and I'm waving my arms and I'm saying, "Nikko! Nikko it's me! It's Mom." He looks and he kind of says yes, but doesn't really say anything and keeps looking around. And I realize he doesn't know who I am.

Nikko didn't know I was there. He couldn't make eye contact. He was in and out of consciousness. I kept trying to get his attention. It's a two-hour, no-contact visit so I can't touch him. Just the sound of my voice would hurt him, and asking him to look at me and give me eye contact was painful for him. I could see how painful it was. I could see that he would literally come in and out of consciousness.

So they unshackle him and he's scared. He's very scared. And I knew that I had a very, very short time to get Nikko back. And that literally everything was depending on this visit. I can't touch him, and there is a dirty piece of glass in between us with those little holes—that metal plate with holes poked in it—and I needed to get Nikko to focus on me. I needed to make eye contact with him, and I needed him to remember who I was. I shouted: "Nikko! Nikko!" I kept calling his name to get him to look at me, trying to get his eyes to, you know, look up to eye level because he couldn't do that—his head was hanging. I was talking very fast and very loud about everything—his childhood, his sisters, the animals in the house. I was doing everything—I'm calling him names, things that I used to call him when he was younger, and I'm not showing fear.

I remember just being very matter of fact about everything and speaking with a lot of force. I remember thinking that he needs to use my strength. And I just keep talking. It's probably twenty minutes into it, and as I'm talking—whatever I'm saying—I would stop and say, "Nikko! Look at me! Nikko, look at me!" And then I'd continue talking. But I'd keep saying it, "Nikko, look at me. Nikko put your eyes on me. Look at me! Give me your eyes. Nikko, look at me."

Very slowly he picked up his head and then he picked up his eyes and moved them across the room until they came to me. I said, "Nikko!" As soon as his eyes met mine I said, "Nikko!" And he said, "Mom? You're here." And I said, "Yes. Nikko, I'm here! I'm right here, Nikko." And his eyes would start falling, and I said, "Nikko, keep your eyes on me. Keep your eyes on me!" And he said, "Mom, you're here." I said, "Yes, I'm here." And I just sat back, and I made him keep his eyes on me and I just smiled, and I let him kind of process the whole thing. And then he smiled.

He knew who I was. I wouldn't let him take his eyes off me, no matter what. I kept talking, and I could see that the more I spoke, and the more I kept his eyes on me—you could literally see the color come back into his face, you could start to see facial expressions. And it was like breathing life into him. They had taken the shackles off his arms—so he could move his arms. I guess he must have hit the box of food with his arms because I wouldn't let him take his eyes off me. And he looked down. And of course I screamed, "Nikko, look at me! Nikko!" And he looked up and he said, "Is this for me?" And I said, "Of course it is." And he had to keep his eyes on me, but he's literally shoving this food into his mouth. I was scared he was going to eat the wrappers and choke.

I was just talking, letting him know that I was there. And he's just shoving this food in his face. You know when children are really hungry and they get one of their favorite meals? They'll sit there, bounce and swing their legs and hum, and they're just so happy while they eat. And that's exactly what was happening with Nikko. I'm there, and he's eating, and it feels good. And he says, "Mom, I don't know if they told you, but I stopped eating." And I said, "Yes, Nikko, they told me. Why? Why did you stop eating?"

Then it was like everything stopped. Nikko stopped bouncing and humming and there was just this blanket of shame. And his head just went down and his eyes went off. And I said, "No, no! Nikko! Look at me! Pick up your head and put your eyes back on me! It's okay." Then I started explaining to him what happens to human beings when they are in severe isolation, that they start to hear voices. Then I went through the basics of what happens to any human brain in this situation. And he picks his eyes up at me and you could see him feeling relief. He just sat back, looking at me, and he's drinking in every word that I'm saying. And you know, I was telling him, "Nikko, you're not crazy. Everything that's happening—hearing voices, the hallucinations, and every single thing is normal. Because this situation that you're in is *not* normal."

IT'S CHANGED THE ENTIRE DYNAMIC OF THE FAMILY

At the end of September 2015, I was told that Nikko's level had dropped because of his outbursts and that they would revisit the idea of him getting visits again in October 2016.[3] I literally counted the days until October 2016. And on September 28, 2016, he went into a medical crisis. He had been through multiple beatings and cell extractions, and he had to be put into the crisis unit, which completely removes visitation from the table. So he's being punished for going into a crisis state.

Every year it happens. He goes into a medical crisis and can't have visits. And it's going to happen again. And when it happens, it will happen worse than the last time. This could be the year that he ends up dead. I am not a dramatic person. I am a realist. I really am. It's so basic what needs to be done, and the fact that I cannot hire an attorney for fifteen, twenty thousand, whatever they're asking—that's a crime. It's a crime what's happening to Nikko. And he will end up dead. He's got another five years. He will not last.

It's destroying the family. My health is failing, the girls are witnessing their mother suffering, knowing their brother is painfully suffering. It's changed the entire dynamic of the family. It's put a strain on my husband and our marriage. It's a crime in itself. My daughters are at the age when they are still sweet and innocent—they're eleven and thirteen—and to rob them of their innocence . . .

It's hell. Nikko suffering is the last thing I think of before bed, it's what I dream of, and as soon as I open my eyes in the morning it's the first thing I think of. It's a very difficult thing to explain, but every part of my life is affected by it. I live in a constant state of panic. I want to be able to give Nikko a hug. I want to smell my son. I want to be able to touch him and make him dinner and make his bed and know that he's in my home and he's safe and he's not being tortured.

---

3. "Level" here refers to security levels within a maximum-security prison. For more on the classification of security levels, see glossary, page 260.

IT'S PRETTY OBVIOUS WHAT I'M DOING

I have a very small house, a small two-bedroom. And you know, I have five foster rescue dogs, plus my four dogs and my ferret and cat, and there's Jackie, Nicole, and Fred. Oh, and I took my nephew in as well. So it's tight. It's tight.

It's pretty obvious what I'm doing. I mean it's not that hard to see. I can't help my son, so I'm running around the state of Florida rescuing animals. I rescued the ferret because it was in solitary confinement. It was in this tiny birdcage. I named her after one of my favorite bag designers— Louis Vuitton. So her name is Louis, and her nickname is Vicious Vera.

I've been working with the ferret every day for the past seven months. You couldn't touch this ferret before. Ferrets have very sharp teeth. They usually don't bite, but this particular ferret was drawing blood. She basically treats Freddy like a piece of meat, but I won't put her in a cage.

She has to have her own space. So she sleeps in my closet. I hate to use the word *damaged*, but she will have the effects of that solitary confinement for the rest of her life. Her personality will be altered forever. But the good news is that she is able to trust as long as you put the work in and you let her know, "I'm here. Even if you bite me and I'm bleeding, I still love you. And I'm here." I can call her and she comes and kisses me on the lips. I'm just consistent with her. But no, I will not put her in a cage.

In early 2017, Heather was featured in an online news video (produced by Mateo) about the impacts of solitary confinement on her and her family. At the time Heather hadn't seen Nikko since October 2015. Following the video's release, she raised enough money through a crowd-funding campaign to hire an attorney. With the pressure from the attorney, Heather was able to secure two ten-minute phone calls and one two-hour visit per month with Nikko. She still can't touch him, however. Their visits take place through glass. Nikko is currently held in solitary confinement in a medical wing at Union Correctional Facility in Raiford, Florida. Heather says he's improving with regular visits and calls. "I have hope now," she says. "But I'm scared he could slip again and I'll lose him before I can get him out."

MICHAEL "ZAHARIBU" DORROUGH

AGE: 64

BORN IN: Cleveland, Ohio

INTERVIEWED IN: Solano State Prison, Vacaville, California

With the exception of the drab prison jumpsuit he wears, Michael "Zah" Dorrough looks like an archetypal college professor. With a slight frame, a full head of hair, and light-brown eyes framed behind prison-issue bifocals, Zah is thoughtful and quiet. He has been in various prisons in the California system since the 1970s and is currently serving a sentence from 1985 for a murder that he says he did not commit. Now in general population, Zah spent nearly thirty years in solitary confinement in various California state prisons.

We visit Zah at Solano State Prison, where he is currently incarcerated. Located in Vacaville, California, Solano sits amid rolling green hills thick with oak trees and rows of eucalyptus and palms. Prison rules prevent us from bringing in recording equipment, so we correspond with him primarily via mail. Through

223

dozens of letters, Zah tells us of his early life in the Watts housing projects in Los Angeles and the horrors of being locked up for decades in solitary confinement for his alleged prison gang affiliations.

GROWING UP IN CLEVELAND WAS SPECIAL

I have been in prison for almost all of my adult life. I think that, sometimes, turning your life around requires that you start your life all over again. Like being reborn.

I was born in 1954. I'm originally from Cleveland, Ohio. I had one sister, Marnetta. She was a dear friend. She passed away several years ago. And I have one brother, Craig, who is still alive. I grew up in a two-parent home. My mother, Thelma, is still alive. My father, Clarence, passed away two years ago from cancer. I was crushed. My parents were my dearest and most trusted friends. They were married sixty-five years.

Growing up in Cleveland was special. I loved to play baseball. I can remember how a buddy of mine and I would get on the bus when we had the money and go down to Municipal Stadium and watch the Cleveland Indians play. I was a huge fan. Block parties were big then. We would block off the ends of the street, someone on each end of the street would bring record players and sound systems, and everyone would bring food, and we would have a party until the evening. During the summer we used to sit out late at night and sing. We all wanted to be the Temptations. We loved Smokey Robinson and the Miracles too, but no one could hit the notes that Smokey hit. The O'Jays were very popular when I was growing up in Cleveland, not just because they were bad, but they were also from Cleveland. They lived around the corner from my grandmother's home. I used to stand out in front of their house and listen to them practice. I think this was pretty typical of how it was growing up in inner cities during that time.

SURVIVING WAS ALL THAT MATTERED

When I was maybe nine or ten the police mistakenly came to our home, then realized they were at the wrong home. I remember one officer saying, "It's just a N----- home," and my mother cursing out the police and my being afraid the police would kill my mother.

I remember the rebellion.[1] It was during the afternoon and several buddies and I were going to a local park to play baseball. It was a quiet afternoon. There were armed National Guardsmen protecting a bank. The bank sat on a corner and we were waiting on the light to change. We were told to keep moving, but we couldn't do so until the light changed. One of the guardsmen walked up to one of my buddies, Anthony, and said, "N-----, did you hear us?" and started to beat him with his rifle.

The streets were a lot different in the 1960s, particularly in Cleveland. Surviving was all that mattered—when and where you will sleep, where your next meal might come from, your next bath. So you think that you must steal from someone in order to eat. You sleep where you can. There was this food place we would go to at night. It's where I started to get into trouble. I started staying out late. We would go to Akron, Ohio, and steal cars and drive them back to Cleveland. I also stopped going to school. And, eventually, I started staying away from home. My family did love and support me, but as I got older, I just seemed to drift farther away from my family. And the more I got in trouble, the farther away I would drift. I think this was my way of keeping that part of my life away from my family.

My first arrest in Cleveland was for robbery when I was twelve. I went to juvenile hall for about three months. It was pretty frightening. I no longer had the shelter of my family. I was around people I knew nothing about. And it didn't take long before I learned that I was in an incredibly racist environment. A very hostile boiling pot.

---

1. The Hough (pronounced "Huff") riots occurred in Cleveland from July 18 to 23, 1966. National guardsmen as well as Cleveland police were stationed on street corners throughout the largely African American neighborhood.

When I came home after juvenile hall my parents began to make arrangements for me to leave Cleveland. My father traveled to Los Angeles to find work, and when he did, my family moved. My father stayed at that same company for forty years. He was a machinist at a company called Western Gear.

It was 1968 and I was fourteen years old. I'll never forget when my family and I moved out to California from Cleveland and the disappointment I felt when I learned that we would not be going back home. But I fell in love with Los Angeles almost immediately. I couldn't believe the energy. The streets were full of life. We also traveled to San Francisco where my grandfather lived and I fell in love with that city too. My grandfather stayed on the corner of Haight and Ashbury in 1968. I loved the idea of people from different cultures and genders being together and loving each other. It was unlike anything that I thought possible. I used to sit on my grandfather's porch and just watch people. I think that experience made it possible for me to see people at their finest. Haight-Ashbury represented to me what humanity was capable of being.

WE'D BE UNCUFFED

I think there were two incidents that defined the direction that my life would take. When I was sixteen there was a fire at my parents' house, and I thought that my mother had been trapped in the fire. It caused me to have a nervous breakdown. I was hospitalized for it. After I ran away from the hospital I'd been committed to, I was kidnapped by what eventually became a rival gang, sat on for about four days, and beaten up on pretty badly.

I wasn't involved in any gang activity at the time. I had no interest in it. The guys who were responsible for taking me were under the impression that I was out of the Nickerson Garden Housing Projects, which was a rival neighborhood in Watts. I was not. At the time the area I ran in was a park, 109th Street Park, in Watts. The park was directly next to the Nickerson Garden Projects, which is why they made the mistake they did. To protect me, my parents sent me to Detroit where I had family, to heal and to be taken care of. I returned to California about fourteen months later. I did make the Nickerson Garden Projects the area that I ran in, and I became a member of the gang that was eventually formed over there, the Bounty Hunters. The Bounty Hunters were formed in response to attacks that had taken place against people in the Nickerson Gardens by this rival gang. We considered it to be our responsibility to protect the Nickerson Gardens Housing Project. Many of us who lived there were fiercely loyal to each other. And regardless of how misplaced some may think this loyalty is, that matters to young people who live in a world in which the deck is stacked.

The gang task force used to arrest some of us out of the Nickerson Gardens. We wouldn't be charged with anything, but we'd be taken down to the police station, kept in handcuffs, and officers would take turns punching us. Occasionally we'd be uncuffed, giving us a chance to fight back. And we would fight back, even though there were three or four officers surrounding us. The choice was to get knocked out fighting back or get knocked out without fighting back at all.

I joined the military in 1973 in the hope of putting my life back together. Well, saying "back together" might be misleading. My life was never together. I was eighteen. I enlisted in the National Guard with the intention of going into the army. My uncle was in the army and at the time it was like my way out of Watts. It really opened me up to the world. It put aspects of my life in perspective for me.

My parents as well as my grandparents, aunts, and uncles raised me to be a responsible thinking and acting person. It was just something about the street, the life, that always got me. When I came home from the military, it was just a matter of time before I found my way back to Watts, the Nickerson Gardens, 109th Street Park, and in particular the Bounty Hunters.

I became a father for the first time in 1973. My second son was born in 1974. I was arrested in 1974 and incarcerated in 1975 for two counts of second-degree murder. A young lady who was very dear to me was raped. I was convicted for the murder of the person who was accused of raping her.

I was also accused of shooting a person in the Nickerson Garden projects who had threatened to bring a rival gang over to the neighborhood. I honestly had nothing to do with this shooting. There were a host of witnesses willing to testify that I was at a party on the other side of Nickerson Gardens at the time the shooting occurred. At the trial, the only witnesses who testified and connected me to the shooting were two guys (they were biological brothers) who'd been arrested for the shooting themselves and agreed to testify against me for deals. My attorney, a public defender, didn't call any witnesses to testify on my behalf, even though they were in the courtroom during the trial. The jury convicted me of second-degree murder. During my sentencing the judge stated that the jury could have certainly found me not guilty. I was sentenced to fifteen years to life.

After that, I received a general discharge under honorable conditions from the military in 1975. My parents said my past had caught up to me. I was sent to San Quentin a month after my twenty-first birthday.

SENT DIRECTLY BACK TO SOLITARY

It's been said that California prisons were perhaps the most violent and brutal in the United States at that time. I certainly believe it. And San Quentin was perhaps the most violent. I remember arriving there. As I got off the bus and was being escorted to the SHU, or security housing unit—it was called "the hole" then—someone was killed. I was convinced at that moment that San Quentin was all that I had heard it was.

In 1978, while I was in San Quentin, several guys and I were engaged in a conversation about baseball. I was an avid fan at the time, particularly of the Giants. There were some officers observing the conversation from a window on the third floor.

I received a chrono a few days later stating that based on the officers' observation, this was a Black Guerilla Family conversation taking place and that I was directing the discussion.[2] The BGF, as I understand it, is a political/military organization that believes in creating a society in which the humanity of everyone is respected, and a "chrono" is a document that explains and identifies an action or decision that was made and why. They are documents that log information used in the "validation" of a prisoner. The chrono I received also stated that I was a captain in the BGF. When I filed an appeal on this and told the reviewing appeals officer that the conversation was about baseball, he laughed. I've always rejected the characterization of my being a prison gang member. I'm always mindful of the fact that it served as the basis for my being buried in solitary, along with others like me.

On one occasion I received a chrono that said I admitted to being a member of the BGF and to being a captain. I never did any such thing. There is hardly any kind of defense against an alleged admission, except to say that I didn't admit to anything. I don't know, nor have I ever been told, what the alleged circumstances were: where I was, who I was talking to, or why I made this admission.

A lot of information is recycled. Informants pass on information to each other, and then multiple informants will use it when they are debriefing.[3] It is, naturally, considered reliable because multiple sources have provided it. And it is in turn used to justify placing supposed gang members in solitary.

---

2. Black Guerrilla Family (BGF) is a prison and street gang that originated at San Quentin as an offshoot of the Black Panthers.

3. In the late 1980s, the California Department of Corrections and Rehabilitation (CDCR) tried to control gang activity in the prisons. If a prisoner was found to be a member of a gang he was "validated" and given an indeterminate SHU sentence. Later, they ruled that if you were inactive in a prison gang for six years, you could leave SHU. The other way to get out was to "debrief"—provide information on the prison gang you were supposedly part of and the names of all the members. If a prisoner was not part of a gang or didn't know the members of one, he might provide random names of prisoners. Debriefing also included providing information on crimes one heard about in prison or any other information that would aid the CDCR or police.

I left San Quentin in 1976 and was transferred to DVI in Tracy.[4] I was transferred back to San Quentin in 1977. After I came back to San Quentin, as far as the CDCR was concerned, I was what they considered me to be. I stayed there until 1983, and spent almost all of my time in the SHU as a validated gang member.[5]

Back then, in each SHU there was what were called strip cells. This was a cell that was stripped of all property: your mattress, blankets, and sheets were taken at breakfast and given back to you at about 9 p.m., if not later. What you were provided really was up to the staff who worked in solitary. You weren't allowed to go outdoors to the yard if you were housed in a strip cell. You were fed on paper trays, and you showered a couple times a week.

I came home on May 30, 1983, Memorial Day. I thought that I was coming home to this woman that I was absolutely crazy about, but she was raped and killed three months before I got out. I was absolutely crushed when I was told that she had been killed. It was one of the few times that I remember my legs giving out from underneath me. I don't remember the details of what happened and I honestly didn't want to know. She was raped, stabbed, and killed by gang members. I should've left California. I was actually told by my parole officer that I should leave the state.

For the first couple of weeks that I was home, I stayed with my parents in Compton. My parents helped me get a job through a friend about a week after I got there. I was working at a place called Jackson Products, in Santa Fe Springs, California.

My youngest son, Roberto, was born in 1985, and that same year I was arrested on a first-degree murder charge. I was charged with being one of three people who were armed with three different weapons in a

4. Deuel Vocational Institution (DVI) is a state prison located near Tracy, California.

5. The CDCR is the largest state-run prisons system in the United States. The department oversees California's thirty-three adult correctional institutions, thirteen adult community correctional facilities, and six juvenile facilities, which house more than 165,000 adults and nearly 2,000 juveniles.

shooting. My alleged codefendants and I were all accused of firing shots into a victim's body. My alleged codefendants and I were tried separately. There was no physical evidence: no guns, fingerprints, bloodstained clothing.

In many ways my trial on this case was much like my trial in 1974. I have statements from a number of potential witnesses who spoke to my former investigator and told him that I wasn't at the scene of the shooting when it occurred. None of these witnesses were called to testify on my behalf. There was a substantial amount of evidence that showed that I was, and am, innocent. After deliberating for almost four full days, the jury convicted me of first-degree murder, but they found that I didn't use a weapon in the commission of the crime. This basically means that the jury didn't believe that I actually shot the victim. In spite of this, I was sentenced to life without possible parole. I was sent directly back to solitary in the SHU at Chino.[6]

THE FIRST EIGHT YEARS OF SOLITARY

It really is hard to define what solitary is like in words. I could probably talk forever about the experience and still not explain it. There's no way that you can be subjected to long-term isolation and not be affected by it.

When I first came to prison in 1975, solitary confinement was very different. There were four major solitary confinement units in California: San Quentin, Old Folsom, DVI Tracy, and Soledad. Every SHU had its own degree of isolation, but for the most part prisoners in solitary were allowed to go out to the outdoor yard that was built inside each unit.

The food was much better then. We were also allowed to have appliances in our cell. And in three of the SHUs we were allowed contact

6. The California Institute for Men is a mixed-security prison that opened in 1941. The facility is often simply called "Chino" because of its location in Chino, California, east of Los Angeles.

visits if we remained disciplinary free for a year.[7] So the degree of isolation that we were subjected to was offset by the number of programs
that were available.

Even then, it was the violence, or potential for violence, that took
its toll on you psychologically. In every SHU, including the SHU in the
reception center at Chino, you knew you were in an environment where
you could lose your life. But San Quentin was the worst. It was overtly
racist in prison, and particularly in solitary, in those years. It was very
common that when cell doors opened, an Afrikan was set up to be attacked by two non-Afrikans. We had to be on guard constantly, every
day. And this meant being awake, dressed, and ready for anything that
might happen before breakfast.

Afrikans are guys who follow certain principles. They study and read
to become critical thinkers who are connected to humanity. "Afrikan" is
a term we use that has to do with shedding the influences of capitalist,
racist, sexist, misogynistic America. That "k" is symbolic of the transformation into a new, critically thinking, person. The term symbolizes our
struggle together and care about each other. Knowing that you were in
such a violent environment, especially if you were an Afrikan, and knowing that the violence was culturally motivated, by staff, certain prisoners,
and the culture of prison, it meant that you had to be hypervigilant. To
live in that state of awareness every hour of every day was enough to create
some serious mental health problems. There were guys who decided they
could not take this, and they chose to be housed in protective custody.

In the late 1980s in the SHU at Tehachapi—and particularly at New
Folsom—there were ongoing incidents of violence.[8] New Folsom was
described as a killing field because of the number of shootings that occurred there. But it was with the opening of the SHU in Corcoran in

---

7. "Disciplinary free" means to have no reported incidents, such as altercations or
contraband.

8. Tehachapi is another name for California Correctional Institution, a supermax state
prison located in Cummings Valley, outside Tehachapi, California.

1988 that the violence really accelerated.[9]

In 1988, they rounded up about thirty Afrikans and placed us in solitary pending an investigation into what was being called "BGF activity." For the entire time that I was in solitary, I was told that the investigation was ongoing. As far as I know it's still ongoing.

I was on the first bus to open up Corcoran SHU and was housed there from 1988 to 1990. It was as racist and as foul a place as any prison I've been to—as totalitarian as well. The inhumanities at Corcoran SHU took place for several years and were kept from public view.

The first eight years of solitary were the most trying. The infamous gladiator fights were being staged at Corcoran when I was there. The administration would house people on the yard together who were classified as enemies with each other. This was done knowing there would be a fight or stabbing on the yard. Prisoners would be allowed to fight, and then an officer in the gun tower would shoot the people who were fighting, sometimes with a nine-millimeter rifle, sometimes with the block gun. The block gun would shoot hard rubber projectiles and at close range could be lethal.

Every day, people were deliberately put into positions that would and did result in fights. Very serious fights, many of which resulted in a number of people, particularly Afrikan people, being shot and killed. I was attacked once by two non-Afrikan people, and even though it was clear that I was being attacked, somehow I was the only person who was shot with the block gun.[10]

I can remember in Corcoran SHU when you were released to the yard, you could take a deep breath and smell cordite in the air. The yard

---

9. California State Prison, Corcoran is an all-male facility located in central California.

10. In 1996, the *Los Angeles Times* claimed Corcoran to be the "most troubled of the 32 [California] state prisons" ("Tales of Brutality behind Bars," August 21, 1996). Inmates were regularly shot and killed. Guards were known to stage fights among inmates, while betting on the outcomes. Prisoners were often shot during these fights or for refusing to fight.

smelled like gunfire. And throughout the day, all day, you could hear gunshots being fired.

WHAT MADNESS FEELS LIKE

The animosities that developed at Corcoran SHU carried over to Pelican Bay SHU.[11] Pelican Bay opened in 1989. I was sent there in May 1990. The IGI (Institutional Gang Investigators) in particular, the so-called gang experts, had complete control over every aspect of the environment.

Pelican Bay was built in the most remote part of California. We were intentionally made to feel as though we were separated from everything. The cells were arranged in pods: seven pods in each building, and eight cells to a pod. The pods were designed in such a way that you could only see and speak to people in the other seven cells in the pod with you. For the first few years the policy was that you couldn't pass anything to another cell, even the cell next to you. When you came out on the tier for yard or showers, you couldn't speak to anyone, nor could you acknowledge anyone in one of the other pods. Doing so would result in your being issued a rules violation report for engaging in gang activity. If you were fortunate enough to receive a visit you were only allowed to visit for one hour, which actually meant only about forty-five minutes.

We couldn't write to our families about the conditions because we didn't want to worry them. It is doubtful that any mail to them would make it out of the prison anyway. The mail was routinely and intentionally held up or thrown away. No phone calls were allowed except for emergencies, and what constituted an emergency was up to the administration—the same people who were responsible for your oppression.

---

11. Pelican Bay State Prison is California's only supermax facility. It is located in Crescent City, just south of the Oregon border. According to the CDCR website, half of Pelican Bay's prisoners are housed in a general population setting, and half are housed in Security Housing Units. Its operating budget is more than $180 million per year.

Part of the constant efforts to isolate us included not allowing phone calls and withholding letters.

There were also the same gladiator-type fights occurring at Pelican Bay. But what made Pelican Bay SHU different from every other SHU past or present was the isolation. I cannot ever remember any SHU that was comparable. Solitary at Pelican Bay really is isolation. You don't see the sky, you see a piece of the sky. Everything was geared toward destroying the humanity of the people housed there. You watched people being driven crazy and even if you didn't know the person, it affected you. There were guys who would get so crazy they would throw feces and urine into your cell.

After decades of being told that you're "the worst of the worst," you have your moments when you question your own self-worth, your sanity. You feel as though no one cares. You are, literally, all alone. It is so damaging that you can start to believe that you have nothing in common with normal people. And there is no way out. This feeling of dread engulfs you. And at that moment, you'd rather be dead than breathing in isolation.

It was after my tenth year in solitary that I became convinced that I'd be in solitary for the rest of my incarceration. There is this black hole that is all around you. The nothingness. Waking up to the same identical thing every single day. And going to sleep knowing what you'll be waking up to. You look up, and you can see a light. It is miles away, but you can see it. You know that if you don't make it to that light, you're going to go crazy. You know exactly what madness feels like and what it looks like.

I've seen a lot in my life. Not much is worse than seeing another human being completely unravel. All of us who were housed in solitary, especially at Pelican Bay, had moments when we actually felt ourselves slipping psychologically. Some of the staff at Pelican Bay were clearly trying to intentionally contribute to driving people with mental health problems crazy. Or get them to debrief. It was really shameful. We saw it regularly, and maintaining our sanity became uppermost in our minds.

It's said that the key to maintaining your sanity in solitary is to stay as creative as possible. And I agree, creativity has its place. But at some point, at least for me, you run out of creative space. We would, for example, constantly switch up on our exercise routines. Instead of doing, say, eight-count burpees, we would do ten count. And then the next month we would do twenty-two count. But they're still burpees.

There were people in solitary who went crazy; people who tried to commit suicide, some more than once. At Pelican Bay SHU, the officers would help facilitate a person losing his mind. We were issued razors during showers, and people would try to cut their wrists while in the shower. They would be taken over to the hospital and put on suicide watch in the suicide cells, strip cells that were freezing cold. Guards would keep the person in the suicide cell for about three days, provide him with a psychiatric consultation, and then put him right back in the same cell he was in before, give him a razor, and the suicide process would repeat itself. I've seen this go on with the same prisoner several times.

TO BREAK PEOPLE

I think that many of us reclaimed our humanity. Fighting back will do that. We did a lot of reading, studying, discussing with each other; those were the kinds of things that kept us as sharp as we needed to be to stay focused. Pelican Bay became a school, a university. The more that we learned and understood about what the challenge really was, the more prepared we became. We were ready for the protest when it was time. We understood that we had to fight that battle. Or there would be no light at the end of that tunnel.

We would complain about our treatment. The complaints started when we first arrived at Pelican Bay and continued over the years that we were housed there. None of the complaints resulted in changes being made, which was the same with Corcoran SHU and other SHUs.[12]

---

12. These complaints eventually led to the class-action lawsuit, *Madrid v. Gomez*, in

A unit was opened up called the Violence Control Unit: VCU. All of the prisoners who had serious mental health problems were moved there. It was still isolation and nothing was done to provide help for anyone who needed it. The VCU simply made it possible for Pelican Bay to hide the people who had problems. In truth they used the VCU to house prisoners who didn't have serious mental health problems in an effort to break them as well.

Over in the VCU staff constantly abused those prisoners. The people with mental health problems would be denied showers. The stench in the building could be overwhelming. Some of the staff who worked the evening shift would make sure inmates didn't get their food. The dinner trays were given to prisoners through a slot. When the officer slid the tray through the slot and the prisoner would come to the door to pick up his tray of food the officer would slam the slot shut, intentionally causing the food to fly all over the cell. The officer would laugh and walk away.

I was housed in VCU for about a month because of a rules violation. Every single day these things happened. There was one officer who came to work and immediately called out to one of the prisoners on the tier where I was housed. He would call this prisoner's name, the prisoner would answer, and the officer would yell back, "Fuck you!" Then the two of them would begin an exchange of insults that would last until the shift change at 10 p.m.

That prisoner had serious mental health problems. The officer was just amusing himself. But when things like this happen day after day it affects you. People who have mental health problems are made worse in solitary. There were guys who would smear themselves in their own body fluids and excrement, eat and drink it.

There were no mental health professionals in the SHU to provide people with any assistance. This was by design. Policy makers at both Pelican Bay and Sacramento weren't interested in anything except the

---

1995, which was brought on behalf of some 3,500 prisoners at Pelican Bay.

outcome that was being produced. The SHU was built for that specific purpose, to break people.

THIS AFFECTED OUR FAMILIES AND LOVED ONES

In 1996, my mother was diagnosed with breast cancer. I submitted a request for an emergency phone call. I was denied the phone call and told that my mother having cancer didn't qualify as an emergency. I was then told that if I agreed to debrief, I would be allowed phone calls whenever I wanted one.

Then my mother had a stroke—the first of two, in 1997. She almost died and the strokes left her partially paralyzed. My father notified me through the mail, and I requested that I be allowed an emergency call after showing the letter to a counselor. I was told that my mother's stroke did not constitute an emergency and my request was denied. A buddy of mine who was housed in the same pod was informed that his wife jumped out of a window on the first floor of her apartment and sprained her ankle. He was allowed to make an emergency phone call.

My father had multiple heart attacks. I was told that this didn't qualify as an emergency. When my grandmother passed away while I was housed at Pelican Bay, the IGI held onto the letter that my parents sent me informing me of her death for forty-five days after it arrived at the prison. I was allowed to make a call almost two months after my mother had buried her mother.

Sometimes we wouldn't receive mail for months, and then one day we'd get three or four months' worth of mail. This affected our families and loved ones. When they didn't hear from us in months, they would think that something was wrong. And when you are in isolation, and you don't hear from the people who have always been there for you, you start to look for what you may have done to cause people to abandon you. My parents were my dearest and most trusted friends, but I still worried I had done something wrong. Then you find out nothing is wrong when that stack of mail shows up in front of your cell. I would feel this sense of relief come over me. Even though I knew, all the while, that it was the IGI doing this, it would still affect me the same way every time. I would always feel as though I'd been abandoned. It's a horrible feeling.

Isolation puts in your head that you are never far from being alone. Every day you wake up and are reminded that you have to be strong and stay on guard so as not to be broken. I did have moments when I wanted to just give up. Not debrief, just give up. I couldn't do it, because if I did, I wouldn't have been able to live with myself.

MOMENTS WHEN I JUST WANT TO BE LEFT ALONE

The system really was rigged in such a way as to use any and all information as a basis to keep us in solitary. In 2006, while I was housed in Tehachapi SHU, I had no information submitted on me in five and a half years. Well, less than six months before I would have been released from solitary, I was called out by the IGI and accused of engaging in all kinds of illegal activity, ranging from ordering the assault on an inmate to providing BGF material to inmates. And of having in my possession BGF training material, codes, names, and addresses of BGF members. My assigned cell was never searched. No evidence existed. In spite of this, and simply because someone told the IGI that I had the information and ordered the assault, it was used to justify my continued retention in solitary for another six years!

The same thing happened in 2012 when I was in Corcoran. The prison administration said there was a letter that contained gang information. But because it was characterized as gang information I wasn't allowed to see the letter or know why they characterized the letter that way. Any challenge to something like this has to be sent to the people who classified the material as gang related in the first place.

As a result of the peaceful protest that occurred between 2011 and 2013, the CDCR agreed to release those prisoners who were in solitary confinement serving indeterminate terms based on their being validated.[13] A special committee was established to accomplish this, and people were released, according to the length of time that they had been housed in solitary, starting with those who'd been housed the longest.

According to the CDCR, I was the one who organized the hunger strike at Corcoran, with a lot of the people on the outside, but it was something we all participated in and contributed to. The longest I went without food was twenty-eight days. After that I had to be rushed to the hospital.

I was released from solitary confinement at Corcoran SHU and transferred here to Solano on November 6, 2015. The biggest adjustment that I had to make in gen pop after being in solitary for so long was not thinking or acting like I'm still in solitary. It never occurred to me that I had to retrain myself to think differently. I've always known that it is constantly necessary to change the way that one thinks. I just never thought or considered that it applied to my being released from solitary to the general population.

There are 250 cells in the building, top and bottom tier combined. As I understand it they have four facilities or yards here, two level 3 facilities (I am housed in one of the level 3 facilities) and two level 2 facilities. The level 2 facilities are dorm living and the level 3 facilities are cells.

My day usually starts at about 5 or 5:30, when I wake up. I'll wash up, make up my bed, and then pray. I'm not much of a coffee drinker, but I'll occasionally have a cup of coffee, and if I have some writing that I need to do, I'll start on it. If not, I'll usually watch the news until breakfast. We usually go to breakfast at about 7:30. I always put in a CD, usually Miles Davis or Stan Getz and João Gilberto/Antonio Carlos Jobim, and listen to it while waiting to go to breakfast.

We're allowed to walk to the dining hall, and I'm able to look at the mountains as I walk. I'll usually make it back to the building that I'm

---

13. In 2013, some thirty thousand prisoners in California prisons went on hunger strike to protest the state's use of indefinite solitary confinement.

housed in by eight. After that we just wait to either go out to the yard or the dayroom. It alternates. When I can go out to the yard, I run. I'm up to running a mile now. I'll usually put in a Michael Franks CD, a jazz artist that I've enjoyed for years. After my run I'll walk around the yard, both to come down off of the running and to speak to a lot of the guys in the yard. I walk for at least an hour.

I'm allowed out to the dayroom every day. In the dayroom area there's a television, several tables and connecting stools, and benches for those who like to watch television. There are also telephones there for use by prisoners to make personal calls. I try to stay as busy as I possibly can. In the general population, at least the food is much better. There is a much wider variety of food served, and that really does make a difference. And, for those who are able to go to the prison commissary, it's well stocked. You're able to draw from your prison account once a month.

Anytime that I receive a ducat, or pass, which is usually a minimum of three times a week, I attend classes. I'm enrolled in several self-help classes and a lifers group and a mentorship program. The programs range from victims awareness to anger and denial management to relapse prevention. The classes have given me an opportunity to find out a lot about myself, although I'm always concerned about anything that has to do with state-sponsored cognitive restructuring. It makes me think they're trying to turn people into slaves.

Here at Solano I still have my moments in which I'll just drift off on the yard and walk by myself. I dig people a whole lot, and I have never considered myself to be an introverted person, but I have my moments when I just want to be left alone. I have my moments when I just won't speak.

I'm continuing to experience this now that I'm in the general population, and I must try to figure out how I can deal with it. If there's something that haunts me, it's those moments when I knew that I was just about to go over the edge psychologically. I cannot describe what it feels like. The only word that comes to mind is *dread*. But it was in those moments that I would find myself looking up from this black hole and seeing a light up at the very top of the hole. It appears when you're most depressed. That hole represents this moment, this one moment in which the dread became so overwhelming that you wish you were dead.

I cannot think of a more depressing feeling than feeling yourself lose your balance. Thinking that you're not going to make it. Even those of us who made it lost something. After years of this, decades even, I just don't think you're ever the same. I'm no longer sure that you can ever go back to whatever normal you may have been. Or considered yourself to be.

I can still remember what that feels like. And I believe that it's what people who commit suicide experience right before they take their lives. I've tried to convince myself that because I'm no longer in solitary, I can and should put it behind me. But I can't. And I should not. Not until the healing is complete.

APPENDIXES

Appendix I. Ten Things You Can Do

1. **Become a friend to someone in solitary.** People in solitary may not have anyone on the outside to write or call, and correspondence with someone on the outside can be a significant source of comfort. To find a pen pal, connect with Solitary Watch's "Lifelines" program. More info is available at http://solitarywatch.com/about-lifelines.

2. **Invite people who have spent time in solitary to speak in your community.** If you are part of a book club, coffee shop discussion group, library meetup, or any other community forum, invite someone who has been in solitary confinement to come speak and share their experiences and thoughts with other community members.

3. **Make demands of local elected officials and candidates.** In most states, the county jail is run by the locally elected sheriff. Attend town halls or write your sheriff a letter demanding that solitary be banned in your local jail. During election time, show up to events to ask candidates for sheriff to state whether they would abolish solitary confinement if elected. Vote accordingly.

4. **Give your money or time to local prisoners' rights and reentry organizations.** These groups are on the front lines of protecting peoples' rights while in solitary and assisting them when they return to the community.

5. **Organize to pass statewide reforms.** State legislatures across the country have passed laws restricting solitary confinement in local jails and state prisons. Contact your local prisoner rights' organization or ACLU to help support existing campaigns to enact new state laws addressing solitary confinement. Join efforts to improve access to quality mental health care funding, both in the broader community and in prisons and jails.

6. **Ask your governor where they stand on solitary.** The heads of most state prison systems are appointed by the state's governor, so what the governor believes about solitary confinement and who they appoint to that position is critical. Call in to radio shows or attend town halls to ask your governor about solitary confinement. Make sure your governor is committed to appointing a corrections director tasked with implementing reforms to solitary confinement.

7. **Volunteer in a prison.** Most prisons have opportunities for volunteers to teach classes inside prisons. There you will have the opportunity to work with and talk to people returning to the general prison population after having spent time in solitary. More broadly and just as importantly, every effort that penetrates prison walls and creates more contact between the outside world and those who are incarcerated increases accountability and transparency.

8. **Support efforts to hire formerly incarcerated people.** Regardless of your vocation, making an active effort to hire

people who were formerly incarcerated not only helps to repair some of the damage done to people in prison, it also helps create a bridge between those who have spent time in prison and those who have not.

9. **Support investigative journalism.** Journalists who have the time and resources to shine light inside prisons will continue to be invaluable in the movement to end solitary confinement. Donate to projects like Solitary Watch and subscribe or donate to other media outlets that cover prisons, jails, and criminal justice issues.

10. **Share this book.** Send a copy of this book to a friend. Snap a photo of an excerpt or quote from this book that most impacted you and share it on social media. Spread the voices of people whose lives have been forever altered by solitary confinement.

Appendix II. Timeline of Solitary Confinement in the United States

Various sources were consulted to create this timeline. In particular, we want to credit the Marshall Project, "Shifting Away from Solitary," and Solitary Watch, "Milestones in Solitary Reform," from which we drew heavily.[1]

1790: As part of a series of reforms advocated by a Quaker group known as the Philadelphia Society for Alleviating the Miseries of Public Prisons, the dirty and overcrowded group cells at the Walnut Street Jail in Philadelphia are converted to house most people in complete isolation.[2]

1816: Auburn State Prison is built in Auburn, New York. The prison requires complete silence, but people engage in group labor, in contrast to the Pennsylvania system of complete isolation.[3]

1821: Warden William Brittin converts Auburn State Prison's group cells to solitary cells, inspired by the Pennsylvania system. Brittin institutes a three-tiered system of classification, in which people in the third tier, considered the most serious offenders, are held in complete solitary confinement without group labor.[4]

---

1. Eli Hager and Gerald Rich, "Shifting Away from Solitary," Marshall Project, December 23, 2014, www.themarshallproject.org/2014/12/23/shifting-away-from-solitary; Amy Fettig and Margo Schlanger, "Milestones in Solitary Reform," Solitary Watch, http://solitarywatch.com/resources/timelines/milestones.

2. "Walnut Street Prison," Law Library—American Law and Legal Information, http://law.jrank.org/pages/11192/Walnut-Street-Prison.html.

3. Judith Anne Ryder, "Auburn State Prison," *Encyclopaedia Britannica*, https://www.britannica.com/topic/Auburn-State-Prison.

4. Ryder, "Auburn State Prison."

1825: The governor of New York ends Auburn State Prison's classification system and use of solitary confinement following numerous suicides, cases of mental illness, and escape attempts by people kept in solitary confinement. Though all inmates now work in groups, they are still restricted to complete silence.[5]

1829: The Philadelphia Society for Alleviating the Miseries of Public Prisons builds Eastern State Penitentiary. Inmates are housed in single-occupancy cells and kept completely isolated from one another. When outside their cells, they are forced to wear hoods to minimize interaction with guards or knowledge of the building.[6]

1842: Charles Dickens famously visits Eastern Penitentiary and writes, "The system here, is rigid, strict and hopeless solitary confinement." He concluded, "I believe it . . . to be cruel and wrong. . . . I hold this slow and daily tampering with the mysteries of the brain to be immeasurably worse than any torture of the body."[7]

1880: Samuel James, a former Confederate major, buys Angola plantation in Louisiana. The name Angola comes from the region in Africa where the enslaved people who were forced to labor on the plantation were originally from. James uses the former slave quarters to house prisoners, whom he forces to work the plantation fields and leases as labor to private companies.[8] Angola later becomes the largest maximum-security prison in the United States.[9]

---

5. Ryder, "Auburn State Prison."

6. "History of Eastern State," Eastern State Penitentiary, www.easternstate.org /research/history-eastern-state.

7. Brooke Shelby Biggs, "Solitary Confinement: A Brief History," *Mother Jones*, March 3, 2009, www.motherjones.com/politics/2009/03/solitary-confinement-brief -natural-history/.

8. "History of Angola," Angola Museum, www.angolamuseum.org/history/history.

9. "Institute Index: A Brief History of the Hell That Is Louisiana's Angola Prison," The Institute for Southern Studies, March 13, 2014, www.southernstudies.org/2014/03

1890: The US Supreme Court, in examining the constitutionality of a person's prison sentence, which included solitary confinement at Eastern State Penitentiary, notes that "a considerable number of prisoners . . . fell into a semi-fatuous condition . . . and others became violently insane."[10]

1901: The state of Louisiana takes over control of Angola prison after public outcry over the brutality inflicted on people by private companies under James's leasing system. Brutality and abuse continue, however, under the new ownership.[11]

1913: Eastern State Penitentiary officially abandons the Pennsylvania system, following years of gradual reforms to the original policy of complete isolation.[12]

1933: The US Army transfers Alcatraz, formerly used as a military prison, to the Federal Bureau of Prisons (BOP). Alcatraz becomes a maximum-security prison that includes the D Block, a solitary confinement hallway in which some inmates spend years.[13]

1963: Alcatraz closes due to high operating costs.[14]

•   A US federal penitentiary is built in Marion, Illinois, to replace Al-

---

/institute-index-a-brief-history-of-the-hell-that-i.html.

10. US Supreme Court, "Medley, Petitioner, 134 US 160 (1890)," p. 134, Justia, https://supreme.justia.com/cases/federal/us/134/160/case.html.

11. "History of the Prison," Angola Museum, www.angolamuseum.org/history/archived-articles/history-of-the-prison.

12. "History of Eastern State."

13. Laura Sullivan, "Timeline: Solitary Confinement in U.S. Prisons," NPR, July 26, 2006.

14. "Historical Information: Alcatraz Origins," Federal Bureau of Prisons, www.bop.gov/about/history/alcatraz.jsp.

catraz. USP Marion will eventually become what is often considered the first "supermax" prison in the United States.[15]

1968: USP Marion institutes the Control and Rehabilitation Effort (CARE) program, through which people were frequently subjected to solitary confinement.[16]

1971: Eastern State Penitentiary closes due to high costs of necessary repairs to the prison.[17]

1983: Two correctional officers are murdered at USP Marion in independent incidents on the same day by members of the Aryan Brotherhood. USP Marion subsequently goes into "permanent lockdown," in which people are kept in solitary confinement for twenty-two to twenty-three hours each day. The Marion model spreads and becomes known as a supermax prison.[18]

1989: Pelican Bay, the first facility specifically designed to be a supermax prison, is built in Crescent City, California. Roughly one-third of the prison's two thousand to three thousand people are housed in solitary confinement in high-security Special Housing Units (SHUs).[19]

1994: A new federal supermax facility, ADX Florence, is built in Florence,

---

15. "Marion Prison," Historical Southern Illinois, Southern Illinois University, www.cs.siu.edu/csday/2009_1/marion_prison.htm.

16. "Marion Prison."

17. "History of Eastern State."

18. "Marion Prison."

19. James Ridgeway and Jean Casella, "Hunger Strike in the Supermax: Pelican Bay Prisoners Protest Conditions of Solitary Confinement," Solitary Watch, June 30, 2011, http://solitarywatch.com/2011/06/30/hunger-strike-in-the-supermax -pelican-bay-prisoners-protest-conditions-in-solitary-confinement/.

Colorado. Prisoners are housed in solitary confinement cells for at least twenty to twenty-three hours each day with limited access to any recreational activities.[20]

1995: A federal judge orders an overhaul of practices and medical care at Pelican Bay supermax in California and holds that people with mental illness must be removed from solitary confinement.[21]

2002: The United States constructs Guantánamo Bay detention camp, also known as "Gitmo," in Cuba to imprison suspected members of al-Qaeda and the Taliban. Approximately 70 percent of the inmates at Guantánamo Bay are in solitary confinement, including some already cleared for release.[22]

2006: The Commission on Safety and Abuse in America's Prisons completes its inquiry and issues its report, *Confronting Confinement*. The report ranks limiting prison isolation as one of its three chief recommendations, urging that prisons and jails "make segregation a last resort," "end conditions of isolation," and "protect mentally ill patients."[23]

---

20. Benish Anver, Gal Bruck, and Richard Wilson, "Written Statement of the American University International Human Rights Law Clinic: 'Solitary Confinement and Mental Illness: An Overview of Conditions at ADX,'" Inter-American Commission on Human Rights, Thematic Hearing on Human Rights and Solitary Confinement in the Americas, American University, March 8, 2013, www.aclu.org/files/assets/au_wcl_testimony_iachr_for_thematic_hearing_3-12-13pdf.

21. Jean Casella and James Ridgeway, "Case Closed on Supermax Abuses at Pelican Bay," Solitary Watch, February 15, 2011.

22. "Solitary Confinement at Guantanamo Bay," Center for Constitutional Rights, May 21 2008, http://ccrjustice.org/home/get-involved/tools-resources/fact-sheets-and-faqs/solitary-confinement-guantanamo-bay#2.

23. John J. Gibbons and Nicholas de B. Katzenbach, *Confronting Confinement: A Report of the Commission on Safety and Abuse in America's Prisons*, Vera Institute of Justice, June 2006, www.vera.org/publications/confronting-confinement.

- USP Marion is downgraded to a medium-security facility, ending twenty-three years of lockdown.[24]

2007: Following a lawsuit, New York State significantly curtails the use of solitary confinement in state prisons for people with serious mental illness and requires the first-ever, limited mental health monitoring of all prisoners in solitary confinement.[25]

- As a result of *Presley v. Epps*, the Mississippi Department of Corrections shuts down Parchman Farm's notorious solitary confinement Unit 32. A "step-down" system is introduced, returning inmates to Parchman's general population; seriously mentally ill prisoners are moved to treatment units. The number of prisoners in solitary confinement drops from 1,300 to 300.[26]

2008: New York passes the first solitary confinement reform bill of its kind, the SHU Exclusion Law. The law, which took effect in 2011, requires the Department of Corrections and Community Supervision to review and report its solitary confinement policies, remove mentally ill prisoners from isolation, ensure that those prisoners' standard of care is higher than that of other inmates, and build a new therapeutic, nondisciplinary prison unit.[27]

---

24. Justin Peters, "How a 1983 Murder Created America's Terrible Supermax-Prison Culture," *Slate,* October 23, 2013, www.slate.com/blogs/crime/2013/10/23/marion_prison_lockdown_thomas_silverstein_how_a_1983_murder_created_america.html.

25. US District Court, Southern District of New York, "Private Agreement Settlement," www.documentcloud.org/documents/682930-shu-exclusion-settlement, document accessed via ProPublica; Christie Thompson, "New York Promised Help for Mentally Ill Inmates – but Still Sticks Many in Solitary," ProPublica, August 15, 2013, www.propublica.org/article/new-york-promised-help-for-mentally-ill-inmates-but-still-sticks-many-in-so.

26. Hager and Rich, "Shifting Away from Solitary."

27. Hager and Rich, "Shifting Away from Solitary."

2010: After a broad-scale advocacy campaign, the state legislature in Maine requires a review and report on the use of solitary confinement. The resulting report uncovers the overuse of isolation and makes recommendations for reform. Maine then cuts the population of prisoners in solitary confinement in half. Now, placing a prisoner in solitary for longer than seventy-two hours requires the personal approval of the commissioner of corrections. The use of disciplinary segregation largely has been replaced with informal punishments, and social programming has been expanded.[28]

2011: The UN special rapporteur on torture calls for a global ban on solitary confinement in almost all cases, with a definite ban on the use of solitary for periods longer than fifteen days and for individuals under eighteen years of age and those with mental disabilities.[29]

2012: The American Psychiatric Association (APA) issues a statement that prisoners with serious mental illness should rarely be kept in solitary confinement and, when they are in such conditions, must receive extra clinical support.[30]

- The Prison Rape Elimination Act (PREA) of 2003, is implemented, limiting the use of solitary confinement for LGBTI individuals and youth.[31]

---

28. Hager and Rich, "Shifting Away from Solitary."

29. "Solitary Confinement Should Be Banned in Most Cases, UN Expert Says," UN News Centre, October 18, 2011, www.un.org/apps/news/story.asp?NewsID=40097#.V2LuZbQrz0s.

30. "ACLU Briefing Paper: The Dangerous Overuse of Solitary Confinement in the United States," ACLU, August 2014.

31. "Prison Rape Elimination Act of 2003," Government Publishing Office, www.gpo.gov/fdsys/pkg/PLAW-108publ79/pdf/PLAW-108publ79.pdf; "Prison Rape Elimination Act," National PRA Resource Center, www.prearesourcecenter .org/about/prison-rape-elimination-act-prea. (The latter source was published in 2012, after enforcement commenced.)

- Massachusetts bans the use of solitary confinement on people with severe mental illness.[32]

- West Virginia prohibits the use of punitive isolation in juvenile facilities.[33]

- Senator Dick Durbin holds the first-ever congressional hearing on solitary confinement.[34]

- The American Academy of Child and Adolescent Psychiatry publishes an official policy statement concluding that, due to their "developmental vulnerability," adolescents are in particular danger of adverse reactions to prolonged isolation and solitary confinement.[35]

- The APA issues its Position Statement on Segregation of Prisoners with Mental Illness, stating that "prolonged segregation of adult inmates with serious mental illness, with rare exceptions, should be avoided due to the potential for harm to such inmates."[36]

- A federal judge approves the settlement in United *States v. Virgin Islands*, which prohibits the housing of prisoners with serious mental illness in isolation and requires that any prisoner in segregation re-

---

32. Hager and Rich, "Shifting Away from Solitary."

33. Hager and Rich, "Shifting Away from Solitary."

34. James Ridgeway and Jean Casella, "First Congressional Hearing on Solitary Confinement to Be Held June 19," Solitary Watch, June 8, 2012, http://solitarywatch.com /2012/06/08/first-congressional-hearing-on-solitary-confinement-to-be-held-june-19/.

35. "Solitary Confinement of Juvenile Offenders," American Academy of Child and Adolescent Psychiatry," www.aacap.org/aacap/Policy_Statements/2012/Solitary _Confinement_of_Juvenile_Offenders.aspx.

36. "Position Statement on Segregation of Prisoners with Mental Illness," American Psychiatric Association," December 2012.

ceive regular review with a goal of minimizing time in segregation. It also requires that prisoners in segregation receive adequate opportunities for out-of-cell time.[37]

2013: US Government Accountability Office issues report finding that the Bureau of Prisons has never assessed the impact of solitary confinement on prison safety or inmate mental health.[38]

- The Justice Department issues a report finding gross misuse of solitary confinement on inmates with mental illness at Pennsylvania State Correctional Institution at Cresson, the first-ever such investigation and finding conducted by the Justice Department's Civil Rights Division.[39]

- Nevada prohibits the holding of children in solitary confinement for over seventy-two hours.[40]

- US Immigration and Customs Enforcement (ICE) establishes a new

37. United States Virgin Islands Golden Grove Adult Correctional Facility, "2013 Federal Court Settlement Agreement in re: *United States of America v. The Territory of the Virgin Islands*," Seventh Compliance Monitoring Report, submitted May 31, 2015, www.justice.gov/sites/default/files/crt/legacy/2015/06/03/goldengrove_mtrrpt7 _6-2-15.pdf.

38. "Bureau of Prisons: Improvements Needed in Bureau of Prisons' Monitoring and Evaluation of Impact of Segregated Housing," US Government Accountability Office, May 1, 2013, www.gao.gov/products/GAO-13-429.

39. "Justice Department Finds Pennsylvania State Prison's Use of Solitary Confinement Violates Rights of Prisoners under the Constitution and Americans with Disabilities Act," Department of Justice, Office of Public Affairs, May 31, 2013, www.justice.gov/opa/pr/justice-department-finds-pennsylvania-state-prison-s -use-solitary-confinement-violates-rights.

40. Nevada Legislature, "Chapter 62B - General Administration; Jurisdiction," section 215, www.leg.state.nv.us/NRS/NRS-062B.html#NRS062BSec215.

policy that limits the use of protective segregation and requires a field office director's approval for the use of solitary confinement over fourteen days. The new regulations apply to over 250 immigration detention facilities.[41]

2014: The US Department of Justice announces the results of an investigation on the treatment of adolescent males at New York City's Rikers Island Jail. The report finds excessive use of force by staff, including "placing adolescent inmates in what amounts to solitary confinement at an alarming rate and for excessive periods of time." Some of the youth suffered from mental illness.[42]

• Colorado bans the use of solitary confinement on inmates with "serious mental illness."[43]

• As the result of a lawsuit settlement, New York bans the use of solitary confinement on inmates younger than eighteen years, becoming the largest prison system in the United States to do so.[44]

---

41. US Immigration and Customs Enforcement, "11065.1: Review of the Use of Segregation for ICE Detainees," September 4, 2014, www.ice.gov/doclib/detention-reform /pdf/segregation_directive.pdf.

42. "Manhattan U.S. Attorney Finds Pattern and Practice of Excessive Force and Violence at NYC Jails on Rikers Island That Violates the Constitutional Rights of Adolescent Male Inmates," Department of Justice, US Attorney's Office, Southern District of New York, August 4, 2014, www.justice.gov/usao-sdny/pr/manhattan-us -attorney-finds-pattern-and-practice-excessive-force-and-violence-nyc-jails.

43. Rick Raemisch and Kellie Wasko, "Open the Door – Segregation Reforms in Colorado," Colorado Department of Corrections, 2015, www.colorado.gov/pacific /cdoc/news/open-door-segregation-reforms-colorado.

44. Benjamin Weiser, "New York State Agrees to Big Changes in How Prisons Discipline Inmates," *New York Times*, February 19, 2014, www.nytimes.com/2014/02/20 /nyregion/new-york-state-agrees-to-big-changes-in-how-prisons-discipline-inmates .html?ref=solitaryconfinement.

- Senator Dick Durbin holds a second congressional hearing on solitary confinement, in which he states that solitary confinement should never be used on children, pregnant women, or people with serious mental illnesses.[45]

- Following the second US Senate hearing on solitary confinement, US attorney general Eric Holder releases a video statement and accompanying press release strongly criticizing the "excessive" use of solitary confinement on children.[46]

2015: New York City pledges to ban solitary confinement for people twenty-one years of age and younger at the notoriously abusive Rikers Island Jail.[47]

- As the result of a lawsuit settlement, Illinois agrees to limit the use of solitary confinement in juvenile facilities and will require that juveniles spend at least eight hours a day outside of their cells.[48]
- As the result of a lawsuit, California agrees to end indefinite periods of solitary confinement and the practice of placing inmates in

---

45. "Opening Statement of Senator Dick Durbin: 'Reassessing Solitary Confinement II: The Human Rights, Fiscal, and Public Safety Consequences,'" Committee on the Judiciary, February 25, 2014, www.judiciary.senate.gov/imo/media /doc/02-25-14DurbinStatement.pdf.

46. Department of Justice, Office of Public Affairs, "Attorney General Holder Criticizes Excessive Use of Solitary Confinement for Juveniles with Mental Illness," Department of Justice press release, May 14, 2014, www.justice.gov/opa/pr/attorney -general-holder-criticizes-excessive-use-solitary-confinement-juveniles-mental.

47. Claire Sestanovich, "NYC Declares an End to Solitary for Inmates under 21," Marshall Project, January 14, 2015, www.themarshallproject.org/2015/01/14/nyc -declares-an-end-to-solitary-for-inmates-under-21#.2ZG6Wrt5R.

48. Julie Bosman, "Lawsuit Leads to New Limits on Solitary Confinement at Juvenile Prisons in Illinois," *New York Times*, May 4, 2015, www.nytimes.com/2015/05/05/us /politics/lawsuit-leads-to-new-limits-on-solitary-confinement-at-juvenile-prisons-in -illinois.html.

solitary solely because of gang affiliation. The state also agrees to review the cases of inmates currently in solitary.[49]

- The Association of State Correctional Administrators (ASCA), a group composed of the chiefs of all state prison systems and large city jails, issues a report on the state of solitary confinement in the United States, and notes that "this Report both reflects and supports ongoing efforts to understand its impact, reevaluate its use, and limit or end extended isolation."[50]

- In a speech given at the NAACP's annual convention, President Barack Obama denounces the practice of solitary confinement in the United States.[51]

- In California, settlement is reached in *Ashker v. Brown*, a class action filed on behalf of prisoners held in solitary. California agrees to far-reaching reforms to reduce the number of prisoners in the SHUs and limit the way SHU confinement is used.[52]

- The Bureau of Justice Statistics introduces its first-ever national

---

49. Priyanka Boghani, "California Agrees to Overhaul Solitary Confinement in Prisons," *Frontline*, September 1, 2015, www.pbs.org/wgbh/frontline/article/california -agrees-to-overhaul-solitary-confinement-in-prisons.

50. Liman Program, Yale Law School, and the Association of State Correctional Administrators, August 2015, *Time-in-Cell: The ASCA-Liman 2014 National Survey of Administrative Segregation in Prison*, www.law.yale.edu/system/files/documents/pdf /asca-liman_administrative_segregation_report_sep_2_2015.pdf.

51. "Remarks by the President at the NAACP Conference," The White House, Office of the Press Secretary, July 14, 2015, https://obamawhitehouse.archives.gov/the -press-office/2015/07/14/remarks-president-naacp-conference.

52. Sal Rodriguez, "Legal Settlement Is Having a 'Transformative Effect' on Solitary Confinement in California Prisons," Solitary Watch, February 8, 2016, http:// solitarywatch.com/2016/02/08/legal-settlement-is-having-a-transformative-effect -on-solitary-confinement-in-california-prisons/.

study of the prevalence of restrictive housing in US prisons and jails. The study reveals that certain populations are overrepresented in solitary confinement, including younger prisoners, LGBT prisoners, and prisoners suffering from mental illness.[53]

2016: President Obama issues new guidelines for use of solitary confinement and new policies for the BOP. The new policies include a ban on restrictive housing for juveniles and the expansion of alternative housing options for people with serious mental illness or inmates in protective custody.[54]

- As the result of a lawsuit, New York announces further reforms to solitary confinement, guaranteeing phone calls and more out-of-cell time for people held in its SHUs as well as measures to reduce the length of time people can be held in solitary.[55]

- Colorado announces that it has abolished long-term solitary confinement, capping twenty-three-hour-per-day isolation to a duration of fifteen days and guaranteeing that anyone held longer than that must have at least four hours out of their cell per day to interact with others.[56]

---

53. Allen J. Beck, "Use of Restrictive Housing in US Prisons and Jails, 2011–2012," US Department of Justice, Bureau of Justice Statistics, October 2015.

54. "Fact Sheet: Department of Justice Review of Solitary Confinement," The White House, Office of the Press Secretary, January 25, 2016. These policies apply only to federal prisons and not state prisons or local jails, where the vast majority of juveniles are held. In January 2016, only 71 juveniles were being held in federal custody versus about 55,000 in state adult and juvenile facilities.

55. Michael Schwirtz and Michael Winerip, "New York State Agrees to Overhaul Solitary Confinement in Prisons," *New York Times*, December 16, 2015, www .nytimes.com/2015/12/17/nyregion/new-york-state-agrees-to-overhaul-solitary -confinement-in-prisons.html.

56. "Senate Passes Ban on Long-Term Solitary Confinement of Inmates with Serious Mental Illness," ACLU Colorado, https://aclu-co.org/statement-aclu-colorado

- On May 3, the Los Angeles County Board of Supervisors votes unanimously to end the practice of solitary confinement at its three juvenile halls and thirteen camps.[57]

- On September 6, the parties in *CLASI v. Coupe* announce that they have reached a settlement that will effectively end the solitary confinement of individuals with mental illness in Delaware.[58]

2017: Oregon passes a law expressly prohibiting solitary confinement of youths as a form of punishment.[59]

- Connecticut passes a law prohibiting solitary confinement for people younger than eighteen. It also requires greater transparency about the use of solitary confinement and mandates instruction for corrections employees regarding the psychological effects of segregation, as well as training in diversionary techniques to prevent situations that would lead to inmates being placed in administrative segregation.[60]

-unanimous-senate-approval-sb14-64-restricting-use-long-term-solitary-confinement
-inmates-serious-mental-illness.

57. Brenda Gazzar, "LA County Ends Solitary Confinement for Juveniles," *Los Angeles Daily News*, May 3, 2016, www.dailynews.com/2016/05/03/la-county-ends-solitary -confinement-for-juveniles.

58. Mindy Bogue, "Solitary Confinement Ended as We Know It in Delaware," ACLU, February 20, 2017, https://aclu-de.org/news/solitary-confinement-ended-as-we -know-it-in-delaware/2017/02/20/.

59. "Senate Bill 82," Oregon Legislature Bill Tracker, https://gov.oregonlive.com /bill/2017/SB82.

60. Christine Stuart, "Law Limiting Connecticut's Use of Solitary Confinement Takes Effect in January," *New Haven Register*, July 13, 2017, www.nhregister.com/connecticut /article/Law-limiting-Connecticut-s-use-of-solitary-11729614.php.

Appendix III. Glossary

administrative segregation/ad seg—A form of solitary confinement mandated by an administrative decision that a person is purportedly too dangerous to be housed in general population. Is often for an indefinite amount of time.

bid—A prison sentence.

the bing—Solitary confinement in jail facilities on Rikers Island in New York City.

burpee—A squat-thrust, full-body exercise.

cell extraction—A process of removing an incarcerated person from his or her cell that often involves a team of corrections officers in riot gear. Electrified shields and pepper spray may be used in order to subdue reluctant and mentally ill people who have covered cell windows, defied orders, or refused to come out of their cells for various reasons.

cellie—Cellmate.

chrono—An informational note by a prison official documenting an official action on a person housed in prison. Items covered in the note may include classification decisions, minor disciplinary offenses, and medical orders.

classification—Assigned by a jail or prison system to denote the risk level of a person housed in prison. Generally, lower levels denote minimum security while higher levels denote stricter security and fewer privileges.

classification committee—A committee often involving prison officials and mental health professionals that decides the classification level of a person in prison.

close custody—A higher-level security prison setting that is often synonymous with solitary confinement.

CO—A corrections officer or guard in a prison or jail.

debrief—To provide information to prison officials that incriminates other prisoners.

disciplinary segregation/D-seg—A form of solitary confinement in which a prisoner is sentenced for a determinate amount of time as a punishment for violating a rule.

ducat—A prison pass for movement within an institution. This pass may allow a person in prison to hold a job and work in certain areas, go to chapel, or attend prison programs.

general population/gen pop/GP—Where the majority of a jail or prison population lives, as distinguished from specialized housing units like administrative or disciplinary segregation units, medical wards, mental treatment units, and other smaller living units serving specific populations of prisoners.

the hole—Solitary confinement.

juvie—Juvenile hall.

level 1, level 2, etc.—*See* classification.

mainline—*See* general population.

Nutraloaf—A bland meal of vegetables and grains baked into a hard loaf and served by jails and prisons as punishment or for situations in which corrections officials believe normal food service poses a threat to safety. It is banned by some, but not all, prison systems.

prison politics—A silent, self-policing etiquette or code of conduct dictating behavior in prison, generally specified by one's racial identification. It is based on fear and intimidation among those housed in prison, including how to dress and who one can interact with and where. Higher-security-level prisons tend to be more "political," with stricter rules and harsher consequences for those who break the code.

programming—Educational and therapeutic instruction, offered either one on one or in group sessions.

protective custody/PC—A form of separation imposed by prison officials to protect a person from threats that other prisoners in the general population pose for that person. In many jails and prisons, prisoners held in "PC" status are kept in the same cells and units as those in administrative or disciplinary segregation.

punitive segregation—*See* disciplinary segregation.

rec/recreation—Opportunity for exercise for people housed in prison.

report—A written description of a disciplinary infraction.

security risk group/SRG—A unilateral designation by a jail or prison official that a person is a member of a group deemed to pose a risk to prison safety. In many jurisdictions, the designation can be used as the sole basis for holding a person in administrative segregation indefinitely.

SHU (pronounced "shoe")/**Special Housing Units**—Common name for the living units where people are kept in solitary confinement under administrative segregation, disciplinary segregation, or protective custody status.

step-down program—A program that gives a person increasing levels of privileges and human interaction as he or she is being transitioned from solitary confinement back to a general prison population.

suicide watch—A process in which a suicidal person is placed in a specialized cell that is usually padded and contains no furniture. The person is monitored with the purpose of preventing self-harm or suicide, usually for a period of twenty-four hours up to a few days.

ticket—A rules violation notice for inappropriate behavior in a prison or jail.

tier—The floor of a multilevel housing unit; for example, "third tier" describes being on the third floor.

validation—When a person housed in prison is officially classified as a gang member. Being validated can lead to indefinite solitary confinement. *See also* security risk group.

yard—Generally means group outdoor activity. Can also mean recreation time for those in solitary.

Appendix IV. Intimacy and Violence in a Supermax Prison

Hope Metcalf

I used to refer to solitary confinement as "no-touch torture." I found it a pithy (but by no means original) phrase to capture the popular narrative of solitary confinement, marked by the *absence* of human contact.

But day-to-day life at Connecticut's supermax prison is all about human contact. For anyone who must survive at Northern Correctional Institution, the relationship between oneself and one's custodians is physical, it is intimate, and it is violent.

So I've come to think that "solitary" is a misnomer. And on that front, at least, I share common ground with my counterparts at the Connecticut Department of Corrections. For the better part of a decade, I have worked with my students in a human rights clinic at Yale Law School to document violations at Northern. We have pushed for broad reforms and also have represented individual clients in efforts to get them transferred to less inhumane institutions where their mental health and other needs could be addressed. In early negotiations with DOC leadership, each time I referred to Northern as "solitary confinement," I got blank looks or scornful shakes of the head. "It's not solitary," one high-level administrator told me. "These guys are no Counts of Monte Cristo. The inmates are constantly talking with each other. And the officers, they talk to these guys dozens of times a day." He paused, "Believe me, at Northern, life is anything but solitary."

At first, I thought this response was just a disingenuous and formalistic sleight of hand. True, our clients didn't suffer the vacuum-sealed existence of Tommy Silverstein, a prisoner at Florence ADX, where he had endured thirty-five years in a soundproof cell, leaving it only occasionally under escort from officers who hid their faces behind full riot gear. But there was no doubt our clients suffered palpable harm from what unfolded behind Northern's walls.

But now—after eight years and hundreds of meetings with dozens of men who wear scars on the inside as well as the outside—I see that my DOC counterpart was, in some sense, telling the truth. Solitary is not about isolation. To insist otherwise is to miss its true purpose and its devastating consequences. In the words of Elaine Scarry, the supermax is the daily "unmaking" of human life, through its ritualized humiliations and physical violence, both actual and threatened.[1]

The violence is etched into the very walls. Speaking in an interview in a 2012 documentary, James Kessler, Northern's principal architect, explains that "when we were designing it, there was a desire that the first experience would make an impression." He then explained that "the limited environment, the lack of stimulus, it's all about the belief that these individuals can change. They put [the prisoners] through this drama. There's nothing soft. It's hard, and they wanted that."[2] The supermax prison's "program," to borrow an architectural term, is to compel its inhabitants to surrender.

I have seen how confinement at Northern distorts perception and breaks the mind. One client shielded his eyes from the bright reflection of my shoe buckle, and another complained about the deafening ticking of my watch. One man, who had spent twelve of the last fifteen years at Northern, had the habit of shouting, the vestiges of spending a decade communicating through air vents and sink drains. And one client, who spoke only Spanish, hadn't had a conversation with anyone in his more than two years at Northern. In our first meeting, his words tumbled out, more like poetry than prose. For nearly three hours, he skittered between biblical teachings

---

1. Elaine Scarry, *The Body and Pain: The Making and Unmaking of the World* (New York: Oxford University Press, 1987).

2. Quoted in Yale Visual Law Project, *The Worst of the Worst: Portrait of a Supermax Prison*, directed by Valarie Kaur, 2012, https://vimeo.com/54826024.

and childhood memories and the trials of the present day, his eyes looking over my shoulders, to some unseen horizon on the concrete wall.

The science is, at this point, conclusive. In the words of Professor Amanda Pustilnik of the University of Maryland, the damage wrought on the brain "make[s] solitary look less like some form of distress, and more like the infliction of a permanent disfigurement."[3] But it is a misnomer—and a misdiagnosis—to classify life at Northern as a form of "solitude." It is torture.

The sense of physical threat for prisoners at Northern is omnipresent, and it is intimate. Basic necessities—food, showers, medicine, toilet paper—are acquired at the mercy of another person. Clients have told me they were afraid to eat their meals—delivered through a metal slot at the bottom of a locked, metal door—for fear an officer may have spit in their food. They had heard threats—or were they jokes? How would they know? Other clients refused to leave their cell for weeks, and their reluctance is understandable. At Northern, each trip out—to the shower, the exercise cage, or medical, or for a legal visit—requires a strip search. Before he submits to ankle and wrist shackles, each man must bend over, lift up his testicles, and cough. Every time.

And these are just the daily requirements for survival. In this atmosphere of hyper-control over the most mundane details, it is hardly surprising that tensions between staff and prisoners often escalate from threats into violence. More than forty years ago, the Stanford prison experiment showed how quickly absolute control can deteriorate into violence perpetrated by the very people—corrections officers—who are tasked with protecting "safety and security." The study's designer, Philip Zimbardo, observed, "We had created a dominating behavioral context whose power insidiously frayed the seemingly impervious values of compassion, fair play, and belief in a just world. The situation won; humanity lost."[4] Disturbed

---

3. Brandon Keim, "The Horrible Psychology of Solitary Confinement," *Wired*, July 10, 2013.

4. Philip Zimbardo, "Revisiting the Stanford Prison Experiment: A Lesson in the

by the harassment and violence against the "prisoners" at the hands of the "officers," he terminated the experiment after just six days.

Northern, like other institutions, masks its violence to outsiders—behind walls and in jargon—while parading it before the prisoners to keep order within. Prisoners who are disruptive or disobedient face the threat of being placed on "behavioral observation status." In practice, this Orwellian term means being forcibly removed from one's own cell by a team of officers in riot gear and then taken down the hall to what prisoners call the "strip cell." There, officers force the prisoners into what the official regulations call "in-cell restraints," but what interrogators around the world call "stress positions." Prisoners are shackled at the legs and wrists, and then a tether chain binds hand to feet. Prisoners are supposed to have freedom of movement, but countless clients have complained of officers yanking the tether just tight enough to force them into a crouched position. They will spend at least twenty-four hours, and we have documented cases up to eight days. Hobbled into the fetal position, they slurp their food from a Styrofoam cup, and, if they are unfortunate enough to have to use the toilet, they cannot even wipe themselves. One client told us how the chains were so tight he had to empty the food on the floor to reach it with his mouth. "Like a dog," he said. Violence permeates everything, even literally emanating from the vents. I have conducted interviews with clients while covering my face with my sweater, trying not to breathe in the mace that hung in the recycled air. "What happened?" I always ask. More often than not, the client shrugs. Just another day.

As political scientist Amy Lerman argues, "Prison is not a 'behavioral deep freeze' and incarceration is not merely a period of incapacitation."[5] Instead, it is itself a place of intense socialization. Or in the case of the supermax, anti-socialization. One client, a petite man in his early

---

Power of Situation," *Chronicle of Higher Education*, March 30, 2007.

5. Amy Lerman, *The Modern Prison Paradox: Politics, Punishment, and Social Community* (New York: Cambridge University Press, 2013), 120.

twenties, was in punitive segregation for two weeks for head-butting an officer. He was angry at himself for "playing their game." "What was the breaking point?" I asked. The young man stiffened, "When he told me, 'I'm going to put a bullet hole in your daughter's head and fuck her.'"

I once asked a captain at Northern what he understood his job to be. He didn't hesitate. "To keep my guys safe." He didn't need to say who "my guys" were: the men (and a few women) in uniform. Then I asked how he knew when a prisoner was ready to leave Northern. "I just know," he said. I pressed him, "How?" He paused. "When he's broken." I wanted to ask, "How broken is broken enough? And how broken is too broken?" But I didn't.

The cruel irony is that some people will break too far, resorting to acts of desperation that the prison deems disruptive and manipulative. I have met men who inserted razors, paper clips, metal battery sleeves— anything that will cut flesh—into the soft hollows of their arms and legs, in the words of one prisoner, "just to feel something." Others banged their heads to the point of unconsciousness, one man wearing a scarred lump on his forehead so pronounced and permanent he looked like a unicorn that had shed its horn.

And yet, somehow, humanity persists.

Within Northern's concrete, pockmarked walls, I have witnessed acts of deep connection and everyday kindness. On visits to meet new clients, I regularly hear, "I don't have it so bad, you really need to check on this other guy." One accomplished jailhouse lawyer, who somehow managed to train himself in the law from a cell at Northern, teaches other prisoners basics of civil procedure and administrative process. He wants them to be able to "fight with the pen, not the sword," as he tells me. A middle-aged client teaches a young man on the other side of the wall how to play chess. They carefully draw out two mirror chess boards, spending hours making moves with numbers and letters, like the old Battleship game. The older man claims he's just glad to have an opponent, and a rookie at that, but in subsequent visits he fusses like an elderly aunt over the young man's choices.

The supermax seeks to unmake prisoners' worlds by putting their pain beyond the reach of human understanding. What follows, then, is the task of retelling and rebuilding.[6] And through words—the narratives in this book, the letters to lovers and friends outside the walls, the poems and songs that no concrete box can hold—the people who survive supermax remake the world. For themselves. For all of us.

Hope Metcalf is the executive director of the Schell Center for International Human Rights and a lecturer at Yale Law School.

---

6. "Whatever pain achieves, it achieves in part through its unsharability, and it ensures this unsharability through its resistance to language. . . . Physical pain does not simply resist language but actively destroys it." Scarry, *Body and Pain*, 4.

Appendix V. Solitary Confinement:
Where Reform Is Headed

Amy Fettig

I am a civil rights attorney and many of my clients are cutters. They slice their arms and legs, hands and feet, and sometimes their stomachs. A few will push straws or sticks into their penises or slice up their scrotums. Some will swallow small, sharp objects that rip them up inside. When we meet I notice the raw, red crisscrosses on their arms and wrists. They will often wear long-sleeve shirts and self-consciously tug at the cuffs in a vain attempt to cover the ongoing carnage wreaked on their bodies. But I know the real carnage is in their minds. I also know that they cut just to feel something, anything at all, because physical pain and blood are somehow better than the terrible numbness of their isolation. They cut to feel human.

You might think my clients are prisoners of war held in some terrible foreign hellhole, or perhaps captives of fanatical terrorist cells. But all of them are in solitary confinement in US prisons, jails, and juvenile detention centers. In the United States, almost nobody survives solitary confinement undamaged, and many don't survive at all. I think of Kalief Browder, arrested for allegedly stealing a backpack at sixteen and put into solitary for two of the three years he spent in jail before being released to the community after charges were dropped.[1] The pain and suffering of those years in jail overwhelmed him, and he took his own life. I think of my client Mariam Abdullah, who was also placed

---

1. Jennifer Gonnerman, "Before the Law," *New Yorker*, October 4, 2014, www.newyorker.com/magazine/2014/10/06/before-the-law; Jennifer Gonnerman, "Kalief Browder, 1993–2015," *New Yorker*, June 7, 2015, www.newyorker.com/news/newsdesk/kalief-browder-1993-2015.

in solitary as a kid. We found her in an isolation cell during a prison inspection in Arizona, a confused and scared seventeen-year-old. We tried to get her out immediately, before it was too late—she seemed to be unraveling in isolation—but the state refused. Instead, they sent her to an adult supermax prison. The pain and desperation she must have felt in that small, lonely cell haunts me. She was dead within weeks.

Solitary confinement costs the lives of tens of thousands of men, women, and children. On any given day in the United States, the best research suggests there are approximately eighty thousand to a hundred thousand people held in solitary confinement in prisons across the country.[2] And that figure does not even include the thousands of other people subject to solitary in local jails and juvenile detention centers.

Like my clients, these people will be shattered by the extreme social isolation and environmental deprivation inflicted by solitary confinement. Yet solitary confinement is a routine—even mundane—practice in American correctional facilities. Its use is pervasive across every state and jurisdiction in the country and commonplace in federal facilities as well. For correctional professionals it is a primary "tool" in the "toolbox" of prison management. In fact, when questioned about the use of solitary confinement, the inevitable answer from corrections staff is that they could not possibly run a "safe" prison without it. But such a response begs the question of what kind of institution requires that people be hurt in order to operate effectively? And why should the American people support any such institution run in their name?

The truth is that we've supported such horrors before—our "peculiar institution" of slavery was treated with the same routinized, bureaucratic indifference to obvious human suffering and cruelty by the vast

---

2. See, for example, The Liman Program, Yale Law School, and the Association of State Correctional Administrators, *Time-In-Cell: The ASCA-Liman 2014 National Survey of Administrative Segregation in Prison*, August 2015; Angela Browne, Alissa Cambier, and Suzanne Agha, "Prisons within Prisons: The Use of Segregation in the United States," *Federal Sentencing Reporter* 24, no. 46 (2011): 46–49.

majority of Americans for much of our history. In the case of solitary confinement, there is likewise a long, well-documented cultural history of its horrors starting with an eighteenth-century report on American prison conditions by Alexis de Tocqueville condemning the practice, followed by Charles Dickens's stunning nineteenth-century critique of solitary confinement in Pennsylvania's Eastern State Penitentiary in his travelogue *American Notes for General Circulation*. In it Dickens states, "I hold this slow and daily tampering with the mysteries of the brain to be immeasurably worse than any torture of the body."[3] By 1890, the Supreme Court described how even short stints in solitary left people "violently insane."[4] In modern times, decades of research and advances in brain science confirm what common sense and basic humanity made plain centuries earlier: solitary confinement is torture.

By any measure the use of solitary confinement in US correctional institutions is a human rights crisis. And yet, up until very recently, few Americans paid any attention to this horrific practice taking place in their own communities and government institutions. Fortunately, the times are changing.

Over the past several years, momentum for reform of solitary confinement and the creation of alternatives to its practice in our prisons, jails, and juvenile detention centers has grown at an enormous rate. In many ways, the reform movement's success at capturing the attention of the media, the public, and state and national leaders is unprecedented for any campaign seeking to end inhumane prison conditions. In the last few years alone, both former president Barack Obama and justices of the Supreme Court have publicly condemned the practice. President Obama even took affirmative steps to push reform by changing policies and practices in the federal Bureau of Prisons and banning the use of solitary confinement on kids held under federal jurisdiction.

---

3. Charles Dickens, *The Works of Charles Dickens: American Notes for General Circulation and Pictures from Italy* (London: Chapman & Hall, 1910), 118.

4. *In Re Medley*, 134 U.S. 160, 168 (1890).

In a historic op-ed in the *Washington Post*, President Obama denounced the practice of solitary confinement in the United States: "How can we subject prisoners to unnecessary solitary confinement, knowing its effects, and then expect them to return to our communities as whole people? It doesn't make us safer. It's an affront to our common humanity."[5] These are powerful words—and likely the first time in US history that a sitting president has called out our inhumane prison conditions. While many might expect backpedaling in the Trump administration, the trajectory for reform at the federal and state level has thus far been unaffected by the regressive nature of the current regime. This is likely because the national reform movement is simultaneously driving systems reform, exposing the harms solitary inflicts on incarcerated people, and focusing on broad-scale culture change.

This current momentum against solitary confinement is no accident. It is the result of long-term investment by a number of groups, savvy organizing, multipronged strategies, innovative corrections management, and intensive and simultaneous engagement with leaders at the local, state, national, and international level. The result is that in state after state and the federal system, both corrections officials and the public are embracing more humane and effective alternatives to isolation. Some reforms have been halting and piecemeal, others more thoroughgoing. Some are driven by legislation or litigation, others by policy or budget.

A significant driver of this movement for change is access to more information about the practice of solitary confinement. For too long this practice existed in the shadows of the American criminal justice system—widely acknowledged but rarely discussed. Many systems did not—and many still do not—collect basic data on how many people are in solitary, for what reason, and for how long. This lack of transparency and accountability extended to the public's knowledge of the practice. Indeed, prior to 2010 there were few media reports on solitary confinement in the

---

5. Barack Obama, "Why We Must Rethink Solitary Confinement," *Washington Post*, January 25, 2016.

United States, despite its pervasive use and corrosive impacts. This began to change with the formation of Solitary Watch, a web-based, single-issue journalism site that creates and collates print and online reporting on solitary confinement and efforts to reform the practice. At the same time, advocacy campaigns nationwide are diligently working to engage media attention through human rights reports, arts collaborations, utilization of social media, local op-eds by community leaders, and engagement with the editorial boards of major news media. As a result of these strategies, the questions of whether solitary confinement is inhumane, inflicts suffering and permanent damage, costs too much, and does nothing to rehabilitate prisoners are now emerging fully in the mainstream media and public discourse. In late 2017, Oprah Winfrey even toured a solitary confinement prison to explore the need for reform.

There is no question that the exposure of solitary confinement as a dire human rights issue in the United States is critical to ending the practice. As a leader in the American Civil Liberties Union's campaign to stop solitary in prisons, jails, and youth detention centers, I am especially grateful that survivors of solitary, their families, and people who work in corrections have raised their voices and told their stories in important books like *Six by Ten* and other mediums so that Americans can know and understand what we have collectively wrought in our criminal justice system. It is not a pretty story, but it must be heard to be understood.

In the next ten years, the reform movement expects to work state by state and at the federal and international level to enforce limits and outright bans on the use of solitary. This will require different strategies, depending upon the culture of each state. We will have to litigate in some places, while supporting legislation and policy reform in others. Engaging with and supporting corrections professionals to change their culture and reject the use of solitary confinement as a one-size-fits-all approach to prison management will also be a key for success. As will promoting alternatives to the use of solitary confinement, along with greater transparency and accountability for all prisons, jails, and juvenile detention centers.

Right now the lack of transparency and public oversight in our places of correction and detention means that conditions within a prison can deteriorate to an extent that imperils the lives and human rights of those who both live and work there without anyone on the outside being aware of what is happening. This is especially true because the public's and the media's right of access to these institutions is extremely limited, and too often, corrections officials are extremely reluctant to open their doors. The result of this overwhelming lack of transparency and accountability in corrections is a complete lack of public outrage about what happens behind bars. In order to stop solitary, we must throw the proverbial prison doors open and look inside with bravery, compassion, and a determination to support the human rights of all. We need light, light, and more light! And we need projects like *Six by Ten* that provide some of the critical rays of sunshine needed to illuminate our dark places.

In the long road toward realizing human rights for all in our complex modern society, one of our first steps is to question the status quo in our criminal justice system. But before we can hope to even understand what the status quo represents, it is necessary to take the time to hear, read, and process the experiences and stories of those directly impacted by that system. Once we learn from their experiences and example, we must add our voices to their call for change—because we are all part of "the system" and, ultimately, the "system" is us.

Amy Fettig is the deputy director of the ACLU National Prison Project.

Appendix VI. Five Demands of the 2011 California Prisoner Hunger Strike[1]

The Prisoner Hunger Strike Solidarity coalition formed in 2011 to amplify the voices of California prisoners on hunger strike. In July of that year, the prisoners in the Security Housing Unit (SHU) at Pelican Bay State Prison (PBSP) began what became a historic hunger strike to protest the cruel, inhumane, and tortuous conditions of their imprisonment and to improve the treatment of SHU-status prisoners throughout California. At least 6,600 prisoners across the state joined in solidarity with the Pelican Bay hunger strikers' demands.

The hunger strikers, led by Todd Ashker, developed the five core demands below. The hunger strike ended when a California lawmaker promised to hold hearings on the conditions within California SHUs. Ashker was the lead plaintiff in a lawsuit challenging conditions at the Pelican Bay SHU that resulted in a 2015 settlement that ended the practice of indeterminate solitary confinement, among other changes.

1. **End Group Punishment & Administrative Abuse.** This is in response to PBSP's application of "group punishment" as a means to address individual inmates' rule violations. This includes the administration's abusive, pretextual use of "safety and concern" to justify what are unnecessary punitive acts. This policy has been applied in the context of justifying

---

1. "Prisoners' Demands," Prisoner Hunger Strike Solidarity Coalition, https://prisonerhungerstrikesolidarity.wordpress.com/education/the-prisoners-demands-2.

indefinite SHU status, and progressively restricting our programming and privileges.

2. **Abolish the Debriefing Policy, and Modify Active/Inactive Gang Status Criteria.**
    - Perceived gang membership is one of the leading reasons for placement in solitary confinement.
    - The practice of "debriefing," or offering up information about fellow prisoners particularly regarding gang status, is often demanded in return for better food or release from the SHU. Debriefing puts the safety of prisoners and their families at risk, because they are then viewed as "snitches."
    - The validation procedure used by the California Department of Corrections and Rehabilitation (CDCR) employs such criteria as tattoos, reading materials, and associations with other prisoners (which can amount to as little as greeting) to identify gang members.
    - Many prisoners report that they are validated as gang members with evidence that is clearly false or using procedures that do not follow the *Castillo v. Alameida* settlement, which restricted the use of photographs to prove association.

3. **Comply with the US Commission on Safety and Abuse in America's Prisons 2006 Recommendations Regarding an End to Long-Term Solitary Confinement.** CDCR shall implement the findings and recommendations of the US Commission on Safety and Abuse in America's Prisons final 2006 report regarding CDCR SHU facilities as follows:

- End Conditions of Isolation (p. 14). Ensure that prisoners in SHU and Ad-Seg (Administrative Segregation) have regular meaningful contact and freedom from extreme physical deprivations that are known to cause lasting harm (pp. 52–57).

- Make Segregation a Last Resort (p. 14). Create a more productive form of confinement in the areas of allowing inmates in SHU and Ad-Seg [Administrative Segregation] the opportunity to engage in meaningful self-help treatment, work, education, religious, and other productive activities relating to having a sense of being a part of the community.

- End Long-Term Solitary Confinement. Release inmates to general prison population who have been warehoused indefinitely in SHU for the last 10 to 40 years (and counting).

- Provide SHU Inmates Immediate Meaningful Access to: i) adequate natural sunlight; ii) quality health care and treatment, including the mandate of transferring all PBSP-SHU inmates with chronic health care problems to the New Folsom Medical SHU facility.

4. **Provide Adequate and Nutritious Food.** Cease the practice of denying adequate food, and provide wholesome nutritional meals including special diet meals, and allow inmates to purchase additional vitamin supplements.

  - PBSP staff must cease their use of food as a tool to punish SHU inmates.

  - Provide a sergeant/lieutenant to independently

observe the serving of each meal, and ensure each tray has the complete issue of food on it.

- Feed the inmates whose job it is to serve SHU meals with meals that are separate from the pans of food sent from kitchen for SHU meals.

5. **Expand and Provide Constructive Programming and Privileges for Indefinite SHU-Status Inmates.** Examples include:

- Expand visiting regarding amount of time and adding one day per week.
- Allow one photo per year.
- Allow a weekly phone call.
- Allow two (2) annual packages per year. A 30-lb. package based on item weight and not packaging and box weight.
- Expand canteen and package items allowed. Allow us to have the items in their original packaging [the cost for cosmetics, stationery, envelopes, should not count towards the max draw limit].
- More TV channels.
- Allow TV/radio combinations, or TV and small battery-operated radio.
- Allow hobby craft items — art paper, colored pens, small pieces of colored pencils, watercolors, chalk, etc.
- Allow sweat suits and watch caps.
- Allow wall calendars.
- Install pull-up/dip bars on SHU yards.
- Allow correspondence courses that require proctored exams.

Signed by

Todd Ashker

Arturo Castellanos

Sitawa N. Jamaa (s/n R. N. Dewberry)

George Franco

Antonio Guillen

Lewis Powell

Paul Redd

Alfred Sandoval

Danny Troxell

James Williamson

Ronnie Yandell

. . . and all other similarly situated prisoners

ACKNOWLEDGMENTS

Our warmest thanks to everyone who shared their stories with us. We're grateful to you for opening your lives, your hearts, your families, and your homes over the years it took to build this book.

Endless gratitude to our managing editors for their navigation and patience. We couldn't have done this without Dao X. Tran wrangling our calendars, offering advice, and tolerating endless bad jokes during weekly calls. Special fist bump to Luke Gerwe for believing in—and helping launch—this project. We're grateful to the other members of the Voice of Witness team: Mimi Lok, Cliff Mayotte, Erin Vong, Claire Kiefer, Alexa Gelbard, and Dave Eggers for their dedication to human rights and education.

Thank you to Amy Fettig, Jessica Sandoval, David Fathi, Bill Cobb, Udi Ofer, Adina Ellis, Alexandra Ringe, and everyone at the ACLU who supported this book.

Thanks to Hope Metcalf, Sameer Jaywant, Steven Lance, Nell Gaither, Pete Martel, Susan Katz, Holly Cooper, Lois Henry, Sara Norman, Raha Jorjani, Susan Goodwillie, and Jennifer Parish. Your guidance, expertise, and perseverance helped us bring together a broad range of stories from across the country.

We're honored to work with Haymarket Books. Special thanks to Brian Baughan for his editorial eye and Dana Blanchard and the rest of the Haymarket Books team for helping bring the book out to the world.

Thanks to the Voice of Witness volunteers who helped make this book possible: Victoria Alexander, Pablo Baeza, Corey Barr, Emma Cogan,

Brittany Collins, Charlotte Edelstein, Katie Fiegenbaum, Justine Hall, Miriam Hwang-Carlos, Mary Beth Melso, Ariela Rosa, Barbara Sheffels, Lucy Wallitsch, Berman Zhigalko, and Kaye Herranen.

Thanks to Cate Malek for her friendship through yet another project, to Sean Havey for traveling to film stories with our narrators, to Adam Hochschild, Heather Ann Thompson, and Eli Feldman for your support and kind words. To Brad Andalman, Michael Hoke, Trevor Gardner, Lisa Guenther, Gus Johnson, Vivian Pendergrass, Paul Skenazy, Joe Stephens, and Leyla Vural for your insightful comments and keen eyes.

Special thanks to Erica Pollack, Elliot and Asher Pendergrass, Nikol Elaine, the Hoke and Pendergrass families, and the McKennas. Your support means more than you know.

ABOUT THE EDITORS

Taylor Pendergrass has been gathering stories about the US criminal justice system for more than a decade. As a civil rights lawyer for the American Civil Liberties Union, Taylor has been counsel in major cases challenging "stop and frisk" policies, deceptive police interrogations, broken indigent defense systems, and degrading jail and prison conditions. His work includes advocating for reforms to solitary confinement and other practices in the New York City jails on Rikers Island. He currently works as strategist for the ACLU's Campaign for Smart Justice, which is dedicated to reducing the US prison population by 50 percent and eradicating racial disparities in the criminal justice system. He lives in Denver.

Mateo Hoke is a writer, oral historian, and mixed-media journalist. He previously spent four years interviewing and researching throughout the West Bank and Gaza for the Voice of Witness book *Palestine Speaks: Narratives of Life under Occupation*, which he coedited with Cate Malek. His work often explores human rights and poverty, though he also enjoys writing about plants, books, and consciousness. His work has appeared in *The Best American Nonrequired Reading*, *Rolling Stone*, *Pacific Standard*, *Lucky Peach*, *McSweeney's*, and *Guernica*, among other outlets. He lives in Oakland.

ABOUT VOICE OF WITNESS

Voice of Witness is a nonprofit that advances human rights by amplifying the voices of people impacted by injustice. We foster empathy-based dialogue and actions that advance human rights through our two core programs: our oral history book series, which illuminates firsthand accounts of injustice, and our education program, which brings these stories, as well as ethics-driven storytelling, to classrooms and communities across the United States and abroad. Visit voiceofwitness.org for more information.

THE VOICE OF WITNESS SERIES

The Voice of Witness nonprofit book series amplifies the seldom-heard voices of people affected by contemporary injustice. We also work with impacted communities to create curricular and training support for educators. Using oral history as a foundation, the series depicts human rights issues in the United States and around the world. *Say It Forward: A Guide to Social Justice Storytelling* is forthcoming in 2019. *Six by Ten: Stories from Solitary* is the sixteenth book in the series. Other titles include:

SURVIVING JUSTICE
America's Wrongfully Convicted and Exonerated
Compiled and edited by Lola Vollen and Dave Eggers
Foreword by Scott Turow

"Real, raw, terrifying tales of 'justice.'" —*Star Tribune*

VOICES FROM THE STORM
The People of New Orleans on Hurricane Katrina and Its Aftermath
Compiled and edited by Chris Ying and Lola Vollen

"*Voices from the Storm* uses oral history to let those who survived the hurricane tell their (sometimes surprising) stories." —*Independent UK*

UNDERGROUND AMERICA
Narratives of Undocumented Lives
Compiled and edited by Peter Orner
Foreword by Luis Alberto Urrea

"No less than revelatory." —*Publishers Weekly*

OUT OF EXILE
Narratives from the Abducted and Displaced People of Sudan
Compiled and edited by Craig Walzer
Additional interviews and an introduction by Dave Eggers
and Valentino Achak Deng

"Riveting." —*School Library Journal*

HOPE DEFERRED
Narratives of Zimbabwean Lives
Compiled and edited by Peter Orner and Annie Holmes
Foreword by Brian Chikwava

"*Hope Deferred* might be the most important publication to have come out of Zimbabwe in the last thirty years." —*Harper's Magazine*

NOWHERE TO BE HOME
Narratives from Survivors of Burma's Military Regime
Compiled and edited by Maggie Lemere and Zoë West
Foreword by Mary Robinson

"Extraordinary." —Asia Society

PATRIOT ACTS
Narratives of Post-9/11 Injustice
Compiled and edited by Alia Malek
Foreword by Karen Korematsu

"Important and timely." —Reza Aslan

INSIDE THIS PLACE, NOT OF IT
Narratives from Women's Prisons
Compiled and edited by Ayelet Waldman and Robin Levi
Foreword by Michelle Alexander

"Essential reading." —Piper Kerman

THROWING STONES AT THE MOON
Narratives from Colombians Displaced by Violence
Compiled and edited by Sibylla Brodzinsky and Max Schoening
Foreword by Íngrid Betancourt

"Both sad and inspiring." —*Publishers Weekly*

REFUGEE HOTEL
Photographed by Gabriele Stabile and edited by Juliet Linderman

"There is no other book like *Refugee Hotel* on your shelf." —*SF Weekly*

HIGH RISE STORIES
Voices from Chicago Public Housing
Compiled and edited by Audrey Petty
Foreword by Alex Kotlowitz

"Joyful, novelistic, and deeply moving." —George Saunders

INVISIBLE HANDS
Voices from the Global Economy
Compiled and edited by Corinne Goria
Foreword by Kalpona Akter

"Powerful and revealing testimony." —*Kirkus*

PALESTINE SPEAKS
Narratives of Life under Occupation
Compiled and edited by Cate Malek and Mateo Hoke

"Heartrending stories." —*New York Review of Books*

THE VOICE OF WITNESS READER
Ten Years of Amplifying Unheard Voices
Edited and with an introduction by Dave Eggers

THE POWER OF THE STORY
The Voice of Witness Teacher's Guide to Oral History
Compiled and edited by Cliff Mayotte
Foreword by William Ayers and Richard Ayers

"A rich source of provocations to engage with human dramas throughout the world." —*Rethinking Schools Magazine*

LAVIL
Life, Love, and Death in Port-Au-Prince
Edited by Peter Orner and Evan Lyon
Foreword by Edwidge Danticat

"*Lavil* is a powerful collection of testimonies, which include tales of violence, poverty, and instability but also joy, hustle, and the indomitable will to survive." —*Vice*

CHASING THE HARVEST

Migrant Workers in California Agriculture

Edited by Gabriel Thompson

"The voices are defiant and nuanced, aware of the human complexities that spill across bureaucratic categories and arbitrary borders." —*The Baffler*

CPSIA information can be obtained
at www.ICGtesting.com
Printed in the USA
BVHW041041021118
531792BV00005B/10/P